ENTANGLING ALLIANCES WITH NONE

Most of the articles in this collection have appeared first in other publications. I would like to thank the respective authors and publishers for permission to reprint them here.

"Thomas Jefferson: The Idealist as Realist," from F. Merli and T. Wilson, eds., *Makers of American Diplomacy* (New York: Charles Scribner's Sons, 1974), 53-79.

"Reflections on Jefferson as a Francophile," *South Atlantic Quarterly* 79 (Winter 1980): 38-50. Copyright 1979 by Duke University Press.

"The Founding Fathers and the Two Confederations: The United States of America and the United Provinces of the Netherlands, 1783-1789," from J. W. Schulte Nordholt and Robert P. Swierenga, eds., *A Bilateral Bicentennial* (New York: Octagon Books, 1982), 33-48.

"The Neocolonial Impulse: The United States and Great Britain, 1783-1823," from Morrell Heald and Lawrence S. Kaplan, *Culture and Diplomacy: The American Experience* (Westport, Conn.: Greenwood Press, 1977), 46-65. Copyright 1977 by Morrell Heald and Lawrence S. Kaplan.

"The Consensus of 1789: Jefferson and Hamilton on American Foreign Policy," *South Atlantic Quarterly* 71 (Jan. 1972): 91-105. Copyright 1972 by Duke University Press.

"Toward Isolationism: The Rise and Fall of the Franco-American Alliance, 1775-1801," from Lawrence S. Kaplan, ed., *The American Revolution and a "Candid World"* (Kent, Ohio: Kent State Univ. Press, 1977), 134-60.

"Jefferson's Foreign Policy and Napoleon's Ideologues," *William and Mary Quarterly* 19 (July 1962): 344-59.

"Jefferson, the Napoleonic Wars, and the Balance of Power," *William and Mary Quarterly* 14 (April 1957): 196-218.

"France and Madison's Decision for War, 1812," *Mississippi Valley Historical Review* 50 (Mar. 1964): 652-71.

"France and the War of 1812," *Journal of American History* 57 (June 1970): 36-47.

"The Paris Mission of William Harris Crawford, 1813-1815," *Georgia Historical Quarterly* 60 (Spring 1975): 9-23.

"The Independence of Latin America: North American Ambivalence, 1800-1820," from Heald and Kaplan, *Culture and Diplomacy,* 66—91.

"Founding Fathers on the Founding Fathers: Reflections on Three Generations of American Diplomatic Historians," from Society for Historians of American Foreign Relations, *Newsletter* 6, no. 4 (Dec. 1975): 1-8.

ENTANGLING ALLIANCES WITH NONE

AMERICAN FOREIGN POLICY IN THE AGE OF JEFFERSON

LAWRENCE S. KAPLAN

*"Peace, commerce, and honest friendship
with all nations, entangling
alliances with none"*

Jefferson's First Inaugural Address
4 March 1801

THE KENT STATE UNIVERSITY PRESS
KENT, OHIO AND LONDON, ENGLAND

© 1987 by The Kent State University Press, Kent, Ohio 44242
All rights reserved
Library of Congress Catalog Card Number 86-27840
Manufactured in the United States of America
ISBN 0-87338-336-2
ISBN 0-87338-347-8 (pbk.)

08   07   06   05   5   4   3

Library of Congress Cataloging-in-Publication Data

Kaplan, Lawrence S.
   "Entangling alliances with none".

   Bibliography. p.
   Includes index.
   1. United States—Foreign relations—1783-1815.   2. United States—Foreign
relations—Revolution, 1775-1783.   3. Jefferson, Thomas, 1743-1826—Views on
international relations.   I. Title.
E310.7.K37   1987   327.73   86-27840
ISBN 0-87338-336-2 (alk. paper) ∞
ISBN 0-87338-347-8 (pbk. : alk. paper) ∞

British Library Cataloging in Publication data are available.

In memory of Albert Hall Bowman

Jeffersonian

CONTENTS

PREFACE

The essays and monographs included in this volume have been written over a thirty-year period and derive in spirit if not in content from ideas conceived and worked out in my doctoral dissertation on Jefferson and France. While many of my initial conceptions have been modified over time, the theme of American isolationism underlies all the chapters. Understanding this particular species of American exceptionalism remains an inspiration in the 1980s even as it was in the 1950s.

This search began in Samuel Flagg Bemis's seminar at Yale in 1948. While its direction did not always accord with his views, I would like to acknowledge with appreciation his support for my studies. A number of scholarly institutions deserve my thanks. The American Council of Learned Societies granted a pre-doctoral fellowship in 1950-51. In later years the American Philosophical Society gave grants in 1967-68 and in 1969-70. As a fellow of the Woodrow Wilson International Center for Scholars in 1974, I had the equivalent of an academic year to work on the Age of Jefferson. In bicentennial convocations in Kent, Ohio in 1976, in Washington, D.C. in 1978 and 1983, in Paris in 1978 and 1986, and in Amsterdam in 1982, I had opportunities to refine my thoughts on the subject.

Two friends in particular deserve more than the few lines that I give them here. Bob Ferrell has been a guide ever since a seminar session in 1948 when he diplomatically suggested that my description of Napoleon Bonaparte as "little corporal" was not only inaccurate but uninspired. Throughout, Al Bowman has taken the time and trouble to read all my writings. His commentary has been critical but always supportive. I want to add a special note of thanks to Bo Heald for permission to incorporate two chapters from our *Culture and Diplomacy* into this volume.

I would like to acknowledge also the role of John Hubbell, colleague in the History Department and director of the Kent State University Press, in encouraging me to publish this book. The work of flattening angularities and minimizing infelicities has been done by my editor at the Kent State University Press, Flo Cunningham. The final typing, accompanied by frequent helpful observations, was done by my special word processor, Marge Evans.

INTRODUCTION

There is little controversy over the most vital function of American diplomacy in the first generation after the Revolution: namely, the securing of a tenuous independence continuously threatened by Great Britain and France. There is consensus as well over the sense of security won by the War of 1812, to the extent that American sovereignty was never to be challenged again in the nineteenth century. Where dispute exists it has been over the meaning of isolationism. This twentieth-century term has particular application to World War I, as noted in chapter 7. The thesis that may be found elliptically, and occasionally specifically in these chapters, devolves on the assumption that the United States sought to maintain its independence by isolating itself from the political life of the Old World. The warnings of George Washington in his Farewell Address, the aspirations of Thomas Jefferson in his First Inaugural Address, and the challenge of John Quincy Adams in the Monroe Doctrine, all speak to the benefits of isolationism from and the dangers of involvement with Europe.

The trouble with the concept of isolationism derives in part from definition. It is obvious that it cannot mean literal isolation from Europe, in the manner of a Chinese wall that Jefferson once wished would serve that purpose for America; Europe impressed itself upon the nation throughout its history by the flow of its culture and by the migration of its peoples. Nor was there any absence of economic connections. While the activities of Chestnut Street, State Street, and Wall Street reflected a more independent financial system after 1815, the volume of American trade with Great Britain increased, particularly in cotton for British factories, while British capital itself was a major factor in the opening of the West, from railroads to mines. Such continuing ties with Europe were more than matched by American concerns with Latin America and particularly with Asia over the next century.

Given these realities it is hardly surprising that scholars in this and earlier generations have discounted or scoffed at the idea of isolationism. A particularly active school of diplomatic historians, identified with Wisconsin historians Fred Harvey Harrington and William Appleman Williams, found no evidence of isolationism in American history. Rather, it has been marked by expansionism at every stage and in more than one form. The drive for markets may be traced to the beginnings of American national

INTRODUCTION

history, and even earlier in its colonial experience. Territorial expansion—the Louisiana Purchase, the Florida acquisition, or the Mexican War—can be identified with a nationalist pressure for conquest of territories, as well as economic exploitation of those lands.

All of the foregoing interpretations of American foreign relations may be valid and persuasive. None of them, however, are incompatible with a view of isolationism as abstention from political or military obligations to Europe, from alliances or from purposeful entanglement in the European balance of power. The Convention of Mortefontaine went part of the way in achieving this separation in 1800; France and the United States were cobelligerents not allies in the War of 1812, as chapters 9–11 reflect. But Jefferson's use of the embargo in 1807 was hardly an abstention from entanglement in the balance of power; rather it was an effort, as suggested in chapters 7 and 8, to exploit an American role in that balance. To the very end of the War of 1812 there were Federalists so anxious to maintain a tie with Britain that their opposition to the war took on the form of treasonous collaboration with the enemy.

What the events of the first four decades of American independence reveal is that the bonds of Europe were too difficult to break. Ideological ties to a French republicanism or political hopes of a French counterweight to Britain, or links to both powers at one time or another to win concessions from Spain in the New World, compromised the ideal of isolationism on the part of Jeffersonians. Similarly, visceral fears for the survival of Britain as the hope of civilization, or economic concerns for markets and credits, obscured a recognition that Hamilton himself fitfully articulated: namely, that the strong American economy he urged through his Federalist program was aimed ultimately at a British competitor. The close financial and economic connections that he urged were essentially temporary expedients to be employed until America could throw off its dependence on Britain. As observed in chapter 5, Hamilton's support for a strong central government in the *Federalist Papers,* like his plan for import duties in 1791, were aimed at Britain far more than at France. Domestic manufacturing would eventually make America independent of British sources. His protective tariff failed in 1791, and his subsequent preoccupation with the Jacobin menace of the 1790s as well as his own ambitions for power distorted these goals and cast aside the particular kind of independence that both Jefferson and Hamilton sought for the United States at the beginning of the Washington administration.

If Jefferson's intimacy with France has outweighed consideration of Hamilton's with Britain in the historiography of American diplomacy, it is in large measure because Jefferson was the dominant figure of his age. His career spanned the entire period of the early republic, and his presence was felt not only at its creation through the Declaration of Independence but also over the next fifty years when his voice would be heard urging Madison toward war in 1812 and Monroe toward an accommodation with Britain in 1823. France was always in his line of vision from its timely support in the revolutionary war to its position as counterweight to British economic control in the 1780s, to its role as protector of republicanism in the 1790s, and finally as unwilling, even unwitting, builder of an American empire in the Napoleonic period. Throughout his long career Jefferson valued his ties with France and savored the way of life he had found there.

Whether these sympathies with Frenchmen and with French philosophy were translated into service to France or to abandonment of America's independence from French politics is another matter. As presented in chapter 1, Jefferson was a pragmatist who seized on a French connection to serve America's search for freedom from European, particularly British, control. It did not mean that he wished to substitute French for British suzerainty. He occasionally lost control of his emotions in the heat of domestic politics or in the heady aftermath of a seeming diplomatic coup, as shown in chapter 2. And his pleasure in things French was as genuine as his dislike for things British. Yet there were always limits to these sentiments. Jefferson valued his British friends and some British institutions, no matter how distasteful he found British cuisine, while his exposure to France as minister led him to recognize limitations among his French friends that inspired despair as well as irritation.

From the earliest days of his public life Jefferson was conscious of the differences between the Old and New worlds. There was nothing innocent about a conception of a happier society in America that needed protection from an exploitive Europe. Britain may have been its progenitor but it was an alien power even in Jefferson's youth, with no more emotional ties, let alone legal claims, to America than the Declaration of Independence or the *Summary Views of the Rights of British America* (1774) indicated. Furthermore, Jefferson would come to share the views of Thomas Paine and John Adams that Europe's dependence upon America's resources would encourage the support of Britain's rivals without granting concessions. Adams's Model Treaty of 1776 hypothecated French intervention at no cost to American interests. The price that America would gladly pay would be switching its trade from Britain to France. A further reward to France would be the effect of Britain's loss of an American empire upon its standing among the nations of Europe.

The course of the Revolution did not work out quite as Jefferson or Adams had hoped. An entangling alliance with France had to be negotiated before French military power would be engaged in America. And in the aftermath of that war both Adams and Jefferson, as diplomatic representatives in Britain and France, respectively, had to cope with consequences which left America nominally independent but in reality a pawn in French statecraft and a victim of British economic reprisal. Chapter 3 reveals their efforts to win Dutch help for the weak and divided Confederation and to use the fate of the Netherlands as an example for the new nation to avoid. Jefferson and Adams emerged from their experiences abroad appreciative of the need for an America strong enough to withstand the pressures of a hostile Old World.

It was easier, however, for Adams to carry his penchant for a strengthened central government into the Hamilton camp than it was for Jefferson. The latter's goals for America never really deviated from either Hamilton's or Adams's, but his concerns about the maintenance of individual liberty against a powerful state separated him from Adams temporarily and from Hamilton permanently. The mood of America as Jefferson returned home in 1790 was conducive to a rapprochement with Britain. With a stronger central government American entrepreneurs could look to Britain for renewal of economic connections, on somewhat different terms from those of colonial days, but on terms close enough to be called "neocolonial," as in chapter 4. This spirit embraced by the Federalist party in the 1790s deepened as Britain was conceived to be the defender of civilization against revolutionary France. For some Federalists the links to Britain would become almost as firm as they had been before 1776; Hamilton himself required a British connection not simply to achieve the kind of economy he wanted for America but to achieve the military ambitions he had set for himself as the decade came to a close. Others were so attached to the former mother country that they lost their American moorings in the War of 1812 and afterwards.

Yet as Washington assumed the presidency, there was among Americans of all factions a consensus based on an America free to develop itself independent of European ties. The French alliance had lost meaning for Jeffersonians as well as Hamiltonians in the early 1790s. As for Britain, Hamilton himself expressed doubts concerning the embrace of the powerful British that were worthy of Adams's or of Jefferson's own concerns, at least until the French revolutionary war in 1793 became a matter of debate in American government. Such is the claim in chapter 5.

The sharp divisions over the course of America's relations with the European powers reached their height in 1798 when the Federalist administration unilaterally broke the alliance with France and seemed poised to place America on the side of Britain through an undeclared naval war with France. Despite all the charges hurled at "monocrats" and "democrats,"

"Francophiles" and "Anglophiles," the distance between the antagonists was never as great as their rhetoric suggested. Adams's own suspicions of Hamilton's political and military intentions, along with his recognition of the futility of engaging in a full-scale conflict with France, helped to bring some perspective to the domestic turmoil of the late 1790s. If Adams was suspicious of Hamilton and disaffected from Britain, Jefferson in turn had increasing doubts about France of the Directory and even about the alliance itself. While the breach between President Adams and Vice-President Jefferson was not to be healed in 1800, the final bilateral termination of the French alliance was accomplished, as shown in chapter 6, with the ungracious acquiescence of the latter.

Jefferson as president was certainly politic in flattening differences between Federalists and Republicans in his inaugural address. He also expressed a belief that France was not trustworthy as an ally for America. It had become just another European adversary after the Consulate to be approached warily and without illusions.

This did not mean that Britain and France were to be placed on precisely the same footing. Britain was simply the primary adversary. The advantage that France could provide the United States, as seen in both chapters 7 and 8, was that of a counterweight against the greater threat. Jefferson feared and distrusted Napoleon increasingly through his presidency; but as long as Britain could manipulate America's economy and as long as its military strength, through the British navy, was the more direct challenger to America's sovereignty, the British menace took priority in his considerations. To cope with this problem, France and French connections could be used to America's advantage. After the success of the Louisiana Purchase, Jefferson was even more emboldened to play off the one European power against the other. It was a dangerous game, as the unhappy history of the embargo reveals. But it was no aberration for the head of a small country to seek its survival in a world war by exploiting such influence as it had to win its national objectives.

While Francophilia plays a minor role in these scenes, Jefferson's tilt toward the French side in the Napoleonic Wars was genuine and carefully contrived. It was based on a perception that France was less dangerous to the health of America than was its adversary. The lesson Henry Adams drew from Jefferson's presidential experiences was that a small power would lose in this contest, as Jefferson did. Adams's picture of the president was a mix of pity and contempt, as Napoleon took advantage of American weakness. Jefferson did overreach himself. He was carried away by the apparent triumph over Louisiana, but he never became a puppet or even an ally of the French emperor.

INTRODUCTION

In his last years in the White House and during his long years of retirement the virtues of isolationism were underscored by the turmoil that American foreign relations underwent in the first decade and a half of the nineteenth century. Frustration over foreign affairs stimulated Jefferson to subordinate his attachment to agrarianism to the building of an American autarchy that would be free of European interference. Manufacture of goods formerly bought abroad, building of roads and canals to distribute them throughout a growing America, and ultimate acceptance of a new national bank to provide credit and strong currency to make an American economy have all been identified with Henry Clay's "American System." It found its inspiration in the trials Jefferson and Madison suffered in dealing with a nation caught up in a European-centered economy and in a European war.

Despite repeated rebuffs from Napoleon, Britain remained the Jeffersonian bête noir. Its defeat, coupled with France's exhaustion, seemed preferable to continuing assaults on the nation's sovereignty. With the failure of the embargo, Jefferson was resigned, as suggested in chapter 8, to war with the British sooner or later. He did nothing to discourage the breaking of ties, and even encouraged Madison to consider a Canadian invasion as a means of fighting a war successfully. Madison was as conscious as his predecessor of the possibilities pitting one adversary against the other. Chapters 10 and 11 present the role Madison wished France to serve as the United States went to war against Britain. If this was alliance, it was informal, temporary, and exceedingly cold-blooded. As in the American Revolution France would help America in achieving success against the British enemy. It was a dangerous gambit that almost ended in disaster for the United States. But unlike the formal alliance with France in 1778, the war ended in a detachment from both Britain and France, which made the War of 1812 a second war of American independence. The result was isolationism from a Europe no longer engaged in wars on the high seas and from a Europe whose markets became less important for the American economy.

Still, the break was not complete. Europe's struggles continued to impress themselves upon America's consciousness in the decade after the Napoleonic Wars ended, but on a lower level and with fewer tensions. The United States could look with some dispassion upon Spain's attempts to repossess its lost empire in Latin America. As chapter 12 explains, the Latin American revolutions against Europe had attracted North Americans as a source of economic opportunity or as a happy by-product of the example set by the United States. But Americans never accorded Latin Americans a sense of seriousness and commitment to their cause. Despite the excitement immediately preceding the issuance of the Monroe Doctrine there was no genuine fear of the kind that had moved Jefferson and Hamilton in the 1790s, that Russia or France or Spain would disturb the balance in the Western Hemisphere. Britain by this time may have been disturbing, but as an economic rival in the area not as a political or military threat to America's security. Rather, it was the opposite. Just as France had been perceived, often inaccurately, as a buffer for the United States, so, more accurately, Britain of the mid-nineteenth century was the unwitting protector of American isolationism. Given Britain's imperial concerns, defense of the high seas and of the American continent against European interference was always in that nation's interest.

The Monroe Doctrine was a fitting symbol for the completion of a political isolationism that had begun in colonial days. By the time Jefferson and Adams had left the scene, they could look with equanimity at Britain's power, economically or militarily. Jefferson and Madison could even envision collaboration over Latin America. Secretary of State John Quincy Adams opposed such collaboration; it might have undermined successful detachment from European commitments. But then again a new involvement need not have resulted from a limited engagement with Britain.

The keys to American behavior may be found in the general reduction of the importance of foreign affairs in American life, including the affairs of Latin America. Over the fifty-year period the idea of Europe's distress becoming America's advantage, as Samuel Flagg Bemis observed over sixty years ago, served to make Europe less threatening as it became less significant. Given the perils that were faced and overcome by the nation, some of them in the first fifty years of its history, its leaders could look ahead after 1823 with recognition that the perils of the next generation would come from the expanding American empire rather than from the world across the Atlantic.

PART ONE:

JEFFERSONIAN BACKGROUND

1

‖ THOMAS ‖ JEFFERSON:

THE IDEALIST AS REALIST

No statesman of the revolutionary and early national periods made a more substantial contribution to the development of American foreign policy than Thomas Jefferson. From his magnificent synthesis of eighteenth-century political theory in the Declaration of Independence to his death fifty years later, Jefferson's idealism, tempered by pragmatic regard for practical realities, played a key role in defining a distinctively American position toward the external world. No one, it might be said, ever blended the moralistic yearnings of the young republic for a new international order with the practical pursuit of national self-interest more effectively than he.

Examination of Jefferson's amazingly varied career and multiple talents highlights the Renaissance quality of his mind and work. For another man any one of his accomplishments would have assured the homage of posterity. Over a span of eighty-three years Jefferson pursued an astonishing range of activities: he was largely responsible for founding the University of Virginia; he was an architectural innovator who helped bring classical forms to the New World; he was an agronomist experimenting with transplantations of rice and silk to the South; he was a theologian who attempted to harmonize Christianity with the temper of the Enlightenment. Above all, he was a scholar in the art of government whose ideas spread through the nation as Jeffersonian democracy. The prestige conferred by authorship of the Declaration of Independence and the power of the presidency ensured dissemination of his ideas in a manner rarely available to political theorists. If his virtuosity did not encompass an appreciation for the intricacies of finance, that shortcoming stemmed less from a lack of understanding the techniques of moneymaking than from a taste that placed spending above getting. Against the bankruptcy of his Monticello estate must be weighed the credit of a life-style that warmed guests in the beautiful mansion with their host's hospitality as much as with fine French wines.

This westerner belonged to an aristocratic family, the Randolphs of Virginia. His father had improved his status by a wealthy marriage. As a member of the governing elite of the colony, Jefferson early experienced British and European influences flowing across the ocean to Tidewater and Piedmont Virginia. While there may have been few artists or scientists at the College of William and Mary in the colonial capital, there were sufficient men and books to initiate the youthful Jefferson into the life of the eighteenth-century liberal mind. He enjoyed the best of both the Old and the New worlds, sharing the excitement of European ideas that ranged from Arthur Young's tracts on scientific farming to the disputed poems of Ossian. Books and papers from European centers found their way to Jefferson's library and to the drawing rooms of Williamsburg and Philadelphia. He was very much a member of the international fraternity of literati that pumped liberal ideas into the courts of Europe and the coffeehouses of America—ideas that ultimately pushed both along the road to revolution. Jefferson's intimacy with scholarly men such as Professor William Small of William and Mary and George Wythe, his law teacher at Williamsburg, and with such sophisticated men of the world as Francis Fauquier, lieutenant governor of Virginia during his student days, were experiences he repeated in Philadelphia and Paris in later years. True, the above names almost exhausted the roster of interesting people in colonial Virginia, but the

4

point is that his circle of acquaintances included some of the broadest intellectual interests there; his six years at the village capital provided him with an extraordinary range of ideas.

At the same time, perhaps more than any contemporary, Jefferson captured the best elements in the transatlantic civilization of the colonies. As an American living close to the frontier he appreciated the richness of his environment and recognized the advantages of a land with few people and abundant resources. The agrarian society he so valued bred equality among its members, fostered self-reliance, and opened opportunities for individual growth that the Old World could never provide; his experiences encompassed facets that Europeans could not share unless they came to America. Jefferson understood what the challenge and opportunity of empty land meant in the life of a man; he could see in a practical way government expressing the will of the body politic. He lived in a society free of most of the oppressive traditions of the Old World. His father had surveyed the lands that became the first political units the son encountered. He understood the strengths and weaknesses of Rousseau's natural man; he knew that the theory of Rousseau and Locke was reality for an American.

Membership in the exclusive group that controlled the colony set Jefferson apart from most of his fellows and conferred special advantages on him. Good fortune allowed him to live a life transcending that of the colonial yeoman, whose scarcity of cash and education limited his freedom to roam physically and intellectually; his appreciation of democracy had an aristocratic base in a deferential society. Granted that class distinctions were slighter than in Europe and lacked philosophical and practical support, Jefferson was, nonetheless, a "gentleman," comfortably fixed in his milieu. He could practice the arts of government as proper and entirely natural functions of his place in society: vestryman in his church, magistrate in the local community, delegate to colonial and national legislatures. Of course, opportunity in the abstract beckoned all men—and it was more than just a pious abstraction in America as compared with other societies—but for men of Jefferson's class there simply was a larger share of opportunity. Others were similarly endowed; his special distinction lay in his genius, in those qualities of mind and spirit that allowed him to range over the whole experience of mankind and distill its essence in lucid prose.

His public career spanned the period from the conclusion of the French and Indian War in 1763 to the end of his second presidential term in 1809, years in which he turned his talents to the creation and maintenance of independence from Great Britain. Jefferson was not concerned with reordering the internal society of America or with indulging private interests. His greatest satisfactions derived from such contributions to political philosophy as were found in the Declaration of Independence or in political practice, from his part in organizing the Northwest Territories, or from the educational theory he bequeathed to the University of Virginia. His primary work, however, was in public affairs, particularly the relations of America with Europe. It could not have been otherwise.

For him, as for all the Founding Fathers, the central event of life was the creation of a nation out of thirteen disparate British colonies. Every step in making the Revolution and in securing it afterwards involved foreign affairs. In such a context, conventional divisions between domestic and foreign affairs lost meaning. In the first generation of the Republic no national leader could escape awareness of the hostile outside world. Europe intruded in every way, inspiring fear of reconquest by the mother country, offering opportunity along sparsely settled borderlands, arousing uncertainties over the aliance with a great power. Unless the new nation settled for a subsistence economy its prosperity rested upon trade with the Old World; the European market held the American economy captive, and no political theory could alter that fact of economic life. There could be no escape from such concerns, any more than from the language Americans spoke, the customs they followed, or the ideas they circulated.

Anglo-American relations dominated American history in the early years of the Republic. Despite a successful military separation, the economic links of tradition proved more enduring than the political, even though many people, Jefferson included, wished it to be otherwise. If an alternative to a British connection existed, it was not to be achieved by retreating into autarchy but by shifting the economy toward France, the wartime ally; it was to France that those leaders suspicious or fearful of British designs turned during the administrations of George Washington and John Adams.

Anglophiles and Francophiles alike, however, held a different view of Spain, the third major European nation whose interests impinged on those of America. For most Americans, Spain presented an object of aggrandizement and exploitation, a weak state whose territories might be despoiled, or at least kept out of the control of other European powers. As Americans looked southward and westward at insecurely held Spanish territory they envisaged a future continental empire of liberty that would free them from the superpowers of the day.

The record clearly reveals the Jeffersonian involvement in foreign affairs. His service as delegate to both Continental Congresses, as wartime governor of Virginia, and as commissioner to France at the end of the war were all linked to French and British influences in American life. During the Confederation period he represented the United States in Paris, attempting to mobilize support for its continued independence. Upon return to America he became secretary of state, the first in the revitalized union, absorbed in assuring survival of the nation in a hostile world. The French Revolution and its subsequent wars dominated his years as vice-president and president. The magnificent acquisition of Louisiana, though not wholly his doing, deservedly is credited to him; and the disastrous embargo of 1807, though not wholly his mistake, if mistake it was, appropriately is identified with him. Success or failure, Jefferson the public man was of necessity a maker of diplomacy.

Jefferson's enemies of every generation make much of what they consider his deficiencies in character. Most dwell on his inconsistency, pointing out that he shifted from one position to another at critical moments out of fear of consequences, instability of judgment, or passion for power. Thus, his movement from strict to loose construction of the Constitution, from agrarianism to support of manufacturing, from fear of executive power to abuse of it in office, from a love of France to distrust and finally to dependence upon that country under Napoleon have all been used by enemies who would dismiss him as weak, cowardly, opportunistic, or worse. His Francophilia has been interpreted as a personality quirk with dire consequences for the country.

Much of the familiar Federalist criticism of Jefferson withers in the face of close examination. A far better case may be made of excessive consistency, of an allegiance to a conception of society long after it had become obvious that the ideal could not be sustained, or of reliance upon economic weapons against Europe after those weapons were turned against him. Jefferson never questioned what he wanted for America; he envisioned a society of cultivated, independent men on terms of equality with one another, keeping government as close to the local level as possible, living on farms rather than in cities because the agrarian life best propagated the good life. Expansionism became part of the plan because an American empire would remove the corrupt and dangerous model of Europe, as it would if the pattern of international commerce could also be reorganized to incorporate the American alternative to mercantilism, free trade. He identified urban commercial society with class conflict, with oligarchic manipulation of politics, and with European financial control over America, most especially Great Britain's economic interests in its former colonies. To combat such dangers, he believed that right reason applied to the right environment would create a society embodying the best blend of the Enlightenment with the frontier.

He never abandoned his vision of the good society. Apparent deviations were responses to external pressures or were expedients, temporary tactical retreats. He shared with other Founding Fathers a belief that alliances with European powers were unnecessary and potentially dangerous to American independence. His musings about a relationship with Europe "precisely on the footing of China," while fanciful, were genuine; and he knew that in an imperfect world less desirable choices sometimes had to be made to attain more desirable ends. Thus, an alliance with France might be made if Britain threatened the nation's independence; the danger of a connection with Europe had to be balanced against the greater damage that defeat or accommodation with Britain might bring. When France took over the Mississippi outlet at New Orleans, Jefferson contemplated a marriage of convenience to the British fleet and nation. Similarly, he recognized that an embargo on trade would require cultivation of manufactures and urban growth in violation of his preference for an agrarian America; when he saw the alternative as acceptance of British domination, he took the risk. No one celebrated the virtues of limited government more eloquently than Jefferson, but he realized that they had to be subordinated to the need for a national government strong enough to enforce the embargo, just as in earlier years the state governments of the Confederation, though in his view better custodians of freedom than a more centralized union, had to give way to the Constitution when the Republic's survival was at stake. In 1803 Jefferson's firm commitment to strict construction of the Constitution conveniently expanded to avoid loss of a vast empire in the West.

Jefferson's statecraft invited criticisms. His means occasionally distorted his ends and diminished the stature of the man who tolerated the distortions. Indeed, he paid for his concessions by witnessing before he died some of the unfortunate consequences he had always feared would follow from the promotion of an industrial society, and his reliance on economic coercion exacerbated international tensions while it created new domestic ones. If he did not also pay for France's exploitation of his too ardent sympathy, it was only because he refused to confess to any errors of judgment in a pro-French policy.

Part of the explanation of Jefferson's flexibility lies in his early recognition of the importance of the external world in American affairs and in his firm belief in the permanent hostility of Great Britain. Preservation of the new nation from the baneful effects of those realities required statecraft; if Jefferson sometimes overrated the efficacy of diplomacy, he seldom underestimated the danger of involvement in transatlantic affairs. Ultimately, of course, Americans sought a solution in withdrawal from the European arena into their own empire, into a peculiarly American isolationism wherein obligations to Europe did not exist. In one way or another nearly every American statesman worked to free the nation from dependence upon Europe.

When Jefferson was secretary of state in the 1790s, his countrymen differed violently about the direction of foreign affairs, especially about the American response to the French Revolution and its subsequent wars. The powerful commercial interests of New England and the seaboard towns looked to Great Britain as a necessary business partner, at least until a viable domestic economy could be created. Many of its leaders equated a pro-British policy with freedom from French ideology and French imperialism. Jefferson and his followers never accepted such views. They believed, at least until after the War of 1812, that Britain intended to reduce America to a position of permanent inferiority in an economic relationship more suffocating than the political connection had been before independence. Like their opponents the Federalists, Jeffersonians responded emotionally to events in France, but they read their import differently. They believed that if the French republic collapsed in its war with monarchical Britain, monarchy if not British rule would return to America.

Jefferson's anti-British animus had deep roots. It grew in part from wartime experiences and received repeated reinforcement during his career. At times his fears approached obsession, but he directed these sentiments more to particular institutions and proponents of policy than to Englishmen per se or to the benign aspects of British culture. However flawed, the British political system surpassed any in Europe; and even when in France desperately seeking help during the Confederation period, Jefferson could in good conscience recommend to French friends that they follow the British political model. If Frenchmen kept in view the example of their cross-channel neighbor, he told Lafayette, they might advance "step by step towards a good constitution." His feelings for English friends remained as warm as his feelings for Frenchmen. He admired the liberal English reformers whose Anglo-Saxon traditions in law and language he claimed for America—indeed, he who had paraphrased Locke's political philosophy could hardly do otherwise.

In some respects this common heritage exacerbated problems between Britain and America, for the mother country lacked the excuse of ignorance for its abuse of freedom and its threats to liberty. Because Britain had extended its heritage to the New World, British behavior became intolerable when it selfishly and abruptly deprived colonists of their right to tax and govern themselves through their own representative bodies. By such actions the ministers of the Crown behaved unconstitutionally. In his *Summary View of the Rights of British America,* presented to the First Continental Congress in 1774, Jefferson had observed that emigrants had come to the colonies as free men, voluntarily adopting the mother country's system of law; they wished to continue their union by submitting to a common sovereign, "The central link connecting the several parts of the Empire thus newly multiplied." All that Americans wished from Britain, he argued, was a restoration of lost liberties, a recognition of their rights as Englishmen. In failing to respond to this understanding of Anglo-American relations, the British invited application of the principles of natural right philosophy, which permitted, even demanded, separation from a ruler who had broken the social contract; for as Carl Becker has said, by 1774 such an interpretation had become "familiar doctrine to all men."

Jefferson and his colleagues thought that if the right of revolution was accepted as natural, circumstances justified it, and they made their case in the Declaration of Independence. Whether they read history and law accurately, the nature of the charges they brought against their sovereign continued to absorb Jefferson's attention for more than a generation. Throughout his public career he saw British policy as part of a plot to subvert American liberties. That plot ranged from the imposition of taxes and the incitement of Indian massacres to destruction of American trade and suspension of the rights of self-government—all for the "establishment of an absolute tyranny over these states." British policy did not change after independence. As Jefferson left office in 1809, he saw the Orders in Council of 1807 as merely another version of the Crown's long-standing attack on "trade with all parts of the world"; impressment was a means of forcing captive Americans "to bear arms against their country"; intrigues among Federalists and Indians were continued royal attempts to excite "domestic insurrections" and to incite "the merciless Indian savages." The hostility that had provoked the Declaration of Independence in 1776 also provided the rationalization for the embargo in 1807.

Of course, experiences in the critical decade after the Treaty of Paris, when he served as minister to France and as secretary of state, had reinforced the Jeffersonian image of Britain as a malevolent force in American affairs. The Orders in Council of 1783, directed against American trade and removing it from imperial preference, corroborated his worst fears. By following the advice of Sheffield rather than the more liberal inclinations of Shelburne the British intended to maintain control over American commerce with minimal reciprocity under their navigation system. British mercantilists abolished subsidies for critical American exports, denied American ships entry into the West Indies, and accepted American goods in Britain on terms no more favorable than those granted European nations. Such was the price of independence, for British ministers correctly anticipated that the impotent government of the Confederation could not implement retaliation by higher duties on British goods or exclusion of British ships from American ports. To many it seemed that Britain had determined to exploit those structural weaknesses and take advantage of the inability of the states to act in concert.

The first minister in London, John Adams, recognized to his despair that Whitehall's policy would enrich Britons at the expense of Americans, and might destroy the new nation in the process. In a brief visit to London in 1786, Jefferson experienced firsthand the contempt for America that the arrogant British had been demonstrating to Adams. His impressions were even darker than those of his Massachusetts friend, for while the king had at times been civil to Adams, he snubbed Jefferson, moving the latter to rage, "That nation hates us, their ministers hate us, and their king more than all other men."

The French connection, so frequently and so pejoratively identified with Jefferson, derived largely from the foregoing emotion and from the problems that evoked it. To escape the web of British mercantilism and to foil expectations of a collapse of the republican experiment, France became a counterweight to British influence and an instrument of American survival; Jefferson saw opportunity, he thought, to use that country's friendship and alliance as a balance to British power and to build more satisfactory commercial arrangements in international trade. He had not forgotten the enormous service that French arms, supplies, and money had rendered in the revolutionary war; nor had he forgotten the self-interest that had inspired that aid. He hoped to exploit such impulses for further service.

Like Franklin before him, he found the task of winning French friendship a highly congenial one. From his first contacts with Frenchmen during the war he had prized the manners and customs they had brought with them; lengthy and spirited talks with Lafayette and Chastellux in Virginia foreshadowed the pleasure he found in French culture and cuisine. While he may not have been quite the traitor who "abjured his native victuals" for foreign food, as Patrick Henry claimed, he did become a lifelong enthusiast for French food and wine. More importantly, he found in Paris a lively appreciation of the American model of the good society which French reformers wished to use in reshaping their own country. When Jefferson became minister he assumed rightly that he would receive the homage his predecessor had won, and he basked in the veneration of the new American society as he followed a scenario limned by that great diplomatic impresario, Benjamin Franklin. Jefferson, like Franklin, sought to exploit the sympathy of the French intelligentsia for America to bend French political and economic policies to the service of the United States.

These objectives monopolized Jefferson's time in France between 1784 and 1789. Initially, the minister concentrated on securing treaty relations with European powers modeled on the 1778 commercial treaty with France. To the new republic political recognition was an important mark of international respectability; the psychic value apparently outweighed the practical. Such treaties seemed to confer legitimacy, almost as if the more agreements one made, no matter how little trade resulted from them, the more certain the permanence of the United States became. Sweden and Prussia signed liberal treaties with America, without affording any substantial material advantages. Those contracts reflected the optimism of 1776 when Americans expected, as Thomas Paine's *Common Sense* suggested, that the world would applaud the new nation's challenge to British leadership in international trade and its arbitrary control of the seas. The next step, expansion of the Continental Congress's Model Treaty of 1776, would be European acceptance of free trade and freedom of the seas, in which the advantage of a small maritime country would be united with the larger conception of a foreign policy following moral law. Philosophes and physiocrats and their American disciples, among whom were Benjamin Franklin and Thomas Jefferson, tended to imbue free trade with nearly mystical qualities; to them it was a panacea for the world's ills, a cure for wars and international rivalries. It followed, as Felix Gilbert has said, "that in a reformed world, based on reason, foreign policy and diplomacy would be unnecessary, that the new world would be a world without diplomats." It also followed that in such a world Americans would reap enormous economic advantage.

Experiences with the French alliance toned down some of Jefferson's expectations for the implementation of such a new order, but despite his awareness of the limitations of treaties and of the shortcomings of European altruism, he continued to believe that the words of the philosophes and the sentiments of French liberal circles could be shaped to American advantage. He spoke the language of the physiocrats when he argued for the removal of trade barriers, pointing out that such barriers on the Continent pushed American commerce into British ports. By appealing to the reformers for support he hoped to serve his country's interests and those of the new international order, the postrevolutionary world that would be governed by the laws of nature. At the same time, while waiting for that new order, he urged upon the ministers in power a full reciprocity of economic policy on the practical ground that all the sacrifices France had made to achieve independence for its ally would be wasted if America returned to the British connection by the back door of economic dependence.

On paper, Jefferson's initial negotiations had some small success. The combined efforts of the physiocrats and the Anglophobes, particularly those in the foreign ministry, overcame many of the obstacles to direct trade. The French lifted import duties on American whale oil as a result of his pleas, and he made spectacular if insubstantial gains in breaking down exclusive arrangements that Philadelphia entrepreneur Robert Morris had made with the powerful syndicate of financiers, the Farmers-General, who controlled the French tobacco market. New trade opportunities opened to Americans.

Few of them lasted, however. The antiquated economic structure of the ancien régime could not tolerate the innovations Jefferson advocated. Suspicious from the beginning of the freer access to their domestic market, the Farmers-General found their prejudices confirmed when they observed that American merchants used their French profits to buy more goods from British manufacturers rather than to reinvest in France. Such a turn of events might have been predicted, for the French lacked both goods and credit to replace the British, even if the tug of habit could have been resisted sufficiently to nudge American importers from familiar connections across the Channel.

Appreciating these obstacles, Jefferson hoped to surmount them by having the French compete with the British in products needed in the American market and by having them develop more sophisticated and flexible marketing techniques. That effort failed. For one thing, even his allies in the foreign ministry, Vergennes and his successors, did not support it vigorously; but perhaps more importantly, it soon became apparent that the allies were working at cross-purposes, with the Americans seeking strength and independence through the French, while the latter looked with equanimity on continued American dependence upon France. Vergennes hoped to exploit the uncertainties of America's future, for as long as the United States could not meet its international obligations, France's role as its protector would remain paramount. In the Quai d'Orsay expectations of continued influence over American policy counterbalanced American dependence upon the British economy and inability to pay the French debts. Moreover, the ministers would be making a virtue of necessity, for no diplomat could make permanent constructive change in the rigid economic structure of prerevolutionary France.

The frustrations engendered by American impotence in foreign affairs and a recognition of the limits on its power of persuasion in the international arena heightened Jefferson's sensitivity to the key events of the last years of his mission to France: the Constitutional Convention in America and the Revolution in France. In his own mind these events were related. Reports from home of dissatisfaction with the Confederation produced conflicting emotions. Suppression of Shays's Rebellion in 1786 and the reputed dominance of Robert Morris's faction in Philadelphia made him despair over the future of the Republic; the avarice of financiers and the anarchy of farmers disturbed him equally, for he saw in both dangerous threats to the safety and security of the nation. Although concerned over the damage demagogues might do to the Republic, he nevertheless retained his sympathy for the complaints of farmers and frontiersmen that stimulated protests against the government.

Rebellion became embarrassing at a time when French reformers looked to the United States as a model. News of transatlantic repression invoked the irony of despotism coming to the New World just as the Old sought to emulate the principles of 1776. In this frame of mind Jefferson reacted to news from Philadelphia. Patrick Henry and James Monroe described the work of the convention as illiberal and aristocratic and fed his initial suspicion of the new Constitution.

Suspicion did not remain the final Jeffersonian position on the federal union contrived at Philadelphia, and he did not return to America in 1790 pessimistic about its future. The views of James Madison and his own recent experiences led him to the conclusion that a stronger government was necessary to assure the nation's survival. Safety in a hostile world required a centralization of power and a unified voice in foreign affairs. He accepted a post as secretary of state in Washington's cabinet on the assumption that the new government would strengthen the nation's hand in international affairs, that it would resolve the problems of diplomacy that the impotence of the Confederation had exposed. Long before the convention assembled at Philadelphia, he had observed that a primary object of his treaty negotiations was to take commerce out of the hands of state governments and to place it under the control of Congress until the states removed the imperfections of the Confederation by a new compact; while the convention deliberated he asserted that the states ought to be "made one as to all foreign, and several as to all domestic matters."

Indeed, one of the unifying forces in Washington's cabinet during much of his first administration was the broad agreement of its members about the need for a strong government and a powerful executive to manage it. Factional antagonisms that later divided the nation—problems of strict versus loose interpretation, of Anglophilia versus Francophilia—existed in embryo at the outset of the Washington era, but in 1790 pressures over the immediate course of the nation's foreign policies overwhelmed them.

Although Jefferson returned home with distrust of Britain and admiration for France, he brought with him no illusions about Franco-American relations. His experiences had revealed important qualifications about the nature of French benevolence. Such optimism as he displayed rested not on any agreements between the two governments or decrees that France had made in America's favor, but on expectations about the more liberal regime that appeared in the making after destruction of the Bastille. As he took up his duties France had not yet revealed the full dimensions of change; in 1790, as in 1787, it still closed the West Indies to American ships and retained its monopoly of American products entering France. Jefferson felt that France had not yet seen its self-interest, had not yet recognized the mutual advantages that would flow from the new politico-economic system proposed by America.

To effect a new relationship with France and to break the old one with Britain required a centralized government strong enough to command the respect of its peers in the international arena. In this view Jefferson was at one with John Jay and Alexander Hamilton. Like the former (who had been secretary for foreign affairs under the Confederation) he believed that if Europeans saw an efficient and well-administered national government, with its trade and finances prudently regulated, they would be disposed to cultivate American friendship rather than risk its resentment. This theme, which Jay stressed in the third *Federalist,* found a harmonious response in Jefferson, and he could even join with Hamilton when the New Yorker asserted in the eleventh *Federalist* that "a steady adherence to the Union" might allow the new nation to tip the scales of European competition in the New World for the benefit of Americans. Thus, a commonly recognized impotence in foreign affairs provided a powerful stimulus for strengthening the powers of the central government. The Founding Fathers, even when they could agree on little else, all sought to exploit European disadvantage for America's advantage.

Historians have not always recognized that Hamilton and Jefferson shared belief in a strong executive able to resist congressional encroachments upon its power in foreign affairs. Jefferson earlier had expressed approval of the constitutional device that freed the central government from the interference of state assemblies on matters of taxation; now with the new government in operation, he thought that the federal legislature's natural tendency to interfere with presidential responsibilities must be resisted. In a memorandum to Washington, presented shortly after he took office, the new secretary of state questioned the propriety of presidential consultation with the Senate about diplomatic exchanges. Arguing that there was no constitutional requirement for such solicitation and that the practice would create an unfortunate precedent, Jefferson interpreted senatorial powers as extending no further than approval or disapproval of nominees. Even then, he envisioned the decision as basically presidential—almost exclusively so, "except as to such portions of it as are specially submitted to the Senate. Exceptions are to be construed strictly." Jefferson's rigid construction of the Constitution in 1790 was hardly distinguishable from that of the Hamiltonians around him, including the secretary of the treasury himself.

If the Jeffersonian vision of American foreign policy began with an executive free of congressional constraints and the shortcomings of the Confederation, it included other elements customarily identified with his great rival, Hamilton: repayment of obligations to foreign creditors through assumption of the debts of previous governments and the promotion of American shipping through an effective navigation system. New England merchants and Philadelphia creditors welcomed these facets of the Hamiltonian program, and, to a point, so did Madison and Jefferson. While it is true that from the outset Jefferson had many reservations about his cabinet colleagues, especially when he suspected them of monarchical tendencies, he could work with them during the early years of Washington's administration. He could tolerate Treasury intrusion into his department by Hamilton's involvement in consular affairs, as long as he believed that Jeffersonian views received a fair hearing. His rivals in the cabinet in those early years were "good men and bold men, and sensible men."

Not even the Nootka Sound affair in the summer of 1790 fully revised that judgment. Although Jefferson strongly opposed Hamilton's wish to grant a British request for the passage of troops through American territory in the event of war between Spain and Britain over the Pacific Northwest, he had no knowledge of Hamilton's intimate connections with British agents. Nor did he adamantly oppose concessions to the British per se. His point simply was that concessions ought to be reciprocal; the United States ought not surrender a bargaining weapon in advance. In their first cabinet debate on foreign affairs Hamilton and Jefferson differed more on tactics than on ideology.

Of course, Hamilton's early hostility to discriminatory legislation against British shipping did evoke criticism from Madison and Jefferson, but not the deep emotional response it was to arouse in 1793–94. Hamilton, after all, had a navigation system, and that was a step in the right direction. It took time before Jefferson's mind converted Hamilton's behavior into a dangerous passion for monarchy and a fatal dependence on Britain.

In part, at least, Jefferson's tolerance for failure of punitive measures against the British may have flowed from the concurrent insensitivity toward America displayed by the liberal regime in France. While the revolutionists had reformed their government under the National Assembly, nothing in those reforms served the interests of the United States. To his chagrin, Jefferson realized that the new bourgeois rulers of France had no more intent than the mercantilists of the old regime to permit liberal terms for American goods in French markets. That realization caught him between anger and embarrassment, for it coincided with a contretemps in relations between the two nations. Madison's navigation law (which failed to discriminate between ships of countries with commercial treaties and those without them) had given rise to a French protest, to which Jefferson normally would have been sympathetic. He recognized that in spirit, if not

16

in letter, it was unfair that British and French ships would receive equal treatment in American ports, and he wished Congress to make special concessions to the French in return for the concessions they had made during his ministry; but French intransigence threatened to undermine support for such an arrangement.

Still, Jefferson sought to exploit the situation. The behavior of the National Assembly freed him from some inhibitions over past French favors and permitted him a degree of flexibility. That France did not see its own advantage in at least removing prerevolutionary restrictions from the West Indian trade seemed incredible to him. His impatience flared into anger when the French consul in New York insisted upon the recall of two consuls whom Congress had sent to the French islands. Jefferson resisted that demand, ultimately winning a minor victory when the American consuls were permitted to remain as "commercial agents." That success signified little and the secretary knew it; he harbored no illusions that an entente had been established between the two countries.

Much of his distress in office, then, stemmed less from the Francophobic character of the Hamiltonians than from the fact that the French refused friendly gestures when they were offered. Neither Madison's persistent attempts in Congress to fashion a navigation system that would benefit French commerce nor Jefferson's illuminating reports on the whale oil and codfish industries (with their clear invitation to France to replace those who had built "their navigation on the ruin of ours") struck responsive chords in Paris. Assuming the impossibility of weaning Americans from British ties, the French middle-class leaders of the Revolution wrote off American commerce. They even revoked the minor concessions that Jefferson had so painfully extracted during his ministry in France. The arrival in 1791 of a new French minister, Jean Baptiste Ternant, did not help matters. Ternant found Hamilton more congenial than Jefferson, so when the latter presented a plan for exchanging with the French full privileges of natives in each other's ports, the negative response did not surprise him. To the minister, free trade seemed to reward Britain at the expense of France.

War in Europe, particularly between France and Britain in 1793, changed the immediate course of Franco-American relations. It revived Jefferson's hopes for a new identity of interests between the two countries, although he recognized the danger of American involvement in the European conflict through obligations incurred in the alliance of 1778. For all his rising anger against Federalists and Britons, Jefferson did not envisage American troops or ships fighting alongside the French in the West Indies or anywhere else any more than did Hamilton. Yet the opportunity for exploiting a new French mood to strike out at British suzerainty over trade and arrogance over maritime claims proved too glittering to resist. The republican government of France opened West Indian ports to American ships and dispatched a more amiable minister to negotiate a liberal commercial treaty based precisely on Jefferson's scheme of mutual naturalization. Small wonder that the secretary's expectations outweighed fears as Europe plunged into the wars of the French Revolution.

There was a link between the worsening of Jefferson's relations with Hamiltonians at home and improvement of his relations with France. From 1793 to the end of the decade, first as secretary of state and then later as vice-president, he saw the republic in peril in America and the republic in peril in Europe. France's part as warrior against British monarchy and imperialism sharpened his antagonism toward British agents in America; increasingly, he saw the Federalist faction as a tool of British interests seeking to restore monarchy to America. Such a goal explained the uses to which Hamiltonian power would be put; it explained the failure of his own efforts to reduce British influence and enhance the interests of American democrats. The whole Hamiltonian program—from funding the national debt and establishing a national bank to Anglo-American reconciliation and a pro-British trade policy—became in his mind part of an enormous invisible conspiracy against the national welfare. The European war unmasked Hamilton's real purpose. Such was the Jeffersonian image of Federalism; of course there was a mirror image of Jeffersonians in the minds of their opponents.

Naturally, this Jeffersonian angle of vision enhanced the importance of France as a counterweight to domestic and foreign enemies. While hardly a new position, its urgency intensified after 1793, and introduced a new and ugly dimension into American debates on foreign affairs and domestic politics. The French republic took on symbolic overtones. According to Jeffersonians, France struggled for more than its own survival—the survival of liberty everywhere was at stake. A British victory would reimpose its rule in America, either directly or through Britain's faithful struggle for republicanism in France; although he deplored the losses, he endured them stoically, even philosophically, regarding his friends as soldiers fallen in the battle for universal liberty. "My own affections have been deeply wounded by some of the martyrs to this cause," he told William Short on 3 January 1793, "but rather than it should have failed I would have seen half the earth desolated; were there but an Adam to an Eve left in every country. Left free, it would be better than it now is." Written a month before France declared war on Britain, this letter expressed Jefferson's deep commitment to the cause of revolutionary republicanism. Given that predisposition, his fear of counterrevolutionary Britain and its supposed American agents intensi-

18

fied. The mild challenge raised by Britain in the Nootka Sound affair of 1790 had become three years later a matter of the life and death of a society.

The immediate problem for Washington's advisers, however, was the position of the United States toward the belligerents. To resolve that difficulty, Jefferson laid down a precedent for recognition of foreign governments: de facto control by the government in power. Possession of domestic power and ability to fulfill international obligations were the tests of legitimacy. Even before Washington raised the question of recognition in the cabinet, Jefferson had spelled out his position in a letter to the American minister in France. As he told Gouverneur Morris on 12 March 1793,

> I am sensible that your situation must have been difficult during the transition from the late form of government to the reestablishment of some other legitimate authority, & that you may have been at a loss to determine with whom business might be done. Nevertheless when principles are well understood, their application is less embarrassing. We surely cannot deny to any nation that right whereon our own government is founded, that every one may govern itself according to whatever form it pleases, & change these forms at it's [*sic*] own will; & that it may transact its business with foreign nations through whatever organ it thinks proper, whether king, convention, assembly, committee, president, or anything else it may chuse [*sic*]. The will of the nation is the only thing essential to be regarded.

Jefferson never questioned that the republican government of France should have its minister received, its financial claims honored, and its role as an ally affirmed; when Washington raised these questions after the execution of the French king and the extension of the European war, the secretary of state immediately perceived the mind of Hamilton guiding the president. It outraged him that America seemed more cautious in its support of a republic than it had been in its allegiance to a monarchy. With feeling he asked, "Who is the American who can say with truth that he would not have allied himself to France if she had been a republic?"

In defending the alliance Jefferson marshaled evidence from many authorities on international law of the seventeenth and eighteenth centuries, from Grotius to Vattel. He won his case, at least over recognition and legitimacy of treaties, if not over neutrality. If his position was based on the moral worth of republicans expressing the will of the people rather than on de facto control of France by the Girondists, realism needs redefinition. The scholars of international law help little in understanding the Jeffersonian position, for they can be cited either way, as Jefferson himself did when he dismissed that "ill understood scrap in Vattel" that Hamilton had used to deny recognition and then a few months later cited that same Vattel to refute the French minister's demand for a more friendly neutrality. For both Hamiltonians and Jeffersonians the nub of the matter seems to have been the legitimacy of a revolutionary transfer of power. For the former, destruction of a hereditary monarchy by revolution stripped from the usurpers all international obligations owed to their predecessors; for the latter, revolutionists merely made legitimate what had been doubtful before by exercising a natural right to alter the form of government.

Neither Hamilton nor Jefferson appeared willing to accept the full implications of de facto government as these had been spelled out in Pufendorf's assertion that the actual possessor of sovereignty, however acquired, was entitled to the allegiance of his subjects so long as no claimant appeared with a better, "more legitimate" right. In the absence of such a claimant, Pufendorf asserted, reason dictated that the possessor should continue to hold power. Although this argument fitted nicely into Jefferson's interpretation in 1793, one wonders whether he would have been so solicitous for recognition of a monarchical government if it had come to power by counterrevolution against a republican regime, whether he would have been so insistent upon receiving ministers and authenticating an alliance if the government in question had been British-sponsored or Anglophile. It is reasonable to conclude that for reasons of morality and national interest Jefferson would have taken Hamilton's stance in opposition to a de facto government if the question turned on the situation of 1814 when a monarchy dependent for survival upon Great Britain replaced Napoleon. Perhaps it was merely fortuitous that the first secretary of state found morality on the side of de facto legitimacy in 1793.

Belief in Federalist subversion of America's republican experiment dominated Jefferson's mind for the remainder of the decade. Obsession with Hamiltonian malevolence led him at times to startling judgments couched in picturesque language. Washington appeared elliptically as one of the "Samsons in the field & Solomons in the council . . . who have had their heads shorn by the harlot England." On another occasion he prepared to leave Monticello for a visit to London (which he expected to find under French occupation) to "hail the dawn of liberty and republicanism in that island." His conviction that the Federalists had accepted a British definition of neutral rights and an inferior position in the British Empire merged with the conviction that they also planned a monarchical government for America. Washington was their captive, and while John Adams resisted Hamiltonian pretensions, the second president was also an adherent of a form of society inimical to Jeffersonian values. So the world seemed to Jefferson, retired in Virginia from 1794 to 1796 and then isolated in the vice-presidency during Adams's administration. A quasi-war with France coupled with assaults upon the liberties of republicans lent credence to a nearly paranoid view of America that Jefferson did not alter until he became president.

Yet even in his moments of deepest despair over the direction of American policy under the Federalists, Jefferson resisted his natural impulses to expand the relationship with France, for he knew the limits of counterbalance. Even as he tangled with his rival over neutrality in 1793, Jefferson had no wish to bring the United States into the European war. His opponents were far less fastidious on isolation when Britain was involved. What Jefferson wanted was a benevolent neutrality that would assist France rather than Britain; with it he wished to pressure the British for commercial concessions in return for abstention from the conflict. He failed. Once a proclamation of neutrality had been issued, the possibilities for manipulating it to the advantage of Britain passed to Hamilton, and he made the most of them. There is, however, no evidence that for all his unhappiness Jefferson would have risked a war with Britain. He, rather than Adams, might have reaped the unhappy consequences of Jay's Treaty—and he might have handled them less well.

Jefferson's disavowal of Minister Edmond Genet during his last year in office and subsequent willingness to let the French alliance lapse at the beginning of his presidency provide an appropriate frame for the comment of France's minister in 1796, Pierre Adet, that Jefferson was an "American and, as such, he cannot be sincerely our friend. An American is the born enemy of all the European peoples." Adet recognized a basic Jeffersonian premise that in the midst of war and revolution he had given his fervent blessings to the French cause—but France essentially was an instrument of policy rather than an object of it. Its society, its people, its culture all evoked a genuine Francophilia. In Jefferson's statecraft with France, however, there were always *arrières pensées*.

In picking up the pieces of the Revolution and making them part of an empire, Napoleon Bonaparte recognized Jefferson's unreliability, though he missed no opportunity to manipulate him. The first consul wisely concealed information about the return of Louisiana to France, anticipating Jeffersonian distress at the prospect of a French neighbor replacing Spain on the Mississippi. More than pressure from westerners or taunts from Federalists moved the president in 1803. France, more than Spain, posed an obstacle to American expansion and had to be removed. With Louisiana safely secured, Jefferson could resume his policy of seeking to balance British power with French. The charges of Francophilia reached their climax in 1807 with the embargo, when the president seemingly fitted his scheme of economic coercion into Napoleon's Continental System. Such an attempted accommodation, however, was hardly a mark of servitude; it was rather a gamble based on the assumption that France posed a lesser

21

threat than Britain. However tyrannical the French emperor might be, his rule would pass away, while the threat of parliamentary tyranny in Britain would remain. Moreover, the British danger hit closer to home by virtue of that nation's control of the sea. "I cannot," as Jefferson phrased it, "with the Anglomen, prefer a certain present evil to a future hypothetical one." The nation's survival required playing one power off against another, while keeping free of entanglements with either. The dismal end of the embargo, and war in 1812, revealed the dangerous defects in that gambit.

Jefferson's handling of foreign affairs appeared to move from one position to another—from alliance with France in the 1790s, to threat of alliance with Britain in 1803, to collaboration with Napoleonic schemes in 1807; from restrictions upon congressional authority over diplomatic appointments in 1790, to assertions of congressional prerogative over neutrality in 1793, to enlargement of presidential power in the enforcement of the embargo in 1808; from an appeal for a Chinese isolation from the world within an agrarian society, to a concurrent encouragement of trade with France in the 1780s, to an advocacy of domestic manufactures during his presidency. The exigencies of politics accounted for some of the shifts, but most were more apparent than real.

The primacy of American independence from the Old World remained a constant in Jefferson's thinking. He preferred an agrarian society to an industrial one; but if he had to accept the latter, he wished for an industrial America cut loose from British controls, performing the role France had failed to provide. To ensure insulation from Europe's troubles he pressed for westward and southern expansion to free American borders from the anxieties of war and to make room for the growth of the Republic. Jefferson's early encounters with division and disunity in the Revolution and Confederation had qualified his dedication to state's rights; his major involvement with them was when he felt impotent to control the central government. While he never denied the virtues he had celebrated in limited government, his early advice to Washington and his own behavior during his presidency suggest that when opportunities for vital action by the executive offered themselves the president ought not to be inhibited by excessive deference to congressional or state authority.

The pragmatic strain in Jefferson's management of foreign affairs, which permitted him to accept conditions inhibiting his freedom of action, also permitted him to shape those conditions to his ideas of the needs of the nation. If commercial ties with Europe were indispensable—as they were—he wished them to be conducted with minimal political entanglements as he preached in his first inaugural. He shed no tears for the demise of the French alliance. If developments abroad served the interests of a small maritime power, he could exploit them without surrendering either American interests or principles. Philosophers of the Old World might be enlisted in the American cause, just as the conflicts among European states might serve American trade or territorial advances. Such sentiments marked Jefferson's view of France and his policy toward it.

Whether Europe or America derived more gain from his dalliances remains debatable. What is certain is Jefferson's consistent belief in the justice of his policies; they were moral by virtue of their American character. For all his expediency he never separated national self-interest from morality in the management of foreign affairs. His determination to recognize the French republic in 1793 rested on justice as well as on utility. Recognition appeased his moral sense while it appealed to his practical streak, much as did his ideas on neutral rights and free trade. A characteristic American approach to international relations has been the casting of national interests on a moral base; Jefferson's contribution was to shape this conceit and to seek a relationship with the external world that followed from it.

2

REFLECTIONS ON JEFFERSON AS A FRANCOPHILE

There have been few aspects of the vast domain of Jeffersoniana which have received more attention than Jefferson's Francophilia. Jefferson's complicated relationship with the French patron, ally, and quasi-enemy of the United States during his long service as wartime governor of Virginia in the 1770s, minister to France in the 1780s, secretary of state and vice-president in the 1790s, and president and adviser to his successor in the first two decades of the nineteenth century has been a matter of enduring interest among scholars and statesmen in every subsequent generation. It is still a subject of fascination for what it may tell about the behavioral pattern of an important public figure as well as about the significance of emotion and bias in the construction of foreign policy.

The term, whether or not pejoratively intended, will always be fastened on Jefferson, no matter how carefully such scholars as Gilbert Chinard, Dumas Malone, and Merrill Peterson have separated myth from reality.[1] Even if Jefferson's Francophilia can be proved to have been wholly in the national interest or exclusively a private matter, there will always be a residual suspicion of weakness in his feelings for France. Patrick Henry struck a sensitive chord, one that could evoke outrage among most Americans, when he observed that Jefferson had "abjured his native victuals" in favor of French cuisine.[2] In some circles a French kitchen in Monticello would be considered a mark of sophistication; in many more his palate would be considered part of that "womanish attachment to France" that Hamilton found to be so reprehensible.[3]

Perhaps it is the longevity of the cleavage between Jefferson and Hamilton that makes it impossible to discard the label. A Francophile Jefferson makes a convenient counterpoise for historians seeking ready means of explaining Jeffersonianism and Hamiltonianism. Politicians find the differences equally useful, and it is no coincidence that among their biographers have been important public men such as Henry Cabot Lodge and Claude Bowers.[4] If Jefferson and Hamilton are symbols of the twentieth-century Democrats and Republicans, respectively, it is understandable that those symbols have continuing consequences. For example, a cost-conscious Republican administration in 1953 could find sufficient funds to light the Lincoln Memorial at night, but not enough to light the Jefferson Memorial. Even more illustrative of the power of symbols was the Republican reluctance to continue the presidential stamp series of 1938 which placed Jefferson on the three-cent stamp. The Eisenhower administration abandoned presidential succession when it introduced the four-cent stamp. Lincoln, not Madison, received the honor. The foregoing information appeared in the Trivia section of the April 1955 issue of the *William and Mary Quarterly,* along with a footnote by its editor, Jeffersonian Douglas Adair, in which he observed that "Republicans who were really staunch to their principles and who were determined not to lick the back side of a Democratic President, could, of course, have stopped writing letters; sent all their letters air mail; or combined the 1¢ Washington and 2¢ Adams."[5]

Twitting politicians might be written off as trivial, but there was nothing trivial about the editor's attack upon Hamilton in that issue. The front cover contained his name and vital statistics—born 1755, died 1804—with the notation inside that this was a bicentennial number. It was apparently a noble gesture on the part of a journal connected with Jefferson's alma mater. But when one looks more closely at the gesture, it turns out to be Jeffersonian riposte to a presidential commission appointed on 11 January 1955 to prepare a celebration in 1957 of Hamilton's birth. At the same time Columbia University was to launch its own bicentennial observance by sponsoring a definitive edition of Hamilton's works. Adair's tribute two years early not only scooped Columbia but underscored the fact that Hamilton had lied about his age. The future secretary of the treasury was born in 1755, not 1757, and concealed the truth so that a sixteen-year-old youth preparing to enter King's College would gain recognition as a *wunderkind* which would not have been to an eighteen-year-old young man.[6]

Against the weight of this record it may be futile to suggest that Jefferson's love of France had no fundamental harmful effects upon his relationship with that country as minister plenipotentiary in the 1780s, as secretary of state in the 1790s, and as president in the first decade of the nineteenth century. On the contrary, he had intended at every opportunity to manipulate France for America's advantage, an intention he had signalled from his first days as a diplomatist. Whatever pleasure he derived from French friends—and it was considerable—he was always aware of their potential influence on the monarchy, the Directory, the Consulate, or the empire. As he told Monroe in 1804, he hoped that suggestions passed on to influential French friends "would do us good if known to their governments, and, as probably as not, are communicated to them." He was confident that he could make "private friendships instrumental to the public good by inspiring a confidence which is denied to public, and official communications."[7]

This was no idle boast. His exploitation of Du Pont de Nemours to inform Bonaparte of American displeasure over potential French occupation of New Orleans in 1802 was a dramatic case in point. It is irrelevant to point out that Louisiana was not ceded because of Jefferson's statecraft, or that the president deluded himself about the extent of his influence. What counted in the Louisiana Purchase, as in the embargo a few years later, was the service Jefferson intended France to render the United States in a world dominated by Great Britain.

Jefferson's ideas were not unique. They went back to a grand design conceived in the Continental Congress which rested on the outside world's recognition of America's economic strength as the key to independence from Britain. As Thomas Paine expressed it in the winter of 1776, "Our plan is commerce, and that, well attended to, will secure us the peace and friendship of Europe."[8]

Ultimately it would do even more. As Europe competed for America's trade, it would permit the United States "to steer clear of Europe's contentions, which she can never do, while, by her dependance [*sic*] on Britain, she is made the makeweight on the scale of British politics." Jefferson shared

26

this vision, which was to materialize in the Continental Congress's Model Treaty of 1776, and expanded on it over the years. France's role in it became increasingly important, first as a military partner and then as an economic partner. He encouraged France to develop an industrial and credit system that could free Americans permanently from British goods and British creditors. It was not that Jefferson considered the end product a perfect solution for the new nation; the ultimate goal was freedom from dependence of any kind, from the controls of any part of the world. But until that day France had a function to perform as a countervailing force that would keep Britain at bay. Such was the meaning of Franco-American collaboration. Its essense was expressed two weeks before his retirement in 1793 as secretary of state in Jefferson's Report to the Congress on the Privileges and Restrictions on the Commerce of the United States in Foreign Countries, a document that Merrill Peterson has called his "farewell address."[9]

Although France never fulfilled the role Jefferson assigned it, its potential governed Jefferson's diplomacy through much of his career, helping to explain his pressure on the ancien régime to ameliorate its commercial restrictions against American products, or on the National Assembly to forsake its mercantilist biases. By the end of the 1790s his economic expectations were gone, but the political need for a strong France to counterbalance British power remained in place, even if illusions of fraternity had disappeared along with the Directory. His linking of Bonaparte with Hamilton as fellow men-on-horseback attests to the low esteem in which he held French republicanism in 1800.[10] Yet France's failure to maintain its revolution did not prevent him from seeking to pit France against Britain on the assumption that Britain continued to be the more immediate threat to the United States. As he confessed in the wake of the *Chesapeake* crisis in the summer of 1807, it was "mortifying that we should be forced to wish success to Buonaparte, and to look to his victories as our salvation."[11] But there was little choice. A few weeks later he repeated that he "never expected to be under the necessity of wishing success to Buonaparte. But the English being equally tyrannical at sea as he is on land & that tyranny bearing on us in every point of either honor or interest, I say, 'down with England' and as for what Buonaparte is then to do with us, let us trust to the chapter of accidents. I cannot, with the Anglomen, prefer a certain present evil to a future hypothetical one."[12]

Jefferson's feelings about France and Britain were rarely presented so boldly as in the above statements. His positions on the Franco-American alliance of 1778 (he gradually but steadily backed away from its commitments) were more characteristic of his style. Like most of his countrymen he welcomed French aid during the American Revolution; his problems as governor of wartime Virginia inevitably pushed aside any reservations he might have had about deviations between the ideals of the Model Treaty of 1776 and the reality of the alliance of 1778. Besides, the obligations of the alliance seemed remote when France was fighting the British on American soil. During his years as diplomat in France in the 1780s or as secretary of state before the outbreak of war in 1793, the alliance was no more than a minor tool in his attempts to pry economic concessions from the ally. It lurked in the background for fifteen years, at most a source of vague uneasiness over its guarantees "from the present time and forever, against all other powers . . . the present Possessions of the Crown of France in America. . . ."[13]

The French West Indies became a problem only when the French National Convention engaged in war against Britain in 1793. It forced Washington to clarify the American position in this conflict in April of that year. Hamilton goaded Jefferson over the validity of the alliance and its obligations. Of the former Jefferson had no doubt; of the latter he stood close to Hamilton despite his inclinations. The secretary of state may have had different reasons, but he wished for neutrality as resolutely as Hamilton. Vulnerability to British economic pressures as well as to British naval power in the Caribbean made an American role in the defense of the French West Indies an impossible goal to achieve even if it had been a desirable one. The most Jefferson would do for the ally was to promote "a fair neutrality" that would serve France as American vessels carried French goods in accordance with liberal understandings of neutral maritime rights.[14]

When neither the British nor the Federalists would concede even this much to France, Jefferson had no weapons with which to fight back. He was handicapped by the overriding necessity to avoid war with Britain over neutral rights. So the "disagreeable pill" Jefferson had been worried about when he mentioned "a fair neutrality" became a poisonous one for Franco-American relations when he had to deny to the French minister Edmond Charles Genet the right to equip and arm privateers in American ports or dispose of French prizes in America. The secretary of state did not flinch from telling Genet that while Article 24 of the Treaty of Amity and Commerce specifically denied a mutual enemy the privilege of fitting ships or selling prizes in the ally's ports, it did not imply that the ally would have this privilege.[15] With all his attempts to avoid damaging or even offending a friend, he was as instrumental as any American in stripping all benefits from the alliance.

Franco-American relations worsened after Jefferson left office. The Jay Treaty with Britain in 1794 made further sport of the alliance as it played with the question of privateers. Almost in parody of Article 24 of the Franco-American Treaty, Jay's Treaty, also Article 24, employed much the same language to deny specifically to the French ally the privilege of army privateers in American harbors. And in Article 25 Britain was to enjoy whatever favors the alliance had given to France. Jay's Treaty distressed Jefferson and his friends. But even as they railed at the growing Anglo-American intimacy nourished by the Federalists and praised the French military efforts against the monarchical forces of Europe, they never accepted the claims of alliance. If the Franco-American alliance came up in their correspondence, it concerned fears that either a French repudiation or a Hamiltonian denunciation of the alliance would be a prelude to war with France and a Federalist alliance with Britain. So long as the alliance existed, even if only on paper, war would be averted. His own role as participant in provocations against France went largely unnoticed except by such perceptive observers as the French minister Pierre Adet who commented in 1796 that "Jefferson . . . is American and, as such, he cannot sincerely be our friend. An American is the born enemy of all the European peoples."[16]

Once the XYZ crisis and the threat of formal war with France had passed, concern about the alliance disappeared altogether from Jefferson's correspondence. Nonentanglement, a theme of his inaugural address, was his recommendation to Elbridge Gerry, newly returned from France, in January 1799: "I am for free commerce with all nations; political connections with none. . . . And I am not for linking ourselves by new treaties with the quarrels of Europe."[17] This was not mere rhetoric either in 1799 or 1801. It expressed a lifelong judgment which only external pressures could change, and then only temporarily. The subsequent Convention of Mortefontaine of 1800 terminating the alliance was signed by President Adams's commissioners, but it could not have gone into effect without the approval of Jefferson as vice-president and president.

At no time in his last days as vice-president when the convention reached the Senate or as president when he had to return the document to that body did he display any opposition on the grounds that it terminated the alliance of 1778. On the contrary, in responding to the importunities of his friends in France, Thomas Paine and Joel Barlow, he disavowed both the old French connection and France's interest in liberal principles of neutral rights which Bonaparte was then seeking to revive in the form of a new anti-British League of Armed Neutrality. His answer to Paine revealed his relief in "the return of our citizens from the phrenzy into which they have been wrought, partly by the ill-conduct of France, partly by artifices practised upon them." The French shared blame with the Federalists for the troubles of the past decade. "Determined as we are," he assured Paine, "to avoid if possible, wasting the energies of our people in war and destruction, we shall avoid implicating ourselves with the powers of Europe, even in support of principles we mean to pursue."[18] Such was Jefferson's response to Bonaparte's invitation to join his League of Armed Neutrality in 1801.

Jefferson's ideas and conduct fitted the growing isolationism of a nation that felt itself to be victimized by intimacy with great powers of Europe. Genuine as his love of France was it did not characterize his French policy, in 1800 or later. By contrast, the Anglophilia of his rival Hamilton, although resting on an equally sincere conception of the national interest, ultimately infected him, to the point where a sympathetic analyst, Gerald Stourzh, could label his behavior as "sometimes treasonable accommodation with Britain."[19]

Nevertheless, Jefferson's benevolent feelings for France did manifest themselves throughout the 1790s in the form of indiscreet suggestions, flashes of temper, and flights of fancy. None of these should excite surprise. He made no attempts to conceal his belief that Europe's violent assault against the French Revolution was a prelude to an assault against the American republic, and that the Federalist leadership was a surrogate for British monarchy. The bond between the two republics in their respective trials appeared vital at this time. These feelings were all the more lively after the Jeffersonians appeared to succumb to Federalist power. Given his sense of isolation among enemies in the Adams adminstration, Jefferson found conspiracy everywhere in quasi-wartime Philadelphia, gripped by the XYZ frenzy. His friendship for France was being used, he felt, to destroy him and his colleagues. The wonder is not that he lost his balance in this difficult time, but that he was still able to recognize as clearly as he did dangers of too close connection with the enemy of his enemies.

The temptations to identify with the France of the Revolution were occasionally more than he could resist. He cheered along with most Americans the triumphal march of the youthful Girondist minister Genet from Charleston to Philadelphia in April 1793: who "offers everything and asks nothing."[20] He was expansive in his first meetings with Genet and seemed to approve of a French invasion of Spanish Louisiana to be staged from Kentucky with American volunteers. Small wonder that Genet thought he had the backing of the secretary of state for this venture. Jefferson admitted that he "did not care what insurrections should be incited in Louisiana" as long as the United States was not directly implicated.[21] His advice did not mean that he would support action involving the United States in hostilities against Spain; it meant simply that the liberation of Louisiana would not be opposed to American interests. The secretary erred in underestimating the brashness of Genet; the happy mood of republican fraternity which surrounded Genet upon his arrival in the United States affected Jefferson and subsequently embarrassed him.[22]

It was a different and gloomier mood that aroused Jefferson a few years later to defend former Minister to France James Monroe's angry vindication of his behavior in France. Monroe was charged by the Federalists with deluding France into believing that Jay's Treaty dealt with settlement of wartime debts rather than acceptance of British interpretations of neutral rights. Secretary of State Pickering laid as much blame as he could for hostile French reaction on Monroe's Francophilic behavior in Paris in 1794 and 1795. Monroe in turn felt betrayed by the Federalists and mounted a monumental apologia 407 pages long and with a sixty-six-page introduction explaining how his service to the country was undercut by the Federalist failure to cultivate France. Had a different policy been followed French aid would have won American claims against Britain. Both a humiliating treaty and a break with France would have been avoided. His efforts failed, as critics found enough ammunition from his own pen to condemn his conduct. While Madison recognized the futility of the effort, Vice-President Jefferson rallied round his friend. Except for some minor criticism of its title, he pronounced Monroe's intemperate attack against Washington "as masterly by all those who are not opposed in principle, and it is deemed unanswerable."[23] Whatever the merits of principle, Jefferson saw in Monroe's position his own fate as pariah and victim. Love of France was far less in evidence than a visceral dislike of the common enemy of the time—the Federalist at home and the British abroad.

It produced from time to time almost inexplicable outbursts which lent themselves easily to distortion by Francophobes. The most notorious was the famous letter to Philip Mazzei in 1796, in which Jefferson indulged in picturesque hyperbole to damn "apostates who have gone over to these heresies, men who were Samsons in the field & Solomons in the council, but who have had their head shorn by the harlot England."[24] There was another such eruption which, while not receiving the attention of the Mazzei letter, was in its implications even more noteworthy. This occurred in a letter to William Branch Giles, a friendly Virginia congressman to whom he wrote in 1795 about his delight at the success of French armies in occupying Holland and about the happy prospect of French armies liberating all of Europe, including Britain. He was so pleased about the new turn of France's fortunes that he was tempted to leave his "clover for a while" to dine with General Pichegru in London where he could help his French friends "hail the dawn of liberty and republicanism in that island."[25] Jefferson had given way to extravagant statements before in private correspondence, when he appeared to prefer a depopulated earth to the defeat of the Revolution, or when he eagerly anticipated the scaffold for kings, nobles, and priests.[26] Some of the most vivid images were pedagogical in purpose, as Dumas Malone suggests, particularly when he was writing to disciples.[27] But to defend, even to glory in, the occupation of England by France seems to be a step beyond blowing off steam among intimates or using hyperbole for instructional purposes. It could be interpreted at the very least as misunderstanding the American interest in the balance of power. Did he mean what he said?.

A close examination of his statement suggests a temporary derangement. Would Jefferson of all people, this abjurer of native victuals, this connoisseur of French food and wine, seriously contemplate dining again in England? Before he had ever visited that island, he had explained in a letter to Abigail Adams in 1785 why the British were such a difficult race: "I fancy it must be the quantity of animal food eaten by the English, which renders their character insusceptible to civilization. I suspect it is in their kitchens and not in their churches that their reformation must be worked, and the Missionaries of that description from hence would avail more than those who should endeavor to tame them by precepts of religion or philosophy."[28] Here is a cri de coeur of the gourmet. His devotion to French cuisine was that of a convert, and his words those of a true believer. Once in France he left behind him "the Virginia tradition of ham, fried chicken, Brunswick stew, greens and batter bread," as Marie Kimball pointed out in her revealing edition of *Thomas Jefferson's Cook Book*.[29] There is room for study of a possible causal connection between Jefferson's culinary passions and the financial troubles of his last years. A taste for Bordeaux was ultimately beyond his means, at least when coupled with his notorious hospitality.

But the question at hand is how serious was he in inviting himself to dinner in London with a French general. Where would they dine? During his brief visit to England in 1786, he had been forced to eat in the London chophouses of the kind described by Boswell a few years earlier, which no self-respecting Frenchman or Francophile could stomach with equanimity. Indeed one of the chophouses mentioned by Boswell, Dolly's on Paternoster Row, was the subject of an uncharacteristic bit of Jeffersonian doggerel, unearthed by Julian Boyd and thoroughly examined in an impressive page-long footnote in volume 9 of the *Papers of Jefferson*.[30] The apparently extemporaneous verse opened with: "One among our many follies was calling in for steaks at Dolly's." Would the fare have improved then years later? Unless French emigrés had opened up suitable restaurants in the interval, or unless Pichegru would have transported his entire kitchen along with his invading army, the incentive to undertake an arduous voyage to England for dinner would have been no greater than a cross-channel trip had been during his ministry in France. Jefferson's impetuous outburst must be judged as an aberration, one from which he quickly recovered.

Still, there may be an unanticipated and for the most part invisible byproduct of Jefferson's Francophilia in the American tradition of recognizing new governments.[31] The secretary of state's position on the recognition of the new French republic in 1793 set a precedent that marked out the United States position from that of monarchical nations concerned with their European conception of legitimacy. "It accords with our principles to acknowledge any government to be rightful," he instructed Gouverneur Morris, "which is formed by the will of the nation, substantially declared."[32] These principles involved essentially effective governance, discharge of national obligations, and general acceptance by the people. These requirements were comfortable for a nation that won its own independence through revolution. Jefferson made direct reference to the problem of legitimacy when he noted to Morris four months later, "We surely cannot deny to any nation that right whereon our own government is founded, that every one may govern itself according to whatever form it pleases, & to change these forms at it's [sic] own will. . . . The will of the nation is the only thing essential to be regarded."[33] Thomas Bailey in his widely read text has called this stand "in effect a corollary of the Declaration of Independence . . . adopted by President Washington and consistently followed by all his successors, with minor departures, until the time of Woodrow Wilson."[34]

Bailey implies that the United States has deviated from Jeffersonian criteria for recognition by the moralistic judgments exercised in the twentieth century with respect to such governments as those of the Soviet Union, Communist China, and Cuba. Certainly Senator William Borah of Idaho believed this to be the case in 1923 when he castigated the Harding-Hughes State Department and by extension the Wilson-Colby State Department before it for violating tradition by refusing to recognize the right of the Russians to change their government as Jefferson had recognized the right of the French in 1793. The excuse of instability which Colby and Hughes had raised against the Bolsheviks in 1920 and 1923 was inadequate; stability was not a strong suit of France in 1793 when the guillotine removed the heads of successive leaders.[35]

Borah did not reckon with the assumptions of Hughes that the administration's stance was in accord with Jefferson's precepts, and that if the United States did not recognize the Soviet Union it was not because of a revolutionary government but because its regime, like that of Maoist or Castroite governments later, did not represent the will of the people, but rather that of a small tyrannical minority intent on destroying America as well as its own people.[36] It is too frequently overlooked that Jefferson's views, while conforming with the self-interest of a state born in revolution, rested heavily on the consent of the governed. To him there was no question that the destruction of the monarchy represented the "will of the nation," just as there was no question in the minds of Secretary Hughes in 1923 or

33

JEFFERSONIAN BACKGROUND

Secretary Acheson in 1949 that the Soviet Union and Communist China respectively were acting against that will.

Hughes may have been closer to the reality of 1793 than Borah; and if so his "Wilsonian" moralism meshes with Jeffersonian sentiment rather than deviates from a Jeffersonian principle. That the principle was built on an objective realization that the legitimacy of another regime was not a matter of American concern or that recognition did not involve approval was undercut by the emotions which the French Revolution had brought to the surface. It was the French republic in peril that moved Jefferson to his principle, in the face of Hamiltonian opposition. One may reasonably speculate about what his idea of the "will of the nation" might have been if the treaties of 1778 had been made with a French republic, and if the new government of 1793 was a British-supported monarchy which had destroyed the republic. I surmise that he would have rejected recognition as resolutely as Hughes did 130 years later.

This speculation threatens to carry the subject of Francophilia too far afield. Jefferson had enough problems coping with the French republic without my raising an imagined monarchy for him to manage. But he solved most of his problems.

Jefferson's affection for France, its people, and its habits was deep and genuine, but was neither boundless nor guileless. His more fervid expressions of attachment appear to pass quickly rather than persist as reflections of considered policy. They were a measure of the strains he had to endure under the Federalist ascendancy, and may have had a cathartic effect upon him. Once the impulse had been purged—approval of a French campaign in America, defense of a disciple unjustly attacked, appreciation for putative French plans for an invasion of Britain—he dropped the issue that had evoked it. His springtime support of Genet did not survive the summer of 1793; his encouragement of Monroe's views in 1797 was little more than a gesture to a friend; and his fantasy about dining with Pichegru in London was not repeated. Good taste as well as good sense ultimately prevailed.

Did Jefferson's widely advertised Francophilia compromise his position as a public man in any way? In my judgment the direct effect was slight, but he provided enough material in his writings nevertheless to keep the question alive for future generations of historians and politicians to debate.

3

THE FOUNDING FATHERS AND THE TWO CONFED- ERATIONS:

THE UNITED STATES OF AMERICA AND THE UNITED PROVINCES OF THE NETHERLANDS, 1783–1789

There is a long-standing sense of kinship between the United States and the Netherlands rooted in a romantic tradition encapsulated in the preface of John Lothrop Motley's *Rise of the Dutch Republic:* "The maintenance of the right of little provinces of Holland and Zealand in the sixteenth, by Holland and England united in the seventeenth, and by the United States of America in the eighteenth centuries, forms but a single chapter in the great volume of human fate; for the so-called revolutions of Holland, England, and America are all links of one chain."[1] This common history and destiny became all the more meaningful when England was temporarily separated from that chain in the American Revolution. The Dutch then became cobelligerents of Americans in that conflict, served as bankers of the new nation after the war, and were perceived as fellow sufferers for the cause of republicanism and democracy throughout the revolutionary era.

The Netherlands, therefore, loomed large in the minds of the Founding Fathers, particularly John Adams, minister to Great Britain and commissioner to the Netherlands, and Thomas Jefferson, minister to France, in the 1780s. Through their eyes such statesmen as John Jay, secretary of foreign relations, and James Madison, leading Virginia critic of the Confederation, perceived events in the Low Countries. The role that the Dutch played both as symbol and as substance in the fashioning of the federal union is worth examining for the example their experience with confederation offered to the Founding Fathers of the struggling transatlantic republic. The bicentennial year of the Netherlands' recognition of the independence of the United States and its signing of a Treaty of Amity and Commerce is an appropriate occasion for a review of their connection.

It is often forgotten that next to France the financial support and fate of the Low Countries preoccupied Adams and Jefferson from their respective perches in London, Paris, and—at one point in 1788—jointly in Amsterdam. They knew better than their colleagues at home the significant position Dutch bankers were occupying in the life of the American Confederation in the 1780s. In Jefferson's case the success of his mission in Paris depended, he believed, upon the ability of the United States to pay interest on its debts to the powerful French patron, and this could be accomplished only through the assistance of Amsterdam bankers. Failure to secure new loans would damage the Republic's credit rating in the world, perhaps irreparably, and could even be a harbinger of the failure of the republican experiment itself. Consequently, they watched with painful fascination the upheaval in the Netherlands, the stuggle between the Francophile and Americanophile Patriot Movement against the Anglophile stadtholderate which in so many ways seemed to be a proving ground for republicanism against monarchy in the eyes of friends and enemies of America.

Self-interest mingled with and perhaps predominated over the appreciation of the Dutch legacy to America when John Adams in his memorial to the States General of 19 April 1781, petitioning for their recognition of the United States, pointed out that "if there was ever among nations a natural alliance, one may be formed between two republics." Their origins "are so much alike, that . . . every Dutchman instructed in the subject, must pronounce the American revolution just and necessary, or pass a censure upon the greatest actions of his immortal ancestors."[2] Although the horizons of his expectations from this "natural alliance" may not have stretched beyond beneficial commercial relations with the Dutch West Indies and loans and advances on generous terms in a joint war effort, such practical considerations did not detract from the importance of the Netherlands to the future of the American republic.

However manipulative Adams's intentions may have been in linking the destiny of the two nations in 1781, guile seemed almost wholly absent a few years later when he sensed the dawning of a new age in the Dutch Patriots' challenge to the House of Orange. In 1786 his language sounded as hyperbolic as Jefferson's was to be over a similar stirring in France: "In no Instance, of ancient or modern history, have the People ever asserted more unequivocally their own inherent and unalienable Sovereignty."[3] Just as for Jefferson in Paris at the beginning of the French Revolution, the achievement of the Dutch would reflect America's service to a new and better Old World.

When this brave new world was stifled at birth, Jefferson's and Adams's mourning for the Patriot cause was deeper than it would have been for a business partner or a military ally. Years later in his autobiography Jefferson recalled with bitterness and regret the fall of Holland, "by the treachery of her Chief, from her honorable independence, to become a province of England; and so also her Stadtholder, from the high position of the first citizen of a free Republic to be the servile Viceroy of a foreign Sovereign."[4] Jefferson's sentiments about the fate of his friends victimized in the Netherlands in the 1780s and in France in the 1790s were in character. Jefferson rarely could abandon a friend. These sentiments took on special significance when they appeared in the comments of the harsher John Adams. Repeatedly he expressed his pity by identifying the victory of the prince of Orange with "rigorous persecutions and cruel punishments of the Patriots in Holland, which are held out in terror."[5] Abigail Adams shared her husband's sorrow. She wrote to their son John Quincy that "history does not furnish a more striking instance of abject submission and depression" than the conquest of the Netherlands "by a few Prussian troops, a nation that formerly withstood the whole power and force of Spain."[6]

Genuine as these moods were, veering from unbridled optimism to the most despairing gloom, they did not characterize the substance of either Jefferson's or Adams's concerns about Holland during their ministries in Europe in the 1780s. Understandably, the dominant theme and most insistent subject of communications across the Atlantic was the state of America's debt to Dutch bankers and the continuing need to float loans in order to sustain the shaky fiscal structure of the Confederation. Given the critical nature of the problem, the attention of diplomats abroad had to center on coping with its implications. Adams had labored under enormous handicaps to initiate loans in the first place, in the face of the unwillingness of the

37

JEFFERSONIAN BACKGROUND

Orangists to embarrass the British by supporting rebellious colonists as well as of cautious bankers concerned about the safety of their investments. Not until the States General had recognized the United States in 1782 were America's sympathizers—and France's friends—in the financial community of Amsterdam able to respond to Adams's importunities. America's chief banker was the van Staphorst family, who also served as the agent of Versailles. Of the 10 million dollars in foreign debt, by 1788 almost half was owed to Dutch creditors.[7] In short, the credit of the United States abroad rested as much in Dutch hands as in those of America's original benefactors, France. The difficulties of a confederal government in New York unable to collect sufficient revenues to pay even the interest on its debts plagued its diplomats abroad throughout the life of the Articles of Confederation.

In this context philosophical speculation about the virtues of Dutch republicanism, or even gratitude for past favors, had to yield to the bleak reality of recommending that Dutch financiers be encouraged to purchase American debts to France on the assumption that defaulting to France would be more dangerous to America than defaulting to private bankers in Amsterdam. As Jefferson put it in 1786, "If there be a danger that our payments may not be punctual, it might be better that the discontents which would thence arise should be transferred from a court of whose good will we have so much need to the breasts of a private company."[8] At the same time Jefferson and Adams were uncomfortable in their knowledge that Dutch speculators had exploitive interests in the American economy. If they were able to buy up the domestic debt as well, they could control the direction of America's economic future. Congress, concerned about the risk of American credit in Holland, turned down the plan.[9]

The problem of excessive dependence was illustrated by the sluggishness of Dutch bankers in floating a new loan in 1786 and 1787 at a time when the Congress of the Confederation could not pay interest on earlier loans. Jefferson was left with the burden of finding ways of meeting unfulfilled payments to French veteran officers of the Revolution as well as the expenses of his own establishment in Paris. The solution suggested in Amsterdam was to seek payment of a year's interest on certificates of the American domestic debt held by Dutch speculators as a precondition for the completion of the current foreign loan.[10] These issues provoked a crisis in 1787 for the two American diplomats, and particularly for Jefferson, who felt intimidated by the intricacies of money questions and who was discomfited further by the prospect of Adams leaving him alone with them by returning to Massachusetts in the midst of the crisis. It appeared that the friends of America in Amsterdam—the Willink brothers and the van Staphorst brothers—had maneuvered the diplomats into a corner.

38

Adams did leave Europe in April 1788 but not before meeting his distraught colleague Jefferson in March at The Hague (where Adams intended to pay a farewell courtesy visit as American commissioner to the Netherlands) and at Amsterdam. There they managed to win a reprieve of three years for the United States in the form of a new loan to meet pressing obligations in Europe. Despite anger on Adams's part and anguish on Jefferson's there was little doubt about the outcome. The Amsterdam bankers had too much at stake to permit the destruction of American credit, as Adams recognized. Moreover, they were well aware that a new government then coming into being in America would repay their investment at full value.

There was a happy ending to the problem of American credit in Holland, and certainly a satisfactory arrangement for those financiers who anticipated the redemption of debts by the new federal government. But they were not achieved before Jefferson, the first secretary of state in the new government, became thoroughly troubled and not a little confused by financial machinations, American as well as Dutch, that he witnessed around him. In New York in 1790 he claimed that he always had been of the opinion that "the purchase of our debt to France by private speculations would have been an operation extremely injurious to our credit; and that the consequence foreseen by our bankers, that the purchasers would have been obliged, in order to make good their payments, to deluge the market of Amsterdam with American paper and to sell it at any price, was a probable one."[11] The secretary of state obviously had changed his mind since 1786, when he thought that such an arrangement was worth making. His education in the mysteries of high finance yielded some cynical insights by 1789. He reported to Jay that bankers would be able to borrow to fill subscriptions just enough to pay interest, "just that and no more or so much more as may pay our salaries and keep us quiet. . . . I think it possible they may chuse [*sic*] to support our credit to a certain point and let it go no further but at their will; to keep it so poised as that it may be at their mercy."[12] Small wonder that Jefferson had an animus against speculators and feared their influence on the economy. It is in this context that he cried out his belief that "the maxim of buying nothing without money in our pocket to pay for it, would make our country one of the happiest on earth."[13]

It was in keeping with his personality that Jefferson's difficulties would be articulated more in generalizations over the evils of speculation than in ad hominem diatribes against the Dutch as speculators. With a more lively paranoic streak to push him, Adams would spell out what Jefferson would only touch lightly. To Adams the troubles over loans were "a mere pretence, and indeed the whole appears to be a concerted Fiction." He wanted to alert Jefferson against "the immeasurable avarice of Amsterdam."[14] Dutch behavior, he claimed, was a product of a national character; they were "a Nation of Idolators at the Shrine of Mammon," he had exclaimed in 1780 when he encountered resistance to his efforts to win Dutch recognition during the war.[15] These slurs were delivered in moments of frustration, but they suggest an unflattering national stereotype functioning in the American psyche. The stereotype appeared more benevolently in Benjamin Franklin's discussion about the facts behind paper money in 1767 when he admonished innocent Americans to observe that "Holland, which understands the Value of Cash as well as any People in the World, would never part with Gold and Silver for Credit."[16] It was a short step from this pejorative appreciation to Franklin's assertion in 1781 that "Holland is no longer a *Nation* but a great *Shop;* and I begin to think it has no other Principle or Sentiments but those of a Shopkeeper."[17]

How much of this sentiment represented the essence of American feelings about the Dutch? How much did it reflect the mood of a crisis, the normal reaction of an impotent debtor to an apparently powerful manipulative creditor? There is no simple answer to these questions. It is worth noting, though, Adams's point that as heartless men of commerce they were even "worse than the English."[18] But the English after all presented more than a legacy of Mammon to Americans. So did the Dutch. In a quiet moment in 1783 Adams confessed that his vexations over loans were as much the product of "clashing interests—English, French, Stadholderian, Republican, and American"—as anything else.[19] And while merchants, bankers, and speculators sought their own advantages from the parlous condition of American finances, the dramatis personae contained Americans as well as Netherlanders. More significantly, there was none of the ideological malice and threat from the major Amsterdam creditors which would have been found among the British or the Orangists.

Similar ambivalent feelings may be found in American views of commercial relations with the United Provinces. Holland's role in the American Revolution as carrier of war supplies and as cobelligerent against Great Britain initially offered ground for optimism over the future of Dutch-American commercial ties. Jefferson had been excited over the prospects since 1776. And as he negotiated for a commercial treaty in The Hague, Adams seemed to share this optimism. He convinced himself at least that Pieter Johan Van Berckel, en route to the United States as first minister of the United Provinces, had concurred in his generalization that those West Indian islands would flourish most "which had the freest intercourse with us, and that this intercourse would be a natural means of attracting the American commerce to the metropolis."[20] Recognizing the inability of France to be flexible in its navigation laws, Adams believed that "we must make the most we can of the Dutch friendship, for luckily the merchants and regency of Amsterdam had too much wit to exclude us from their islands by treaty."[21]

Reality soon intruded to return Adams and his colleagues to their more normal skepticism. The Netherlands, it was obvious, was not different from any other European nation. If the most-favored-nation clause in the commercial treaty of 1782 had any meaning it was only in the symbolic value granted by the fact of an agreement itself, not by a Dutch departure from the restrictive economic system of Europe.[22] Madison was convinced that the British example would dominate Europe. Given the weakness of Congress's power to regulate commerce under the Confederation, France and the Netherlands would do as the British had done: play off one state against another, thereby encouraging disunion as they freely discriminated against American shipping.[23] On occasion the Dutch even appeared more obdurate than their European rivals. Hamilton indulged in the conventional stereotype when he observed that the Netherlands' "pre-eminence in the knowledge of trade" has led them to adopt commercial regulations "more rigid and numerous, than those of any other country; and it is by a judicious and unremitted vigilance of government, that they have been able to extend their traffic to a degree so much beyond their natural and comparitive [sic] advantages."[24] Jefferson seemed to agree with this judgment when he noted gloomily that "Holland is so immovable in her system of colony administration, that as propositions to her on that subject would be desperate, they had better not be made."[25] John Jay added that the Dutch fear of competition made it "look as if the Dutch regret our having found the Way to China, and that will doubtless be more or less the Case with every Nation with whose Commerical Views we may interfere."[26]

But these comments were hardly final judgments of American policymakers during the Confederation about the role of the Netherlands in America's future commercial relations. They were manifestations of unhappiness over the weakness of both the American confederation and its potential European partners which permitted Britain to exploit American trade without fear of retribution. To the end of this period Jefferson still nursed hopes that France or Holland would eventually replace Britain as America's chief trading partner, if only out of their self-interest. Hence, he deplored the actions of individual states in violating treaty agreements with the continental nations and deplored the provision in the Articles of Confederation that permitted states to pass their own navigation acts;[27] they would provide excuses for Europeans to continue in their old ways. He continued to assume that British excesses and arrogance in their control of the American market would stimulate the Dutch or French to liberalize their trade policies with the United States. Although hoped-for lower

41

freight rates and reduced tariffs from their European allies never materialized, the Americans persisted if only because increasing British hostility fostered the illusion of impending change.[28]

Unwilling or unable as it was to respond to American pleas, the United Provinces shared a community of economic interest with the United States which was visible to Louis-Guillaume Otto, the astute secretary to the French minister to the United States from 1779 to 1784. "The Americans' connections with the United Provinces," he wrote, "will remain all the more firm, as they are based on a large conformity of political principles, on an equally strong passion for commerce without a great deal of rivalry, on a similarity of mores and customs, and perhaps also an equally strong hatred for England."[29] Otto envisaged a role for his nation in its benevolent interest in exploiting Dutch and American Anglophobia to link the two republics each to the other and both to France.

The French diplomat was correct in identifying continuing American antipathy toward the former mother country. He failed, however, to anticipate the inability of France to play its part as defender as well as exploiter of the two smaller countries. In 1785, when Otto was writing his memoir, France appeared to waver in its support of the Francophile Dutch Patriots as the Austrians threatened war with Holland over the firing on an imperial ship on the Scheldt. At that time a coalition between France and Prussia on behalf of the Dutch was in the making against Austria and Russia, with England as a neutral in this conflict. Unsuccessful French mediation left the Netherlands with a war penalty of 10 million florins. Two years later the partners in the diplomatic minuet shifted. Austria would play a small role in concert with France against a more powerful British-Prussian combination which was far more serious both to the Dutch and to the Americans.

In 1787 Prussia invaded Holland to avenge an insult to the princess of Orange, the king's sister, by the Francophile Patriots. The Patriot party, a combination of aristocrats and democrats, intellectuals and businessmen, looked to America for inspiration and to France for sustenance. Once again France failed its Dutch friends; the French, intimidated by British influence with the stadtholder and by the ineptness of the Patriot defense, repudiated their alliance. The aristocratic elements among the Patriots then deserted to the Orangists, and the pro-American republicans were sentenced to defeat and exile.

The impact of this event upon Jefferson and Adams was traumatic. It underscored the growing concern about the interference of the major powers in Dutch affairs which was the subject of so much of Jefferson's correspondence to America from 1785 to 1788. If the Netherlands' plight moved them it was not only because the victims were identified as friends of America and the oppressors as supporters of the Anglophile stadtholder; it was also because the troubles of the Dutch confederation could become the troubles of the American confederation; civil war invited foreign intervention.

Jefferson initially displayed considerable sangfroid when the crises began in 1785. He regarded the kindling of the "lamp of war" in the Low Countries as a species of European power politics which would be worrisome to Americans only because peace terms with England had not been fully executed. "That done," he felt, "their wars would do us little harm."[30] Even the Prussian occupation of Holland on behalf of the stadtholder did not fully jar him; he recognized as much as any diplomat the distressing state of France's finances, and understood intellectually their reasons for conciliation.[31] As late as October 1787, after the stadtholder had been reinstated and Britain was obviously triumphant, he still would write that it was "possible, and rather probable," that France would eventually go to war to restore the Patriots to power and humble England once again.[32]

But this was the last shred of wishful thinking. He was no longer above the scene in the summer of 1787 as he reflected on Holland's fate—"a British navy and Prussian army hanging over Holland on one side, a French navy and army hanging over it on the other."[33] No longer did he look upon a foreign war as outside America's concern. He recognized in the summer of 1787 that any war threatening to damage the position of the French ally would endanger the United States.[34] And when France formally announced to the British its intention not to fulfill its obligations to its Dutch ally, Jefferson's panic was complete. He was moved to note an "important lesson, that no circumstances of morality, honour, interest, or engagement are sufficient to authorize a secure reliance on any nation, at all times, and in all positions. A moment of difficulty, or a moment of error may render for ever useless the most friendly dispositions in the king, in the major part of his ministers, and in the whole of his nation."[35]

The experience of the Netherlands was a powerful argument to American witnesses of the evils of the balance of power and the inadequacies of alliances with great powers. Europe is a dangerous place, and its history a warning to America. While there may be temporary advantages in joining one side or another, or occasionally imperative reasons for it, it is always perilous and never to be sought after by the smaller power. "Wretched indeed is the nation in whose affairs foreign powers are once permitted to intermeddle!" Jefferson exclaimed in 1787.[36] Holland was that wretched nation, a "frog between the legs of two fighting bulls," as Adams saw it.[37] And but for the grace of God and the width of the Atlantic Ocean the fate of Holland could be America's as well.

Yet with all the empathy felt for the failed Patriots by Adams and Jefferson there was concomitantly a smugness, a sense of superiority that derived from the Dutch status as Europeans. If they failed, part of that failure was their own doing. Americans at home shared this conceit. The source of many of their impressions of the United Provinces in the 1780s were two diverse personalities: Charles W. F. Dumas, a diplomatic agent for both the French and the Americans and a devoted client of the Patriot cause; and Gijsbert Karel van Hogendorp, a nephew of Minister Van Berckel and advocate of the stadtholder's position. Although the former was closer to Jefferson and Adams personally and professionally, the youthful van Hogendorp presented sufficient counterbalance to Dumas to stimulate American doubts about the anti-Orange forces.[38] There was division among the Patriots between aristocratic regents who wished only to reduce prerogatives of the House of Orange and the more democratic elements who wished to render magistrates more responsive to the popular will and to emulate the activities of the American Revolution, and this was well known to American observers. It was the ineptitude of the latter and the fickleness of the former that colored their judgments. Adams characterized the friends of America as "unskillful and unsuccessful asserters of a free government" who knew too little about history and less about the government. "They have, therefore," mourned Adams, "been the dupes of foreign politics and their own indigested system."[39]

If it was not a case of "plague on both your houses," at least there was a distancing of Americans from even the best-intentioned of the Dutch allies. Distinctions between Orange and Patriot were blurred, for if their old friends the Patriots were to be pitied, "so are their deluded Persecutors."[40] Weighing van Hogendorp against Dumas, Jefferson claimed to be "disposed to wish well to either party only as I can see in their measures a tendency to bring on an amelioration of the condition of the people, an increase in the mass of happiness."[41]

These caveats, however, did not exclude the possibility of reclaiming and rehabilitating the "poor Patriots of Holland," as Washington called them.[42] It was just that their rescue would have to be accomplished by removing them to America and to freedom.[43]

Despite the Olympian tone adopted by the American diplomats, the fate of the United States in 1787 was hardly as secure as their language made it seem. Was the American confederation in better shape than the Dutch? Would the new constitution just then being framed be the solution for the ills which beset the Congress of the Confederation? The statesmen on both sides of the Atlantic could not be certain of the outcome. While the United Provinces was an example to them as they went about creating a federal union, the example was susceptible to differing interpretations.

The initial lesson for Jefferson was the threat to liberty inherent in the elevation of a monarchical prince which made even a weak and divided federation a happier arrangement. The prince of Orange was "a half king, who would be a whole one," as he wrote Abigail Adams, a villain in the sense that George III was to the American colonies.[44] Employing a bestiary image he was to use frequently in the future, he warned against hereditary magistrates and wished "to besiege the throne of heaven with eternal prayers to extirpate from creation this class of human lions, tygers, and mammouts called kings."[45] Benjamin Franklin shared Jefferson's fears, from his base as delegate to the Constitutional Convention in Philadelphia. To him "a single head," the projected federal president, may be sick or malevolent, or responsible for the destruction of a country, as in the case of Holland under the stadtholder, the "Source of all the present Disorders in Holland." If the United States did need a strong executive, he should be, as the stadtholder was not, subject to impeachment.[46] Jefferson's concern about the conditions for an American presidency was even stronger; he worried over the length of the executive's term and the danger of indefinite tenure. The behavior of the stadtholder "would have sufficed to set me against a Chief magistrate eligible for a long duration, if I had ever been disposed towards one."[47]

Advocates of the Constitution conceded that the stadtholderate contained monarchical qualities but either dismissed them as inapplicable to the American executive on the grounds that the president was to be elected periodically or converted the model into an argument against confederation. Madison made a point in the Virginia convention of locating the evils of the stadtholder in the structure of the Dutch confederation itself. Given its inherent weaknesses, he claimed that the prince at least served to keep the faltering nation together.[48] In New York, Alexander Hamilton went further in ascribing merit to the stadtholder; only he was in a position to give "energy to the operations of this government which is not to be found in ours."[49] So, unhappy as the experience of the Dutch may have been, at least its system contained a leader with authority lacking in any officer of the American confederation. The Constitution, according to this line of reasoning, would grant the new president those powers which had made the stadtholder effective while withholding those which could make him a tyrant. Even Jefferson and Franklin ultimately accepted this judgment.

Consistency was not a dominant element in the roles which the United Provinces played for America at the time of its Constitutional Convention and the ensuing debates in state ratifying conventions. It served as a useful metaphor, mentioned, in fact, no fewer than thirty-seven times in 1787 and 1788, to be summoned, as were the Amphictyonic Council and the Germanic confederation, to serve debaters' points.[50] Whether the elaborate re-creation of Dutch history, as presented by both sides at the conventions, was accurate was immaterial. What counted was the usefulness of Dutch history—real, imagined, or just misinformed—as grist for argumentation. Nor did it matter if the precedent reflected favorably or unfavorably upon the Netherlands. At one time, Madison noted Holland's failure to make constitutional changes after four attempts; at another, its success in getting its way with the other provinces through the corrupt influence of its wealth. In the former instance, Holland was the victim of the principle of unanimity; in the latter, the bully of the smaller members of the confederation.[51]

In the end the Dutch proved to be a more serviceable foil for the Federalists than for the anti-Federalists. Not that the enemies of the Constitution did not try to build up a Netherlands in their own image. One method, employed by William Grayson in the Virginia convention debates, was to claim that Dutch problems were not the consequence of misgovernment: "Holland, we are informed, is not happy, because she has not a constitution like this. This is but an unsupported assertion." Moreover, the Dutch had "a fellow-feeling" toward Americans, according to the Virginian, and were willing to continue to loan money to the United States because "they were in the same situation with ourselves." As proof he suggested that their willingness to allow American debts to pile up stemmed from the fact that they have not yet paid their debts to France dating back to the days of Henry IV.[52] Melancton Smith in the New York convention took a similar tack in claiming that the Netherlands, despite so many defects, "yet existed; she had, under her confederacy, made a principal figure among the nations of Europe, and he believed few countries had experienced a greater share of internal peace and prosperity."[53] These were vain gestures. The anti-Federalists' defense of the Dutch experiment was no more successful than their defense of their own Articles of Confederation. There was a consensus among most of the Founding Fathers that the Netherlands was a species of failed confederacies—Greek, German, Swiss—which the American confederation too closely resembled.[54]

But the Dutch republic was not simply a negative model which the Founding Fathers of the federal union sought to avoid. If they were ignorant of or indifferent to the inner workings of Dutch history and government, their knowledge of the events of their own time was full and accurate and important to them. Madison and Monroe, Washington and Jay, knew explicit details from Adams and Jefferson, and their responses were far more perceptive and compassionate than they would have been if the Netherlands were only another case study of an aristocratic republic. The words of the American diplomatists in Europe as well as those of their correspondents at home betrayed an anguish over the sufferings of a kindred people with kindred institutions.

These sentiments were reciprocated in full. Inevitably, considerable Dutch sympathy for the American cause in the revolutionary war had been dictated by an opportunity to capture lost West Indian trade, by anticipated land speculation in the Ohio and Susquehanna valleys, and by the expectation of profits from American securities. But there was additionally a political and ideological content to the economic gamble Amsterdam financiers and businessmen made in their American investment. It was not coincidental that the leading figures in these transactions, such as the financier Nicolas van Staphorst and the tobacco merchant Jan de Neufville, were participants in the Patriot Movement. They equated the victory of America over Great Britain with the defeat of the Anglophile Orange forces and regarded the emancipation of America from the British Empire as a replication of their own secession from the Spanish Empire in the sixteenth century. George Washington was William the Silent redivivus.[55]

There was probably greater sentimentality about the relationship on the Dutch side than there was on the American. The latter were frequently annoyed at the Dutch goals and methods, were convinced that their ambitions were beyond their capacities, and were skeptical of their ability to acquire the kind of self-government Americans possessed. Yet their annoyance appeared to mask fears that American behavior might have been the same in their situation, or even could be in future situations. Hence, the sufferings of Holland provided "a crowd of lessons," as Jefferson put it: "Never to have an hereditary officer of any sort: never to let a citizen ally himself with kings: never to call in foreign nations to settle domestic differences: never to suppose that any nation will expose itself to war for us, etc."[56]

More than fear of a common fate inspired their reactions. The friendship with Patriot leaders evoked emotions greater than the sum total of American self-interest. Adams and Jefferson were deeply affected by the similarities in the direction the Dutch Patriots, or at least the Americanophile segment of them, were traveling. They wished them well even as they doubted their potential to succeed. And when they failed, their American friends beckoned them to be born again in the New World. There they could participate in a political and social order to which they could only aspire in the Old World.

PART TWO

FEDERALIST FOUNDATIONS

4

THE NEOCOLONIAL IMPULSE:

THE UNITED STATES AND GREAT BRITAIN, 1783-1823

Of all the nations confronting the new republic in 1783, none was more important or more threatening to its survival than Great Britain. The reasons for a continuing intimate relationship were obvious. The American language, literature, and economy maintained ties with the Old Country that no political separation could rend. The reasons for hostility were equally obvious. By the terms of the peace treaty of 1783, the United States was obligated to repay debts to British creditors without the power to redeem this promise, and to "earnestly recommend" that the states restore properties confiscated from Loyalists without power to enforce its recommendations, no matter how earnestly they might be made. Within American borders, British troops still remained at seven posts, giving rise to temptations for the stronger power to test the weaker's strength within the next generation. Similar temptations affected the economic connection. British markets and British credit continued to dominate American commerce after the war. These temptations were not to be resisted until the British were prepared to accept the United States as a permanent member of the society of nations, beyond the patronizing acknowledgment of its existence in Article I of the Treaty of Paris. This acceptance would not take place until another war had been fought.

While the pattern in the first generation of independence is complicated, one may discern in it a classical Creole relationship on the part of both Americans and Englishmen. Envy and resentment coexisted with admiration and affection. Americans both imitated and rejected the parental model, while Englishmen both patronized and despised their American clients. In this context, the conventional distinctions between Hamiltonian and Jeffersonian attitudes toward Britain are often blurred. For example, Jefferson's Anglophobia, though genuine and deeply felt, became virulent only when events fed his periodic fears of British reconquest of America by their arms or by their followers. Nevertheless, he always recognized British virtues, particularly their superiority in the arts of governance over the rest of Europe, which belonged to a heritage he claimed for Americans. After the War of 1812, he was willing to contemplate an informal entente with Britain against French or Spanish designs on Latin America. Even at the height of his Anglophobia, he had the prudence to keep Federalist Rufus King as minister in London and to exploit French concern about the British navy to extort concessions in Louisiana.

What united all Americans of this time in their views of Great Britain was the recognition that the relationship was important, for better or worse. For the United States, a foreign policy toward Britain was shaped by the political and economic insecurity of the new nation, a condition aggravated by British power. British posts in the Northwest threatened American control of the frontier; Britain's rule of the seas affected the fundaments of American international commerce; British credits determined the extent of America's economic expansion. Here is sufficient justification for the national schizophrenia over the British, which would have existed even if the special psychological scars from the recent war had fully healed. Anglophobes would have one method of dealing with the British challenge, Anglophiles quite another.

For Britain, the American issue was of far less importance. America was only one part in the British imperial scheme. It is true that the American market and resources were of increasing significance to the British economy. Even in the 1780s, in the midst of the disarray of the Confederation, Great Britain exported 10 percent of its products to the United States, and this figure was to rise to one-third of its total exports by 1801. Nevertheless, the British could afford to indulge their prejudices and resentments against Americans, reasonably secure in the knowledge that the United States was unable to strike back effectively. It could be punished for its revolution and restricted in its role as a competitor without damaging either Britain's market in America or Britain's position as a belligerent in wartime. Successive British ministries acted on these assumptions until the War of 1812.

Diplomatic, commercial, and cultural agents were busy on both sides of the Atlantic to promote partisan views of the proper Anglo-American posture. British mercantilists, fearful of American movement into the fur country of the West, and manufacturers worried over American rivalry did their best to keep the ministry to a hostile American line with the assurance that the republican experiment was bound to fail. To counter these pressures, Americanophiles, ranging from banking partners of American firms to West Indian nabobs dependent upon Carolina provisions, and from free traders following the advice of Adam Smith to libertarians of the order of Richard Price and Joseph Priestley—scientists and divines of rationalism— urged a policy of accommodation with America, noting the benefits a reconstituted Anglo-America would yield.

The different governments of the United States in the postwar period were similarly importuned with advice either to support a Britain under attack from the French Revolution or to strike out at the country which still held posts in America and discriminated against American commerce. Given the greater relative importance of the relationship to Americans, lobbying was understandably more intense in New York, Philadelphia, and Washington than in London. Anglophile propagandists not only made their arguments heard from official positions but occasionally precipitated crises which a softer stance might have averted. Indeed, they fostered misjudgments in England which laid the groundwork for the resumption of war in 1812, long after they had lost all influence with the government.

A reasonable point of departure in any examination of the Federalist relationship with Britain is the Creole complex, which affected the behavior of both parties. For the British, this took the form of a "supercilious assumption of superiority," as H. C. Allen has phrased it.[1] Even when the British court finally accepted an American minister, the latter observed that American concerns "would not be answered with high language, but with what would be more disagreeable and perplexing—with a contemptuous silence."[2] The minister was John Adams, whose sensibilities were easily

ruffled. But his perceptions are echoed repeatedly in the diplomatic relationship, including an offhand notation of his son, John Quincy, that two
of his British counterparts at Ghent "had the English prejudice of disliking
everything that was not English."[3]

American irritation over manners and deportment was reciprocated in
full by Englishmen of every generation. In fact, there was a remarkable
consistency about the views of Englishmen in America, particularly in the
diplomatic community. The hostility of Harriet Martineau and Charles
Dickens, so celebrated in the nineteenth century, may be found in almost
every envoy to Philadelphia or Washington. Since most British official visitors in the first two generations after independence were influenced by the
most disaffected segments of the Federalist party, their distaste was understandable. Still, it often appeared vehemently rather than as just a reflection of the views of American Tories. Even when George Hammond, the
first British minister to the United States, married an American, his dislike
of the people as well as the climate was such that he never returned to the
United States after his service ended. Those British representatives who did
enjoy some popularity outside the circle of Anglophiles did so at the cost of
repressing their genuine feelings. In the case of Augustus Foster, the result
of this exercise in restraint was to offer Americans a "bland exterior,"
which turned out to be an offense in itself.[4] The energy Foster expended in
controlling his amusement or repugnance over the uncouth behavior of the
natives may have been one of the blocks that made him unresponsive to the
threat of war during his ministry in 1811 and 1812. Even the most popular
of ministers in the early national period, Sir Charles Bagot, could not stand
the environment of Washington. He managed to confine his distress over
life in America to confidential communications. As his successor, Stratford
Canning put it: "I consider my residence in America as a second and
rougher period of education; one's passage through it is not unattended
with the privations and annoyances of school, but I do not quite despair of
being able . . . to look back upon it as I now do with thankfulness on the
restraints and disciplines of Eton."[5]

Those who sought to give meaning to a new Anglo-American community either failed to win approval for their recommendations of conciliation
from official policymakers or succeeded unwittingly in distorting the position of their own country in their communications with leaders abroad.
The British friends of America belonged to the first category, while the
American friends of Great Britain fitted the second category. Of the two,
the American Anglophiles had more power and influence in their government, but they ultimately committed more mischief than service to their
cause by fostering illusions in London about American attitudes and plans
at critical moments during the French Revolution and Napoleonic Wars.

No comparable illusions about British positions were raised by Americanophiles in Britain, although they were as earnest and as zealous in promoting the American cause as were their Federalist counterparts. British friends of America were numerous and steadfast, if not as influential. The Whig tradition had a pro-American stamp. Such prominent figures as Charles James Fox, Edmund Burke, and even Lord Shelburne vied with one another in their criticism of their government's American policy during the revolutionary war. Regrettably for the Americans, these sentiments may have been widespread, but they were rarely translated into permanent service to their friends.

From the Treaty of Paris to the Treaty of Ghent, British ministers treated Americans with condescension, contempt, or malevolence. They would concede nothing except under duress, they forced American commerce to conform to their regulations with few gestures of reciprocity, and they injured American pride even when the exigencies of war with France made American trade more important than it had ever been. Great Britain never opened the West Indian ports legally to American shipping, refused to send a minister until 1791, and did not evacuate the Northwest posts until after Jay's Treaty had been signed, and then only after that treaty had yielded the same advantages that France had received in the alliance of 1778. Moreover, the French wars were the occasion for greater restrictions on American trade as the British navy enforced an illegal blockade and put forth unilateral interpretations of maritime law. Throughout this period, Great Britain practiced a policy of impressing into the British navy sailors who were charged with desertion to the American merchant marine or navy.

Relations between the two countries were not uniformly hostile. Bradford Perkins has marshaled impressive evidence to show a genuine rapprochement between the two nations between 1795 and 1805.[6] Foreign ministers Grenville and Hawksbury displayed some appreciation of American sensibilities and participated in propelling the United States for a time into a period of prosperity as neutral America serviced belligerent Europe. During the quasi-war with France, Great Britain winked at American trade with its own West Indies and permitted fraudulent trade between the French and Spanish West Indies and Europe, through its *Polly* decision in 1800, wherein shipments from West Indian colonies were supposedly Americanized by being reshipped from an American port. At the height of fraternization, weapons were even supplied to the Americans, while both parties talked of collaborating in an attack on Latin America. Nor did the election of a Republican president necessitate an abrupt change. In 1803 Jefferson wrote of "marrying ourselves to the British fleet and nation" unless France made the necessary concessions in Louisiana, and Rufus King, the Anglophilic minister to Great Britain under the Federalists, retained his post for two years because the Jefferson administration valued his access to the Court of St. James.[7]

Nevertheless, the price for accommodation with Britain was ultimately too high—subordination to its economy, and acquiescence in its war of attrition with France and, especially, in the role of the inferior in the Anglo-American relationship. If there were periods of remission between 1783 and 1814, they were expediential and short-lived. As the normal British mood of condescension and contempt was intensified by wartime resentment of American profiteering from Europe's troubles, the dominant Jeffersonians mirrored these feelings. To Jefferson and Madison, Britain's discrimination and hostility were a species of the same attitudes that had determined the Revolution itself. The Republican solution, going back to 1789, was to liberate the nation from British economic control even if the French substitute was not suitable. Until long after his presidency, Jefferson felt that England had reconquest in mind and believed that the Federalists, or at least a substantial number of them, participated in schemes for the reestablishment of the British Empire in America.

The ultimate breakdown of relations in war was unwittingly fostered by those Americans who had tied their fortunes to Great Britain. It was their view of America that made the British behavior toward the nation more than a matter of revenge for the Revolution or protection of special economic interests. If British governments disparaged republicanism as an ineffectual system or if they saw themselves as the saviors of the West and guarantors of America's economy, they did so in response to the intelligence that streamed across the ocean for more than a generation from public and private correspondents, on paper and in person, from figures as influential as Alexander Hamilton, secretary of the treasury and adviser to Washington, and Timothy Pickering, secretary of state under Washington and Adams. Representing the wealth and power of New England and the seaboard cities, the Anglophile party controlled American politics in the 1790s and dominated British thinking about America long after it had lost political control.

The Jeffersonian charge that the Federalist elite attempted to create a society modeled on the mother country and in subservience to its interests has considerable merit when one observes the impressions received in Great Britain. For two generations, British ministries operated on the assumption that America would yield in a crisis and that the opposition to Federalism was unable to manage power properly if it ever acquired it. But the charge requires refinement to account for motives. Only a small minority would defer automatically to British wishes. For such Federalists as Hamilton, Morris, and particularly John Adams, the support of Britain was to serve American objectives.

56

In Hamilton's mind, only Britain could provide both the instruments of economic advancement and territorial expansion. Hence, his advice to Washington in 1790 to permit British passage through United States territory in the event of a war with Spain over Nootka Sound in the Pacific Northwest was cool and calculating in origin. If he would accommodate Great Britain, it was because he feared that a denial would be ignored and British forces would then move into Florida and Louisiana without American approval, thereby enhancing British influence along the borders to a dangerous degree. Moreover, by "rendering New Orleans the emporium of products of the Western Country, Britain would, at a period not very distant, have little occasion for supplies or provisions for their Islands from the Atlantic States; and for their European Market they would derive from the same source copious supplies of Tobacco and other articles now furnished by the Southern States: Whence a great diminution of the motives to establish liberal terms of Commercial Intercourse with the United States collectively."[8] If this was Anglophilia, it lacked both an emotional and ideological base.

Yet Hamilton's behavior went beyond this advice to the president. In his anxiety to counter the secretary of state's recommendation to use the Nootka Sound controversy to extort concessions from Great Britain, he sought out George Beckwith, a British agent in Philadelphia, and with the authority of his rank assured the Englishman that the expeditionary force dispatched against the Indians was not intended for use against British posts. Such information undercut the attempts of Jefferson and Gouverneur Morris, Washington's special emissary in London, to exploit the crisis to remove the British from the Northwest and to win commercial concessions in the West Indies. Knowing that the United States would not side with Spain and would not impose a punitive tariff stiffened the British at a moment the ministry might have yielded. By his secret communications to Beckwith, Hamilton gave the British confidence to postpone the very benefits his demonstrations of friendship were supposed to achieve. The most that the cabinet would concede was the dispatch of an official minister, George Hammond, whose instructions specifically precluded a commercial treaty or any serious changes in the Anglo-American relationship. So, no matter how cold-blooded Hamilton's motives may have been, the results of his actions at this moment fitted the role of agent or dupe implied in the title of Julian P. Boyd's book, *Number 7*, the code term applied to Hamilton in Beckwith's dispatches.[9]

With the beginning of the French revolutionary wars in 1792, the emotional dimension of Anglophilia dominated the Federalist outlook on the world even as Great Britain's treatment of American commerce took a turn for the worse. If ever retaliatory action was in order, it was early in 1794 in the aftermath of repressive British orders in council which illegally block-aded France and unjustly seized American ships carrying goods to or from the French West Indies. Chief Justice John Jay was sent to London to protest not only British violations of American neutral rights but also the continuing problem of British troops in the Northwest, now aggravated by British anti-American propaganda among the Indians on the frontiers. Only the Jay mission saved the British from Madison's strict navigation laws, which would have imposed retaliatory duties on British imports. But rather than modify the Federalists' Anglophilia, the party under Hamilton was fastened more firmly than before to the belief that Great Britain was protecting civilization from assaults from atheism and anarchy originating in the French Revolution and extending to France's republican friends in America.

Such considerations moved Hamilton to intervene once again to affect British policy toward the United States. Given the depth of American anger, the British feared an American membership in a new League of Armed Neutrals as much as they did a duty against British shipping. While Jay was deep in negotiations in London, George Hammond, the British minister in Philadelphia, was able to report Hamilton's judgment that "it was the settled policy of the Government in every contingency, even in that of an open contest with Great Britain, to avoid entangling itself with European connexions, which could only tend to involve this country in disputes wherein it might have no possible interest, and commit it to a common cause with allies, from whom, in the moment of danger, it could derive no possible succour."[10] Secure in the knowledge that the United States would not join a revived league with or without Hammond's information Foreign Minister George Grenville was free to ignore Jay's implied threats and to fashion a treaty that yielded little of substance to the American position on neutral rights.

How much the spirit of abhorrence of France animated this private com-munication and how much, in the case of Hamilton, the service to Britain rested on continued expectations of British commercial advantages or on a common purpose against Spanish America will always be open to specula-tion. Certainly, other Federalists made no bones about their identification with the British cause, particularly after the French Revolution became identified with French imperialism in the quasi-war between France and the United States from 1798 to 1800. The independent Gouverneur Morris, who had displayed conspicuous annoyance with Englishmen during his mission in 1790, was sufficiently affected by the threat of the French Direc-tory to serve voluntarily as an observer and propagandist for Great Britain during visits to Prussia and Austria in 1796 and 1797. He urged Grenville to identify the war with the idea Federalists had always associated with the conflict, namely, a crusade against anarchy: "This kind of crusade will not indeed be so wonderful as that which was produced by the preaching of Peter the Hermit, but may answer better purposes."[11]

Anxiety over the possibility of a French victory moved Minister William Vans Murray in Holland and Rufus King in London to serve the British cause in diplomatic ways. Neither statesman was as hopelessly infatuated with the British as some of their more rabid colleagues who had never experienced Englishmen firsthand; King and Murray were of the moderate strain, closer to President John Adams in mood and seeing with Adams the dangers of a full-scale American war with France, which Hamilton and Pickering did not choose to see. Yet King was willing to turn over to his friend Grenville the private correspondence of Murray on the matter of the counterrevolution which Dutch Patriots hoped to make against their French-controlled regime with British help. With King as his intermediary, Murray became Grenville's agent in arrangements with the Dutch underground. Although hopes of Anglo-Dutch cooperation foundered on Britain's insistence upon the restoration of the stadtholderate, the clandestine involvement of American diplomats and the easy acceptance of these activities by Whitehall suggest the role assigned to Americans of whatever rank in the British official mind. The nuances of difference between an independent Adams Federalist and a devoted Hamiltonian went unexamined. For Great Britain, American behavior, even when occasionally indecorous as in King's protests against impressment or obstreperous as in his stand on prerevolutionary debts to British creditors, was still that of the Creole: useful, slightly contemptible, and taken for granted. There was little in Federalist service to the empire to dispute this judgment.

Regrettably for both countries, the advent of Jefferson to power did little to modify Britain's policy toward the United States. French power under Napoleon was more formidable than under the Directory, and the British governments understandably had less appreciation for the sensibilities of Americans under conditions of greater stress. If anything, resentment over America's profiting from her trials helped to produce new frictions and gave Britain justification for its measures. George Canning, foreign minister and leading British antagonist of Jefferson's second administration, asserted in 1808 that "the Strength and Power of Great Britain are not for herself alone, but for the world," and America should be properly appreciative.[12] Augustus Foster was more candid: America should beware. "The two greatest Commercial Nations in the Globe cannot move in the same Spheres without jostling one another a little; where we were aiming blows at the French Marine, we want Elbow room and these good Neutrals wont give it to us, & therefore they get a few side Pushes which makes them grumble."[13]

This mood of truculence toward the United States was translated into a series of offensive actions dating from the Essex Decision in 1805, which denied Americans indirect trade from the West Indies to the Continent, to the Orders in Council of 1807 which denied Americans any trade with Napoleonic Europe unless American ships yielded a middleman's profit paid to Britain through special license fees. All of these decrees were accompanied by the rise in impressment and the expansion of the definition of contraband. Great Britain appeared to be determined to use the crisis with France to destroy rival American shipping interests. In the face of Britain's challenge and Naploeon's counteraction in the Berlin Decree of 1806, which placed the British Isles under blockade, and the Milan Decree of 1807, which ordered any American ships licensed by the British to be seized, the Jefferson administration instituted an embargo on trade with Europe that was specifically aimed at Great Britain.

Great Britain had purposely provoked the Anglophobia of the Jeffersonians to a degree that exceeded the tensions of 1793. The difference in 1807 was that the Jeffersonians were in power and, unlike the earlier years, were in a position to put into effect an anti-British policy. But the British ignored the hostility and expected the same conformity with their interests they had received from the Federalists. It was not that they were unaware of Jefferson's attitudes, particularly after the Louisiana Purchase had ended the skittish detente with Britain which the administration had been apparently moving toward in 1803. They claimed to have exposed clearly the service of Jefferson to France, and they attributed the punitive elements in their decrees to Jefferson's Francophilia. The president, in their view, was either an unreconstructed servant of French revolutionary ideology or in such fear of Napoleon that he subordinated his independence to the emperor's wishes.

The result of such information, freely and extensively offered by Federalist newspapers, correspondence, and visits, was not the modification of British behavior in deference to American Francophilia or American anger. The message that Canning and his associates received was that Jefferson was an enemy but an impotent and inefficient enemy. They could share with the Federalists contempt for the resolution of the Jeffersonians and for their ability to execute an Anglophobic policy successfully. Rather than look upon the embargo as a shrewd and potentially destructive mode of warfare against Britain's wartime economy, they chose to listen to the Federalist diatribes and concluded that the embargo was a last desperate action of a coward unable to strike out in conventional warfare. Moreover, the weapon Jefferson selected would, if pursued, destroy America by ruining its economy and dividing it as a nation. So New Englanders assured the ministry as they volubly opposed measures to close their ports and conspired to separate their section from the Union. England could take comfort in the knowledge that true Americans supported the mother country's fight to defend civilization, American and English. The minority of French sympathizers would eventually be turned out of office. In the meantime, their gestures were too feeble to be taken seriously. Such was the view of America from Parliament, a view formed a generation earlier and unchanged in the Napoleonic period.

Against the massive British confidence built on Federalist prejudice the British voices of opposition could scarcely be heard. As in 1783, distaste for Americans and their revolution prevailed, as well as a continuing unwillingness to have them profit from their new position at British expense. Just as economic advantage had joined with a sense of national interest to give victory to Lord Sheffield's arguments in 1783, so the arguments of Admiralty lawyer James Stephen in his pamphlet, *War in Disguise; Or, the Frauds of Neutral Flags,* found a ready audience in 1805, the year of Trafalgar. Neutrality, he claimed, really never existed; the American neutral trade served France, since most of the cargoes transported to the Continent carried French goods under the fraudulent re-export trade from American ports. Let British seapower stop this trade. If raw materials or manufactured products reached the Continent, there should be a British profit from such trade. Such was the rationalization for the revocation of the permission to "break" a voyage. Stephen's philosophy was justifiable as a vital measure that prevented the enemy from receiving contraband goods as well as a means of forcing British products onto the Continent. Whether or not officially inspired by the Pitt ministry, this pamphlet had Pitt's blessing. The prime minister had seen it before publication and advised a private printing.

The hypocrisy, as much as the hostility, of British policy aroused Americans. Conceivably, the emergency would have elicited many concessions even from Jeffersonians. The abortive Monroe-Pinkney Treaty, drawn up by two diplomats with impeccable Republican credentials, repeated the formulas of the Jay Treaty on neutral rights and even remained silent on impressment in exchange for some relaxation of the issue of broken voyages. Jeffersonians on the scene had some understanding of Britain's problems. Despite his long Anglophobic record, Monroe recognized that there were limits beyond which Great Britain could not go, "when the very existence of the country depended on an adherence to its maritime pretensions."[14] But the insolence of Stephen's approach to Anglo-American relations undid the steps toward reconciliation implicit in Monroe's treaty as it confirmed the malevolence which Jefferson had always believed was the main characteristic of British feeling toward America.

The few Englishmen who tried to stem the tide of economic war and expose the sophistry of the arguments in its favor were isolated and ignored in Parliament. Lord Grenville was unable to work with the followers of Fox to moderate, if not reverse, the orders in council. New men appeared in the Commons to serve as spokesmen for America, and some of them, such as Samuel Whitbread and Alexander Baring, were forceful and articulate. But they lacked prestige and power. Whitbread, a former brewer, also lacked familial connections, and his rigorous criticism could be written off as the posturing of a self-made man. Baring, the most persuasive and resourceful of the critics, was a member of an influential banking family with close American connections; his wife was the daughter of Senator William Bingham of Pennsylvania, and he had financial ties with the Philadelphia house of Willing, Morris & Company. Indeed, he was too closely linked to the United States and vulnerable to charges that his devotion to American causes was more a matter of private than public welfare.

The fears of Whitbread and Baring were realized in 1812. War did result from the divisions between the two countries. The Jeffersonians generated none of the moderating forces that led to accommodation under the Federalists. President Madison's war message referred specifically to Britain's "carrying on a war against the lawful commerce of a friend that she may better carry on a commerce with the enemy." The predictions of economic disaster also seemed verified. Instead of profiting from America's discomfiture, British planters and merchants encountered the beginnings of an American manufacturing base created by the nationalism British enmity had fostered. Even if the British depression of 1810 could not be blamed wholly on the American problem, the decline in commerce with the United States certainly worsened it. The friends of America, Cassandras to the end, at least had the satisfaction of crediting the qualified removal of the offensive orders in council on 17 June 1812, to the distresses they had foreseen.

At the same time that the Americanophiles seemed to find vindication for their stand in London, there was a change in the tone and even the substance of the advice given by friendly Federalists from Washington and Boston. Federalists of an earlier day, such as John and John Quincy Adams, reflected the growing nationalism in America. While many of them abhorred the idea of war with England, their fears were less for the fate of England than for the suffering an unprepared America would endure, as Rufus King saw it, or for the special advantages France would gain from an intimacy inspired by a common enemy, as Theodore Sedgwick recognized.[15] While deploring the behavior of Jefferson's successor, Madison, they were willing to express their disagreement and even distress with British rigidity toward the United States.

The activity of Harrison Gray Otis, a Massachusetts congressman and firm supporter of England, represented the new direction of the more moderate Federalists. In 1811 he tried to persuade the ministry to make partial concessions which could be made with minimal sacrifice of British security. "The American Cabinet is doubtless weak and perhaps not very well affected towards your Country," he wrote. "But you must allow in return that John Bull, though a good sailor, soldier, and in fact on the whole a good fellow, is a bad negotiator and politician." While many Americans were intimidated by France and prejudiced against England, the more intelligent "tremble for the prosperity and fate of Great Britain, and consider her justly as the Bulwark of the liberties of this country and mankind."[16] A year later he urged the Parliament to repeal the orders in council even if the Berlin and Milan decrees had not been genuinely revoked. Otis was convinced that the French would repeat their provocations in the future and awaken Americans to the real enemy of their country. If the ministry did not respond on the grounds that Napoleon's conciliatory gestures toward America were a sham, "the scrupulous adherence of your Cabinet to an empty punctilio, will probably unite the whole country in opposition to your nation, and sever for generations, perhaps forever, interests that have the most natural ties of affinity, and men who ought to feel and love like brethren."[17]

These good pieces of advice were communicated directly to Prime Minister Spencer Perceval by Harrison Gray Otis's Loyalist uncle in London. They were also published by an opposition paper, the London *Morning Chronicle,* and republished on 28 April 1812, by the Boston *Centinel.* The London *Evening Star* on July 13th of that year, before news of Madison's declaration had reached England, suggested that the Otis letter had hastened the repeal of the orders in council, although the validity of this claim was somewhat weakened by the revelation that the editorial was written by Gray himself. He had paid a pound for the privilege. It was further vitiated by the caustic reply Perceval had made to Gray in February 1812, in which the prime minister made it perfectly clear that British policy was based on motives far more complex than the "punctilio" noted by Otis.[18]

A brusque rejection of Otis's offices probably would have followed from more discreet approaches to the ministry. The moderate Federalists did not fit into the pattern of American reaction the British had been accustomed to find. Friendly warnings that hinted at unity in America or fault in Britain were more than counterbalanced by the familiar information supplied to Minister Augustus Foster in Washington or to London correspondents of such High Federalists as Timothy Pickering. As the Boston *Independent Chronicle* pointed out, "In every measure of government, the federal faction have rallied in opposition and urged the Ministry to persist in their Orders."[19] Many of this group welcomed rather than deplored the prospect of war in the expectation that the crisis would destroy the Madison administration. Foster's dispatches disclose conversations with Federalists who wanted Britain to push the government into war to expose its weaknesses. If Madison fought he would collapse; if he retreated he would be disgraced. Alexander Hanson, influential editor of the Baltimore *Federal Republican,* informed former Minister Francis J. Jackson in March 1812 that "the only way to dislodge the prevailing party from the post of power is by saddling them with a war which they have neither the means [nor] the ability to conduct."[20] Given these goads to war, Britons in Washington or in London could be excused for believing that either Americans would not fight, no matter what they said, or could not, no matter what they did.

With the coming of war, a case can be made that the Federalist information and British contempt for American behavior were both confirmed. With some success, Federalists of New England made strenuous efforts to prevent recruiting of troops, to refuse financial service, or to resist British incursions into their territory. Some of the more rabid enemies of Madison attempted to use the war as the occasion for separating from the Union and making a separate peace. The conduct of the war from Washington offered few reasons to expect victory from the Republicans. While the peace commissioners were at Ghent in the difficult days of the fall of 1814, New England Federalists were openly preparing for a meeting at Hartford to promote "a radical reform in the national compact," in the words of the Massachusetts General Court. At the same time, the governor of that state, Caleb Strong, was secretly employing an agent to visit General Sir John Sherbrooke in Halifax with oral instructions to find out in what ways Britain would help Massachusetts in the event of a clash between the state and the federal government. Sherbrooke promptly asked Lord Bathurst, secretary for war, about the course of action he should take in response to Strong's queries. Had peace not followed almost immediately, the British general would have been authorized to give logistical support to Massachusetts but no specific promise of troops.[21]

What was noteworthy about this exchange was the eagerness of Bathurst to have Sherbrooke sign an armistice with Massachusetts at that particular point. Only two weeks before the conclusion of the Treaty of Ghent, the secretary for war sent four dispatches to Sherbrooke concerning the options open to the general in the event the treaty aborted. Given this information, it is hardly surprising that the British had some reasons for confidence about the future of their war in America no matter what happened at Ghent. As Liverpool observed to the foreign secretary, Lord Castlereagh, one day before the treaty was signed: "The disposition to separate on the part of the Eastern states may likewise frighten Madison; for if he should refuse to ratify the treaty, we must immediately purpose to make a separate peace with them, and we have good reason to believe that they would not be indisposed to listen to such a proposal."[22]

There is no doubt that the divisive actions of a Federalist minority played a role in the contingency planning of the British government in 1814. Secretive though their behavior was, there is also no doubt that some of the zealots were building hopes for a new government from the defeat of American armies in America. Should the Hartford Convention not meet their wishes—and it did not—they were prepared to continue treasonable negotiations with the British, which were made acceptable by their consistency with preachments they had been making for a generation. Such luminaries as Pickering, Gouverneur Morris, and Charles Carroll counted on British General Sir Edward Pakenham's anticipated victory in Louisiana to serve their purposes. As Pickering put it, "From the moment that the British possess New Orleans the Union is severed."[23]

The trouble with the scenario the High Federalists visualized was that events did not break as they envisioned; New Orleans did not fall, and the Union was not severed. Furthermore, the invasion of Louisiana was undertaken a month after the British and Americans had concluded their treaty at Ghent. With all its opacity, the cabinet was ultimately more perceptive than its American advisers. Although the failures of American arms early in the war appeared to confirm British contempt for the intelligence and strength of the Republicans, they began to perceive before it ended the reservoirs of strength American nationalism could tap. They had the sense to realize that the enormous effort that would still be needed to defeat Americans was not commensurate with the results to be gained. In making peace in 1814, British diplomats exhibited a grasp of reality that their Anglophile friends overseas never acquired.

The realism Great Britain displayed in bringing the war to a close characterized both sides of the Anglo-American relationship in the next generation. The experience of war and the even more impressive recognition of American economic power sobered many of Britain's emotions about Americans. In Foreign Minister Castlereagh, Charles Webster found "the first British statesman to recognize that the friendship of the United States was a major asset to Britain, and to use in his relations with her a language that was neither superior nor intimidating."[24] The new rapprochement

FEDERALIST FOUNDATIONS

developed partly from the disappearance of both the Federalists and neutral rights from the scene, and partly from a fresh appreciation of a community of interests vis-à-vis Europe. If America had not come fully of age, it had emerged from a colonial status in the official mind of Great Britain.

5

THE CONSENSUS OF 1789:

JEFFERSON AND HAMILTON ON AMERICAN FOREIGN POLICY

The dramatic, even melodramatic, confrontations of the personalities of Thomas Jefferson and Alexander Hamilton have attracted so much attention in their time and afterwards that observers of the first generation of the Federal Union frequently reduce the diplomacy of the Washington administration to the level of a duel between the two great cabinet members. The nature of their antagonism lends itself to a Manichaean contrast between good and evil. Depending upon the angle of observation, Jefferson or Hamilton was the wise defender of American interests against the cunning servant of a foreign power, either France or England. Thus, the Hamilton-Jefferson duel has its counterpart in Anglophilia and Francophilia, and the control of American foreign policy was made the object of their activity. Victory for Hamilton meant the triumph of an Anglophile, aristocratic, mercantile elite; victory for Jefferson meant the ascendancy of Francophile, democratic, agrarian masses. The polarity is conveniently absolute.

Historians have contributed to the sharp division between the two men, not because of particular partisan bias—although this is occasionally present—but frequently because of the enormous difficulty of providing independent judgments of the actors in this period. No matter what the intentions of the scholar may be, his search for objectivity becomes entangled in the web of traditional evaluations. When Paul Varg determined that Hamilton was "above all a realist who fatalistically accepted the existing framework, and dedicated himself to obtaining the best bargain possible," he automatically placed himself in the Hamiltonian camp. If Hamilton was the realist, then as Varg concluded a paragraph later, Madison was the "idealist in foreign policy," a pejorative description of a man who "never felt it necessary to balance goals with the power available."[1] By contrast, Albert Bowman and Cecilia Kenyon identified Hamilton as the idealist who, according to the latter, required a patriotism from the people he did not expect from the advantaged classes and, according to the former, formulated his foreign policy not on conditions as they actually were but on what he wanted them to be.[2] Realism in these views was on the Jeffersonian side. Both men, as Bowman saw them, "recognized the value of neutrality, but Hamilton would have surrendered it to Britain's demand . . . while Jefferson would have used it as a diplomatic weapon against all Europe."[3]

The temptation to categorize is irresistible; the historians themselves are prisoners of the past. Even when scholars attempt, as the foregoing have, to strip the situation of its emotional undertones, the language of the familiar controversy seems to impose itself upon the writers. This is not always the case; other writers flaunt their biases in a way that presents no difficulty to the reader. When Gilbert Lycan asserts that Hamilton was unfairly deprived of credit for the Louisiana Purchase[4] or when Julian Boyd entitles a book *Number 7: Alexander Hamilton's Secret Attempts to Control American Foreign Policy,* the reader has no difficulty in identifying the authors with the main stream of the hagiographical tradition in the study of American foreign policy.

What is missing in many of the analyses of the conflict within Washington's cabinet are not only the nuances vital in the understanding of the conduct of foreign policy but also important dramatis personae whose roles are either given perfunctory mention or who are wholly submerged in the rivalry between the secretary of state and the secretary of the treasury.

John Jay, Gouverneur Morris, and Washington himself appear too frequently as pawns of Hamilton; while Madison, Monroe, and William Short emerge as extensions of Jefferson's personality. John Adams in the beginning of the Federalist period at least behaves as some species of sport or crank, except when he is clearly on the outer edge of the Hamilton circle. To assert that these influential and complicated personalities have been slighted is not to deny that scholars have attempted to give them consideration in their writings. Dumas Malone, the most authoritative of Jefferson's biographers, scoffed at the notion that Madison and Hamilton parted ideological company only upon the return of Jefferson to America.[5] John C. Miller, a leading student of Hamilton, made clear the legitimate claim of Washington as a prime mover in foreign policy, rather than as a befuddled conservative led docilely to his positions by the dominant Hamilton.[6] But despite impressive disclaimers, the other statesmen of the period, even when the stamp of their personality is felt, are placed on a Jeffersonian or Hamiltonian field rather than accorded separate ground of their own.

Another approach to foreign policy might subsume the difference among cabinet members under a substantial consensus broad enough to encompass all the members of the Washington administration and most of the Congress as well. Irrespective of personality conflicts and future ideological affiliations the leaders of the government agreed that the Confederation had failed to support a viable American foreign policy. They all looked upon the reconstituted Union as an opportunity to extract vital concessions from Europe which had been unattainable in the past, from the relocation of boundary lines to the expansion of trade.

In this light Washington was the spokesman for a nation. Those factions for whom he did not speak had retired in confusion from the national scene. The Jeffersonians were not drawn from those groups. The sheer extent of agreement in Philadelphia rendered the president unprepared for the fierce differences over the national mandate which developed in subsequent years. His mind, never quick, could neither comprehend fully the protean nature of the cabinet struggle nor accept its implications for American politics. Unwittingly, Washington contributed to Jefferson's problems by virtue of his own bent for foreign and military affairs. Hamilton, on the other hand, owed much of his freedom of operation to the president's lack of expertise in financial matters. Moreover, the vast areas of Hamilton's activities, including consular affairs, provided the secretary of the treasury with a measure of influence with the president and the Congress that would have aroused the animosity of a secretary of state, especially one who was his senior in age, distinction, and service to his country. The absentee Virginian, fresh from his laurels in France, had reasons other than ideological to build an opposition to Hamilton. Jefferson was jealous of the younger man's prestige and power in the new government.

The transfer of a personal distaste for each other's manners and mannerisms to ideas and policies was neither automatic nor immediate. Certain forces brought Hamilton and Jefferson together despite a variety of misgivings on the part of both men. Each had his reservations about the Constitution which in other circumstances could have separated them from the outset. To Hamilton the document was insufficiently responsive to the need for a secure governing body and hence excessively susceptible to the ravages of democracy. To Jefferson, viewing the Constitution through the eyes of Mason and Monroe, the document encouraged incipient monarchism through presidential re-election and implicitly threatened civil liberties through its silence on a bill of rights.

Although hindsight reveals wide philosophical gaps from the outset, it often overlooks the agreement of the two secretaries to act in concert under an imperfect Constitution which they both recognized to be the best possible instrument of government available in that year.

Jefferson's experiences in France offered no reasonable alternative. His reports from Paris throughout his service as minister clearly reveal how unstable a support the French government would be to America's foreign policy. For the optimistic Jefferson this insight took time to assimilate. He had left for France in 1784 to join Adams and Franklin in treaty making with European powers, with high hopes for French assistance in the war with Britain; the hopes persisted into the postwar period when he realized how valuable the ally could be in countering continuing British malevolence toward the United States. His initial triumphant reception in Paris as the successor of Franklin convinced him at least of the benevolence of the French intelligentsia. And in the next five years he could take pride in the treaty he signed with Prussia in 1785 as well as in the work of Adams in the treaties with the Netherlands and of Franklin with Sweden, in 1782 and 1783 respectively. Above all, Jefferson had the right to bask in some self-congratulations over the influence he exerted among friends who were to lead a revolution in the year of his departure from France, 1789.

All these small triumphs, while gratifying to the ego, did not conceal from the minister the essential failure of the United States to win over France and Europe to the new liberal conception of international economy that he had envisioned at the end of the revolutionary war. Jefferson had undertaken initially "nothing less than a diplomatic mission to convert all Europe to the commercial principles of the American Revolution," in the words of Merrill Peterson.[7] This was not to be. Favorable treaties with Sweden and Prussia, countries with few prospects of serious trade with the United States, were not the answer to America's difficulties. What was needed was a massive breakdown of the mercantilist thinking and practices of the Old World to permit the new nation to redirect its commerce away from British channels. The goal was not merely the securing of greater economic benefits for Americans or the achieving of any abstract principle of free trade. These objectives were simply instruments for ending British control over American affairs, economic and political. Nothing that Jay in New York or Adams in London informed him about British attitudes after 1783 gave him any reason to doubt the peril facing the United States if she failed to meet this challenge.

If Europe disappointed, at least France should have responded to America's need. To this end Jefferson employed all his many charms to move such men as Lafayette and Du Pont and such groups as the physiocrats, with their concern for free trade, to change French economic policy toward the United States. France must extend the few concessions made to American economic interests and capture for herself the lucrative commerce Britain had enjoyed for over a century. To do this, new laws had to be enacted. The links implied in the mutual acceptance of a liberal doctrine of neutral rights and most-favored-nation treatment must include, according to the reasoning of the American minister, the free entry of American products into the French market in exchange for French supplies and manufactures.

Jefferson had no chance for permanent success on the eve of the collapse of the ancien régime. Hapless France would not help herself, let alone a distant and uncertain ally. Even when a ministry—finance or foreign—was willing to yield to America's importunities, as in the case of the decree of 1784 which would permit American ships legal entry to the West Indies, it would retreat under pressure of angry French merchants fearful of American competition. Vergennes was in substantive agreement with almost all of Jefferson's arguments, but there was little he or any other minister could do to effect a remedy. Such concessions as America did win turned out to be inadequate palliatives, and no one recognized this problem more clearly than Jefferson himself.

All his experiences in France confirmed the importance of a vigorous central authority in the United States if the respect of Europe and the proper behavior of Great Britain were to be secured. Debts had to be paid, reciprocal agreements had to be met, navigation laws had to be enforced. Could the Confederation manage these tasks? It might have been Jay or Adams writing when Jefferson claimed in 1785: "You see that my primary object in the formation of treaties is to take the commerce of the states out of the hands of the states, and to place it under the superintendence of Congress, so far as the imperfect provisions of our constitution will admit, and until the states by new compact make them more perfect."[8] By 1787 he was even more sensitive to the incapacity of the Confederation to control the actions of the states and to the effect that incapacity had upon the conduct of foreign policy. Although his correspondence during the debates over the Constitution reveal serious doubts about the new instrument, "he never doubted," as Dumas Malone has observed, "the wisdom of putting diplomacy in federal hands."[9]

Hamilton in New York had other reasons for objecting to the weaknesses of the Confederation, but none of them related to any special service he wished to confer on Great Britain. The incipient chaos in a government that could not pay its debts and that could not enforce its ordinances demanded change. He was a prime mover in the movement to call a convention with power to revise the Confederation. All told, he identified a dozen defects in the Articles, all of them growing out of the excessive limitations upon executive power. Obviously, the Jeffersonian objectives of a French counterweight to British power did not inform Hamilton's actions, but the nation's ability to prevent a state—Connecticut for example—from levying heavier duties on imports from Massachusetts than from Great Britain would have the blessing of both men.

Hamilton's praise of British monarchy as the model for the Constitution makers was not the measure of his view of the federal union. He could accept the document without king or aristocracy just as Jefferson was able to live with a president eligible for indefinite reelection. Hamilton's concern for energetic government was directed against future rebellion of the Shays variety, an object hardly shared by the minister to France at this time. But as Hamilton pointed out so clearly in Number 24 of the *Federalist Papers* a government capable of military establishment would cope with the increasing dangers from Britain and Spain whose colonies posed a threat, separately or in "future concert," to the United States. Jefferson as well as Madison could have associated himself with the author of these views. Similarly, there is a harmony in 1789 that blends the Hamilton who looked forward to a close American link to the British mercantile system and the Jefferson who sought a French factor to break that very link. The latter was not seeking a dependent role for the United States; his America would exploit the French ally for the advancement of American commerce. And the former, with all his admiration for the British way of commerce, sought not merely the present profit for America from a special relationship with Great Britain but envisioned a future in which an American industrial machine would rival and prevail over a British competitor.

Both outlooks project independence of British and French influences as well as cultivation of a policy designed to win security and prosperity for the new nation. If the common ground on which Hamilton and Jefferson stood in 1789 collapsed under them by 1793, it was the course of European events more than incompatible philosophies that accounts for the breakdown. The French Revolution fashioned new meanings for France and England in the minds of the two secretaries, indeed in the minds of a considerable part of the country. Hamilton increasingly found in Great Britain the model of the good society, the font of America's commercial growth, and the protector against French imperialism. His Anglophilic tendencies had been evident in the 1780s but they were to be deepened and widened by the European changes. For Jefferson France was to become even more than before the counterweight to British commercial power as she added the new function of bellwether of republicanism in a hostile monarchical world. The Anglo-French War of 1793 pushed the country and the two men into actions which had not been anticipated five years earlier. Given the joining of Hamiltonianism and Jeffersonianism into an American system of political economy a generation later, the observer may claim that Anglophilia and Francophilia were the source of the divisive passions which marked the 1790s rather than agrarianism and mercantilism. A foreign policy still tied to the fortunes of Europe, which neither statesman had desired in 1789, dictated the direction of American politics.

The place of foreign policy and the management of diplomacy were important issues to the framers of the Constitution, even if they were not central to the worries of the nation at large. The proper conduct of foreign relations lay implicit in the elaborate distribution of powers among the three branches of government. Each could check the other two, but all of them contained ingredients which reinforced a national authority over foreign affairs of an order so conspicuously absent under the Confederation.

In clear, if negative, terms Section 10 of Article I of the Constitution denied to the states the power to "enter any treaty, alliance, or confederation," or to "lay any imposts or duties on imports or exports," or to "enter into any agreement or compact with another State, or with a foreign power, or engage in war, unless actually invaded, or in such imminent danger as will not admit of delay." Some of these inhibitions were drawn directly from the Articles of Confederation; but unlike the latter, the new basic law specified measures for their enforcement, to end once and for all the dangers inherent in thirteen sovereign states. To administer foreign policy an equally clear mandate went to the president in Section 2 of Article II. As head of the executive branch of government he could make treaties and nominate and appoint ambassadors and consuls "by and with the advice and consent of the Senate." The most explicit of all the powers given to the judiciary concerned foreign affairs. Section 2 of Article III extended to the judicial power "treaties made, or which shall be made," and to all cases affecting ambassadors or consuls. Finally, Article VI announced to the world that "all debts contracted and engagements entered into, before the adoption of this Constitution, shall be as valid against the United States under this Constitution, as under the Confederation" and that the Constitution, including treaties made in its name, "shall be the supreme law of the land."

Small wonder that every statesmen with experience in foreign affairs rallied to the support of this document. It addressed itself precisely to those troubles which had exposed the impotence of America under the Confederation. Its allure was powerful enough to quiet the suspicions of southern politicians who had been aroused over Jay's treatment of the Mississippi Valley. When Patrick Henry invoked Jefferson's reservations about the Constitution to support his case that central power would be inimical to southern liberties, Madison quickly countered by pointing out to the Virginia ratifying convention that Jefferson's objections did not involve rejection of the Constitution; he had merely wanted improvements.[10] Besides, as Madison emphasized, Jefferson's backing and filling over the document never applied to foreign affairs. Jefferson in August 1787 had made clear that "I wish to see our states made one as to all foreign, and several as to all domestic matters."[11] A few months later he expressed his appreciation to Madison for the tax powers that would be given to the federal legislature to free it from the interference of state assemblies.[12]

The American minister to Great Britain was even more fervent in his blessing of a stronger central government. Adams's experiences in London had been more painful and more humiliating than anything Jefferson suffered in Paris. It was in London after all that the principle of the *alternat* was officially excluded from the American treaty—the custom of having each contracting party be first-named in its own copy of the treaty. Under strict instructions from Whitehall, David Hartley had signed his name first on both copies of the Treaty of Paris, while the Americans followed in alphabetical order.[13] Here was a supreme symbol of American inferiority which John Adams was not likely to forget or forgive. The Constitution, however, could help to reduce its significance.

John Jay, one of the signers of that treaty, was also one of the three propagandists of the *Federalist Papers* working for the passage of the Constitution through the New York ratifying convention. While his specific contributions were few quantitatively, all of them reflected the expertise he had acquired as the Confederation's foreign minister. He wrote only five of the eighty-five essays, but after Hamilton's introductory paper the next four were Jay's handiwork and each of them related to the necessity of frustrating Europe's ability to divide the Union against itself. The fact that this theme was established so early in the presentation suggested the priority Hamilton, Madison, and Jay gave to the problem. Jay advised in *Federalist Paper* Number 4, that if Europeans "see that our national government is efficient and well administered, our resources and finances discreetly managed, our credit re-established, our people free, contented, and united, they will be much more disposed to cultivate our friendship than provoke our resentment." But if they see America weak and fragmented, the nation would be exposed "not only to their contempt, but to their outrage."

The new secretary of state, successor to the secretary of foreign relations, would not only subscribe to the foregoing sentiments, but he would agree as well to the benefits of union outlined by the secretary of the treasury which would confound "all the combinations of European jealousy to restrain our growth." Hamilton's paradigm of a hostile Europe competing with the United States in commerce of every kind and envious of America's potential strength, expressed in *Federalist Paper* Number 11, was close to Jefferson's perception of Europe's pretentions of superiority over America, almost in the same language Jefferson used to rebuff the ideas of Buffon and Raynal when he was in France:

> Men, admired as profound philosophers, have, in direct terms, attributed to her inhabitants a physical superiority and have gravely asserted that all animals, and with them the human species, degenerate in America—that even dogs cease to bark after having breathed awhile in our atmosphere. Facts have too long supported these arrogant pretensions of the Europeans. It belongs to us to vindicate the honor of the human race, and to teach that assuming brother, moderation. Union will enable us to do it.

If Jefferson and Hamilton shared anger over the pseudo-scientific slanders of the French philosophes, they shared as fully in the initial building of a fabric of government sturdy enough to implement the promise of the Constitution. The two men had not met until Jefferson returned to the United States early in 1790 to assume his office, but the absence of immediate friction was due more to a common outlook on national problems than to Jefferson's notorious reluctance to involve himself openly in any feud. The secretary of state could even accept treasury's personnel force of some seventy men, with functions in consular affairs intruding into his department, in contrast to his small staff of five, with limited duties, as long as he could accept Washington's assurance that his office was the more important and the more distinguished.

Jefferson appeared as ready as Hamilton to act on the principle that the executive branch should have maximal independence, at least in foreign affairs. And his blessing was not merely by indirection. In April 1790, shortly after taking up his duties, he presented a memorandum on the powers of the Senate over diplomatic appointments. His theme was that such a transaction was altogether executive and almost exclusively so, "Except as to such portions of it as are specially submitted to the Senate. Exceptions are to be construed strictly."[14] As for the president's question on the propriety of consulting the Senate on which countries should be approached about diplomatic exchanges, Jefferson asserted that there was no constitutional requirement for soliciting such advice. He felt it impolitic to set a precedent. The Senate's powers extended no further than the approval or disapproval of the person nominated by the president. In displaying this loose construction of presidential authority the secretary of state put himself in a position indistinguishable from that of his conservative predecessor, now Chief Justice Jay, whom Washington had consulted on the same issue.

Given this attitude, Jefferson and Madison were not hostile to the Hamiltonian program as they first understood it. The raising of revenue through a tariff, the repaying of obligations through federal assumption of the debts of the previous governments, and the creation of a navigation system to promote American shipping were not objectionable to the secretary of state. The liquidation of the foreign debt was welcomed by Madison. Even Jefferson's negative views on the federal assumption of state debts, in exchange for a federal capital on the Potomac River, were visible only after the event; he was the broker to the arrangement initially.[15] Jefferson in 1790 may have had doubts about the implications of many of Hamilton's positions, but he was able to concede that whatever differences prevailed then, his opponents were nonetheless "good men and bold men, and sensible men."[16]

Nowhere were the similarities and differences over foreign policy more clearly expressed in the early years of the Washington administration than over the Nootka Sound crisis of 1790 between Spain and the United States. Boyd has pointed out that Hamilton had weakened America's bargaining power with the British by assuring their agent that the United States would not support Spain's position in the Pacific Northwest.[17] Such misinformation stiffened Britain's resistance to concessions which Jefferson hoped might be made in return for permission for British troops to use American territory in the event of war with Spain. Had Jefferson known the extent of Hamilton's dealings with Great Britain at this time, he might have understood the reasons for them no matter how vigorously he would have deplored his rival's actions. In advising Washington to give British forces passage, Hamilton was acting on the assumption that if the United States failed to do so, Great Britain might seize Louisiana and the Floridas on her own. Such a consequence would increase British influence along American borders to a dangerous degree, as well as damage future Anglo-American commercial relations.

By rendering New Orleans the emporium of products of the Western Country, Britain would, at a period not very distant, have little occasion for supplies or provisions for their Islands from the Atlantic States; and for their European Market they would derive from the same source copious supplies of Tobacco and other articles now furnished by the Southern States: Whence a great diminution of the motives to establish liberal terms of Commercial Intercourse with the United States collectively.[18]

If this was Anglophilia it was severely qualified by the secretary's calculations. Fear, not friendship, moved Hamilton.

It may be claimed that before the end of 1790 Jefferson and Madison, each working on the other's fears, discovered in Hamilton's program a divergence from the common good and in his person an arrogance that annoyed them at every turn. Funding of debts appeared to be a device to enrich speculators at the expense of the agrarian South; and the blunting of Madison's efforts to construct a navigation system appeared to be the product of a dangerous attraction to monarchical Britain. Yet, it is questionable if the conclusions of conspiracy suggested above were fully articulated, even though the foundations for them were being laid. It was not just the intellectual opacity of President Washington that made him fail to perceive irreconcilable differences in the cabinet. If they existed at all, they related to means, not to objectives. For the president in his first two years in office the consensus of 1789 over America's relations with the outside world persisted. And most of the evidence that suggested otherwise belongs to a later stage of the Hamilton-Jefferson rivalry.

Briefly the consensus reasserted itself in the afterglow of the heated presidential election of 1800. The Convention of Mortefontaine ending the quasi-war with France was the occasion for surprising agreement between the two statesmen over the uneasy detente with the French. The Francophile Jefferson, newly elected to the presidency, and the Francophobe Federalist leader who had built much of his program in that decade on hostility to France both cautiously accepted the convention despite their common fear of trickery on the part of the first consul, Napoleon Bonaparte.

Although neither the administration nor its critics recognized the full dimensions of the first consul's guile in 1800, Federalists and Republicans alike sensed some of the dangers which could emerge from dealing with the new French government. Jefferson expressed his distaste for the "dictatorial consulate" which he identified with Hamilton, "our Buonaparte," who he felt was capable of destroying American republicanism with the same kind of coup the French general delivered. Suspicious from the start, the president-elect called the convention a "bungling negotiation,"[19] but did nothing to prevent it from becoming the law of the land, even after Bonaparte had made his own interpretation of its meaning. Moreover, such criticism as Jefferson had of the convention itself was not for ending the alliance or for limiting the possibilities of financial compensations from France but rather for the difficulties the convention might produce in America's relations with Great Britain! Here was a reluctant tribute to Adams's service. Neither his former Francophilia, which should have pushed toward the renewal of the alliance, nor his present dislike of the new French leadership affected Jefferson's acceptance of the convention. The nation needed disentanglement from France, and it needed continuity in its commercial ties with Great Britain. President Jefferson understood these realities.

Hamilton did not lag behind Jefferson in recognizing the importance of the convention. Unlike most American statesmen in 1800, he saw through Bonaparte's game with the freedom of the seas, noting that the convention "plays into the hands of France by the precedent of those principles of navigation which she is at this moment desirous of making the basis of a league of the northern powers against England."[20] But when the question arose over the acceptance or rejection of the arrangement, Hamilton concluded that the solution at Mortefontaine was the least harmful of all the potential threats inherent in the Franco-American relationship, just as Jefferson was in some respects the lesser of the two evils which were then confronting the Federalists in the congressional choice of president.

This mood of internal accommodation was based, not on affection, but on a realistic evaluation of the nation's needs. They were much the same as they had been in 1789. As for the troubles in the intervening years, President Jefferson in his First Inaugural Address observed that "during the throes and convulsions of the ancient world, during the agonizing spasms of infuriated man, seeking through blood and slaughter his longlost liberty, it was not wonderful that the agitation of the billows should reach even this distant and peaceful shore." Although Jefferson and Hamilton each had a hand in roiling the waters—and would again in the near future—they both paid tribute to the virtues of their own early counsels: namely, the support of a strong central government capable of maintaining freedom from European entanglements and profits from European commerce.

6

‖TOWARD
‖ISOLATIONISM:

THE RISE AND FALL OF THE
FRANCO-AMERICAN ALLIANCE,
1775–1801

Isolationism has always held an elusive quality for American diplomatic historians. The term itself is no older than the 1920s, and fittingly is identified with a revulsion against the entanglements of world war.[1] This rejection of Europe was undergirded by an earlier religious image of a New World arising out of the failure of the Old, sitting apart on its transatlantic hill. These Calvinist expectations of a New Jerusalem in turn received reinforcement from the secular thought of the Enlightenment, which contrasted the simple, egalitarian, free society of eighteenth-century America with the complex, class-ridden, war-plagued societies of Europe. As a consequence of this bifurcated vision of the world Washington's Farewell Address of 1796 became an enduring symbol of America's isolation. His message was directed against the French alliance of 1778, the first and only entangling political commitment to Europe the United States made until the framing of the North Atlantic Treaty in 1949.

For all but a few ideologues tied either to the mother country or to the wilderness, isolationism meant a freedom to enjoy access to all ports interested in receiving American products. It meant further a freedom from subservience to any foreign power, of the kind which had forced them into the service of a maternal economy or of dynastic wars in the past. Finally, it extended to a self-image of virtue and innocence that would be protected by advancing principles of peaceful relationships among nations.

The alliance with France violated these conceptions of America's position in the world. Conceivably, the potential contradiction between the profession of isolationism and the making of alliance lies in confusion over the meaning of "alliance." It may be resolved, according to Felix Gilbert, by accepting an eighteenth-century understanding of alliances which embrace both commercial agreements and military obligations.[2] There were no genuine distinctions between a treaty of commerce and a treaty of alliance. So when the Founding Fathers spoke of a foreign alliance as a desideratum, they could reconcile their wish for a commercial connection with refusal of political bonds. There is evidence enough in the language used by policymakers during the life of the twenty-three-year alliance to buttress this thesis. Both the French and Americans intertwined the provisions of the Treaty of Amity and Commerce with the claims of the treaty of alliance in the 1790s. And the Model Treaty of 1776 lumped political and commercial considerations together.

But there is also abundant evidence that the men who framed foreign policy during the Revolution recognized clearly the distinctions between the two kinds of treaties. They wanted France to be obligated in the Model Treaty without cost to themselves. They failed to entice the French under these terms, and they knew they failed. If they accepted political and military entanglement it was because they felt they had no choice. The most they could do would be to limit the potential damage subservience to France's national interest would have. None of the framers was surprised to find France willing to limit American territorial claims in peace negotiations in 1782, or to keep West Indian ports closed to American ships in the 1790s, or even to make the United States, if possible, an equivalent of the Cisalpine Republic. Napoleon Bonaparte was not only the end product of France's revolution in this period, but the logical extension of fears they had always entertained of foreign control.

That a successful defiance of England would require the help of Europe was understood even before separation was made official. The Continental Congress established a five-man Committee of Secret Correspondence on 19 November 1775, "for the sole purpose of corresponding with our friends in Great Britain, Ireland, and other parts of the world."[3] Since the voices of America's friends in and out of Parliament had either been stilled or had turned away from the colonies, the "other parts of the world" became an immediate object of attention. The most notable part was France, England's familiar enemy, which had been periodically testing colonial discontent for ten years to see how it might be turned to its own advantage.

The French court's interest was not ephemeral. Vergennes, the foreign minister, welcomed the dispatch of Silas Deane, a former delegate to the Congress from Connecticut and merchant connected with Robert Morris's firm in Philadelphia. It was not coincidental that Morris was a member of the committee which presented the Model Treaty of 1776. Deane was joined by Arthur Lee, the committee's agent in London and colonial agent from Massachusetts. He was the brother of Richard Henry Lee, another member of the Committee of Secret Correspondence. The scene was set then both for the supply of munitions, weapons, and equipment to the colonies by indirect means from the French and Spanish crowns which permitted a vital and massive infusion of energy to the colonial war effort and an opportunity for fiscal confusion and personal profit for the American agents involved in the transactions. In all these dealings the substance was commerce, not politics; trade, not military obligations.

The function France was performing should have fitted perfectly the message of Thomas Paine in his *Common Sense,* when he expressed a few months later that "the true interest of America is to steer clear of Europe's contentions, which she never can do, while, by her dependance [*sic*] on Britain, she is made the makeweight on the scale of British politics." More than this, he asserted that "Our plan is commerce, and that, well attended to, will secure us the peace and friendship of Europe." It also reflected the thinking of John Adams who had been the prime mover in the summer of 1776 in drawing up a model treaty. His Plan of 1776 operated on the assumption that Europe would sue for America's trade and would promote America's independence to secure this advantage as well as to weaken British colonial power. France was the vital cog in the plan that would serve the war effort but without the price of entangling reciprocal obligations. Adams's language could not be plainer: "I am not for soliciting any political connection, or military assistance, or indeed, naval from France. I wish for nothing but commerce, a mere marine treaty with them."[4]

As a consequence of a confidence bordering on truculence the American Model Treaty of 1776 elaborated on liberal ideas of international law and freedom of the seas, ideas appealing to the philosophers of France and to the naval competitors of the great seapower of the day. More controversial in tone was the self-denial Article 9 would impose on the French, forcing the king to promise that "he shall never invade, nor, under any pretense, attempt to possess himself of any of the territories of the mainland which had been French or Spanish in the past."[5] Almost grudgingly it seemed, the French would be permitted to keep whatever West Indian possessions they acquired by virtue of joining the Americans.

Such euphoria as this plan reflected dissipated rapidly in 1776. The war went badly for American arms and American morale. While the surreptitious aid given by the French and Spanish was substantial, it did not produce the desired effects on the war effort. As a result, the demands on France moved from commercial support to military assistance to a promise of reciprocal political and military obligation, in return for open adherence to the war. It was the Americans, and not the French, who became the suitor for an alliance. An increasingly nervous awareness that the world was not so well ordered as the Paine scenario had implied informed the advice given the ministers in France by the Committee of Secret Correspondence and its successor, the Committee of Foreign Affairs. Deane and Lee, joined by Franklin late in 1776, were permitted to relax the requirements for French aid. They were to assure the French of no future allegiance to Britain, of no trade advantages to any other power greater than to the French benefactor, and an additional agreement to make no termination of war, should the French enter it, without full notice to the French partner.[6]

As American confidence in its own power weakened, the commissioners' importunities became more frantic. The American distress abroad was compounded by the rivalry between Arthur Lee and his family on the one side, with Silas Deane, supported by Franklin, on the other. While this controversy ultimately became a major cause célèbre in the Continental Congress, ruining both Deane's and Lee's careers, it is worth noting that their position on the French alliance differed in no significant way before the treaty was made. Both men were willing to offer promises along with vague threats to move the French from their cautious stance. Deane warned the French that without sufficient help the Americans would be forced to reunite with the British. An independent America, on the other hand, would make France a successor to Britain in the domination of world commerce.[7] Arthur Lee pursued a different tactic when he appealed to the French to witness America standing up to Britain and serving them by striking out at Britain's pretensions. "We are left like Hercules in his cradle, to strangle the serpent that annoys all Europe."[8]

The French foreign office listened and bided its time. Port officials returned British prizes Americans brought too openly into French cities. There was no acknowledgment of the declaration of American independence, even as supplies and soldiers found their way to America from France. It required the victory at Saratoga in the fall of 1777, and more important, signs of British accommodation to America's early war aims before France was willing to make an alliance formally and accept the price of war for its pains. And when the treaty was finally concluded, the brave words of Adams and Paine were forgotten. Not only did the United States reassure the French about the termination of the war and about commercial benefits, but a specific entanglement was made in Article 2, which was not to be found in the Model Treaty, in the form of mutual guarantees "from the present time and forever, against all other powers, to wit, the united states to his most Christian Majesty the present Possessions of the Crown of France in America as well as those which it may acquire by the future Treaty of peace. . . ."[9] Thus the commissioners made an agreement which bound the United States for an indefinite future to the defense of a foreign power's territory in America, a sure guarantee of involvement in the European balance of power in any subsequent quarrel between Britain and France.

The American response was one of relief and gratitude. The Congress considered the treaty officially on 4 May 1778, and ratified it two days later with little commentary beyond directing the commissioners "to present the grateful acknowledgements of this Congress to his most Christian majesty for his truly magnanimous conduct respecting these States in the said generous and disinterested treaties."[10] The only question raised by the commissioners concerned the mutual prohibitions of duties on exports between the United States and the French West Indies. These articles were removed.

The appreciation was genuine and appropriate. France's decision for alliance was a decision for war with Britain, and it confirmed American independence, if not victory on the battlefield. Given the turmoil of the Congress, the divisions within the new nation, and the uncertainties of the military results, France gave the United States a remarkable gift—that of a successful conclusion to the Revolution. It agreed to renounce its concerns with former colonies in the New World, and to maintain "effectually the liberty, Sovereignty, and independance [sic] absolute and unlimited of the said United States, as well in Matters of government as in commerce."[11] In the short run the benefits outweighed any debits.

Generous as the French were, their interest in the success of the United States was always subordinated to their greater interests in their financial status, maintenance of the monarchical principle, and cultivation of their more important alliance with Spain. If America could achieve its objectives in war without clashing with France's other concerns, the French ally would gladly be of service, as long as the paternal guidance of His Most Christian Majesty would govern American behavior. But when it became apparent first to the new peace commission abroad—John Adams, John Jay, and Benjamin Franklin—and then to the Congress that France was prepared to accept less than the borders the United States wanted or the fisheries New England demanded, the relationship soon became uneasy. From the French side came charges of ingratitude as Minister Gerard was caught up on the side of Deane in the Lee-Deane dispute, and as his successor had to pursue French interests by influencing public opinion through the subsidized journalism of Thomas Paine and Hugh Henry Brackenridge.

American restiveness was more openly expressed. A generalized anti-Gallican and anti-Catholic sentiment had its center in New England, but its vibrations were felt throughout the states. Friends of France like Jefferson were sorely disappointed over the quality of French military assistance. Distrust over the purposes of French aid was widespread from the beginnings of the alliance, as secret negotiations among the European powers between 1778 and 1782 evoked suspicions first of French disinterest in America's transappalachian ambitions, and then of the ally's collaboration with the British and Spanish in an attempt to confine the United States to the Atlantic littoral. These suspicions were justified, and most of the French *arrières pensées* about America were exposed before the war ended. Even more open were the pressures exerted by French officials in America to bend Congress's policies to France's wishes. Luzerne, in the best manner of a patron chiding a client for his errors, made Congress revise its instruction to the American commission abroad from a general statement that the commission be guided by "the advice and opinion of the French peace negotiators" to a more specific mandate that it "undertake nothing in the negotiations for peace or truce without their knowledge and concurrence."[12] Since the Court disliked John Adams, his appointment was broadened to include first two and then four commissioners.

But ironically as the war drew to a close, the Congress became more compliant rather than more resistant to French designs. The explanation for docility was not in the venality of politicians on the payroll, even though that roll was long, illustrious, and well padded. It lies more in the increasing awareness of the fragility of the Confederation and in the psychological and financial drain of the long war with Britain. To men such as Robert R. Livingston, the first secretary for foreign affairs of the Confederation, and Robert Morris, its superintendent of finances from 1781 to 1783, there was no substitute for French support in this period.

Morris, in his critical capacity as finance minister, reveals this dependence clearly. Buoyed by the Franco-American victory at Yorktown, he expressed his surprise to Franklin in December 1781 that the United States made so many purchases in Holland. "If everything else were equal the generous conduct of France towards us has been such that I cannot but think every possible preference ought to be given to the manufacturers of that nation."[13] Whether this sentiment reflected the state of his personal investments more than the national is less material than the importance he gave to the continuing French financial support. At the same time he recognized the price of this support. A few months later, after Congress heeded his advice, he had second thoughts about the relationship and urged merchants to draw upon Spanish and Dutch creditors rather than on Frenchmen exclusively. In July 1782 he lamented that France had not granted all aid as loan rather than as gift because "I do not think the weight of the debt would be so great as the weight of an obligation is generally found to be." No matter how assiduously Morris may have been pursuing his private welfare, he understood the public's as well.[14]

As for Livingston, he was alarmed at the freewheeling behavior of the commissioners who wandered over Europe denouncing the ally, dickering with the enemy, and ignoring the will of the Congress. Jay, prodded by Adams, had exposed a secret French memorandum which presumably would have ended the war, with the British and Spanish sharing territory between the mountains and the Mississippi, while Franklin concluded a separate agreement with the British which left the French no alternative but to accept. Jay's letter chafing at congressional fetters discomfited Livingston. Jay insisted on the Americans accepting British terms if they were appropriate: "we are under no obligation to persist in the war to gratify this court. But can it be wise to instruct your commissioners to speak only as the French minister shall give them utterance."[15]

Livingston was not alone in his nervousness. He represented the sense of the Congress preoccupied with financial cares and with the impediments to governance. While Hamilton could admit that it was "not improbable that it had been the policy of France to procrastinate the definite acknowledgmt. of our Independence . . . in order to keep us more knit to herself & untill her own interests could be negotiated," he preferred to compare French benevolence with British malevolence.[16] Jay and his colleagues had erred in not showing preliminary articles to the ally before signing and in working out a separate and secret article on Florida boundaries with the British. There was a churlishness implicit in the commissioners' behavior. On balance, as Madison suggested, the total role of France deserves gratitude, not reproach.

Congressional reaction was not simply shock over the improprieties of their representatives abroad. It represented as well fear over French displeasure. John Mercer of Virginia was particularly exercised over the Florida issue, for fear that an angry France would turn around and join Britain in a punitive attack on the United States. Jay's indiscretions played into British hands by creating divisions between the allies, from which only the British could profit. The secret Florida article, enlarging that territory if it fell back into British hands, may have been deliberately contrived by Britain "not for the sake of the territory ceded to her, but as a means of disuniting the U.S. & France, as inconsistent with the spirit of the Alliance."[17] As for France's retribution, Luzerne remonstrated with Livingston and congressmen about the behavior of the commissioners. The king "did not think he has such allies to deal with." In answer to a question about France's intention to lodge an official complaint to the Congress, "M. Marbois [France's chargé d'affaires] answered that Great Powers never *complained* but that they *felt* and *remembered.*"[18] And this ominous note emerged before the knowledge of the secret article had reached the French. As for a congressional rebuke to the envoys, the Congress consoled itself that the ministers did not literally break the treaty and that France was not directly involved in the Florida border problem. So while the commissioners were reprimanded for ignoring congressional instructions, it was done in such a way that their sensibilities would not be ruffled and that the "perfect harmony and confidence" of the ally would be maintained.[19]

Embarrassed as Congress was over this issue, it is questionable if its fears were essentially military or political in nature. The American delegates were neither as naive nor as dependent as the French had hoped. Their problem was fiscal, and the one response they feared most was the rupture of the pipeline of credits and supplies from France to the American economy. Morris raised the question in January 1783 when he informed Congress of a multi-million livre gap between American commitments and American credits, and asked if he should take the risk of France refusing to honor bills. Congress decided to move on the assumption that even if peace came quickly, "France would prefer an advance in our favor to exposing us to the necessity of resorting to G.B. for it; and that if the war sd. continue the necessity of such an aid to its prosecution would continue."[20] In short, Congress displayed much the same kind of *realpolitik* Franklin showed to Vergennes when the latter had upbraided the American diplomat for faithlessness to the alliance. Franklin replied by asking for more funds from the French to repair the damaged ties. The major difference was that Americans at home found it less politic to rub French sensibilities quite as raw as Americans abroad were prepared to do. Ultimately a committee was appointed to consider application for more loans on the grounds that the monies used for the army's disbanding would leave a sense of gratitude to the French among ex-soldiers. The alternative, as the French were subtly reminded, was internal convulsions among unpaid veterans which would not serve France's interests.[21] So much for American subservience to the claims of the alliance.

The treaty lost much of its significance to both parties after the war ended.[22] France had too many other problems plaguing its society in the 1780s to place any priority on its American investment. With few immediate benefits on the horizon, subsidies to American journalists were no longer necessary, even if they could have been afforded. France's complaisance over America's inability to repay its debts reflects the comfort the government was able to take in a weak and divided nation that had only France to turn to for support, no matter how attenuated the relationship should become.

Actually, France and things French prospered enormously during the Confederation. Appreciation for the French role in the Revolution took the form of a rise in interest in the French language and culture. Whatever the political differences and dynastic ambitions of the Crown, France had proven itself a friend, and French friends of America wanted America to succeed as a model for the less favored parts of the world. The lionizing experiences of Franklin and Jefferson in France, and the influence they had on the budding French revolutionaries were flattering to all Americans. In this light the alliance was a symbol of a sentimental bond, rather than a contractual obligation. The duties of treaties, even the fulfillment of trade concessions, were of less moment than the adulation of Lafayette, Brissot, or Chastellux. It was even possible for Frenchmen less worshipful of Americans to wish the United States well, even as they wished them weak and dependent upon France's favor.

What Jefferson, in particular, had wanted from France was a commercial relationship with political overtones. Concessions in admission of American tobacco and whale oil would advance not only the interest of Virginia planters and New England fishermen, but would also shift the American commerce from British to French channels. As minister to France and later as secretary of state, Jefferson regarded France as a counterweight to the dangerous irredentist British power, political and economic. In failing to achieve these objectives, he recognized that political instability and fiscal ineptitude more than political hostility accounted for the frustrations he met.

But even as he sought French assistance, Jefferson recognized the dangers of entanglement. France's failure, after the Revolution, to liberalize American commerce with the West Indies or its earlier unwillingness, as guarantor of the Peace of Paris, to help Americans push the British out of Northwest posts or to defend American shipping in the Mediterranean against Barbary pirates might have evoked stronger reactions from Americans. If they did not, a subliminal recognition of a counterpart guarantee to

87

FEDERALIST FOUNDATIONS

French possessions may have checked their anger. There was an underlying uneasiness over the French relationship experienced by American leaders of every persuasion. They agreed that the weakness of the Confederation required drastic remedies to cope with a hostile world. Madison and Jefferson, as well as Jay and Morris, believed that France as well as Spain and Britain was part of that world. For James Monroe the quarrel between him and Jay over the abortive treaty with Spain in 1786, which would have closed the Mississippi River to American shipping, excluded France; for both men France's role was that of Spain's patron. Similarly, Jefferson could join with Jay in deploring Franklin's consular agreement with France of 1782 for its apparent grant of excessive privileges to French consuls in America; they smacked of extra-territoriality.[23]

Although the alliance survived, it lacked vitality. When its implications were considered, they frightened American statesmen. The language of the Constitutional Convention and of the *Federalist Papers* tells the feelings of the framers about entangling alliances, and it tells also of the continuing consensus of future Jeffersonians and Hamiltonians. Francophilia had no constituents in the Convention at Philadelphia in 1787, as far as political ties were concerned. Within the Confederation the differences in foreign affairs had never been between proponents and antagonists of alliance; rather, they were between xenophobes hoping to remove all foreign connections and nationalists who wanted central power to manage those connections better. Monroe and Elbridge Gerry belonged to the former category in this period; their answer was to minimize foreign relations. Gerry looked upon the French edict discriminating against American trade in the West Indies as symbolic of American impotence in international relations. The only solution for the United States was withdrawal.[24]

No such pessimism dominated the convention and the defenders of the Constitution. While the *Federalist Papers*—particularly Jay's early contribution—hypothecated the consequences of the dissolution of the Confederation and the subsequent intervention of foreign powers, they also cited the Constitution as the instrument to dissuade hostile Europeans from intervening. Not the French alliance, but American internal power, would save the nation. If alliance was mentioned, it was pejoratively. Jay wrote in *Federalist* Number 5 that if the nation broke into rival units, it is likely that "each of them should be more desirous to guard against foreign dangers by foreign alliances, than to guard against foreign dangers by alliances between themselves. . . . How many conquests did Romans and others make in the character of allies?" In Number 4 he had specifically identified France, along with Spain and Britain, as potential foreign allies to tempt rival American republics. There was no distinction here between present ally and late enemy.

The record of the first few years of the Federal Union in which Jefferson and Hamilton shared power in the cabinet discloses no significant shift in sentiment over the French alliance. While Hamilton and his followers moved quickly toward an appreciation of a strong British commercial connection and thereby to a depreciation of the French treaties, Jefferson did not find the Treaties of Alliance or of Amity and Commerce equally important to him. It is not that he advocated the termination of the connections. The threat of British reconquest and commercial enslavement appeared stronger to him than before, and France's role as a weapon to break loose from Britain's economic control appealed to him and to Madison in the House of Representatives. Moreover, the early phases of the French Revolution inspired pride in American contribution to France's political enlightenment. But the sluggish response of presumably liberal France to the secretary of state's overtures revived all his suspicions and annoyances. Revolutionary France should have none of the old regime's excuses for failing to accommodate the economic needs of the United States. When the National Assembly imposed special duties on all foreign ships carrying commerce to France, Jefferson found this "such an act of hostility against our navigation, as was not to have been expected from the friendship of that nation."[25]

Many of these feelings receded when France and England went to war in 1793. France, now a republic, was challenged by British monarchism. And when Hamilton emerged openly as the powerful American champion of British interests, the role of France assumed a new character to the Jeffersonian. The alliance was pushed into the forefront of a cabinet debate, by virtue of Hamilton's goading Washington into a proclamation of neutrality in the European war. The secretary of the treasury welcomed the Anglo-French crisis as an opportunity to break with France and realign American policy formally toward Britain. He could not have found a more sensitive issue with which to challenge his political opponents—Jefferson, Madison, Monroe, and the Republican leaders of the North, George Clinton of New York and Alexander Dallas of Pennsylvania. For neutrality was their object, as well as his, but it was an objective they did not wish to publicize in any way embarrassing to or injurious to the French war effort. Initially, they were willing to settle for a proclamation, provided that the word "neutrality" was excluded from the text.[26]

What they wished to avoid was the potential conflict between the obligations of the Treaty of Alliance, which could bring them into war in defense of the French West Indies, and American vulnerability to British economic and naval power, which would make war a disaster for the United States. Consequently, they spent their energies in the spring of 1793, where possible, on the more acceptable subject raised by Hamilton: namely, the illegitimacy of the French republic as an excuse for breaking the alliance and refusing to accept its envoy. As Jefferson indignantly wrote to Gouverneur Morris in Paris, "We surely cannot deny to any nation that right whereon our own government is founded, that every one may govern itself according to whatever form it pleases. . . ."[27] Madison, under the pen name of "Helvidius," asked his readers to "suppose" that conditions had been reversed— that American congressmen had all been killed, that an interregnum resulted in which the states of South Carolina and Georgia were in danger of being overrun without the interposition of French arms. "Is it not manifest, that as the treaty is the treaty of the United States, not of their government, the people of the United States could not forfeit their right to the guaranty of their territory by the accidental suspension of their government; and that any attempt on the part of France, to evade the obligations of the treaty, by pleading the suspension of government, or by refusing to acknowledge it, would justly have been received with universal indignation, as an ignominious perfidy?"[28] More than illogic and ingratitude was involved. Monroe uncovered a Hamiltonian plot "to separate us from France & ultimately unite us with England."[29]

All of the above sentiments were echoed and reinforced by the numerous democratic societies which sprang up throughout the country in 1793. Whether they were the heirs of the Sons of Liberty or spawns of the French Jacobin societies, they served to promote friendship with France and fidelity to the alliance.[30] Their primary note, and that of Jeffersonian leadership as well, was that France was fighting America's battle abroad. And America's service to the alliance would not be belligerency, but economic aid for which neutrality was a prerequisite. But it would be "a fair neutrality," in Jefferson's words, in which American vessels carried goods to France from the West Indies, unimpeded according to liberal understandings of neutral rights, with produce for France and profit for America. Jefferson admitted that it would still be "a disagreeable pill to our friend."[31]

The Jeffersonians deluded themselves in believing they could have both neutrality and the alliance. It is customary to blame the indiscretions of Genet, the youthful French minister in 1793, for spoiling the delicate relationship between the two countries. But could the claims of the alliance, under the circumstances, have permitted the kind of neutrality Jefferson preferred? The British navy obviously had no intention of permitting what they called contraband goods to move from French colonial ports in American ships, even if it would stimulate resentment in the United States. The French would have permitted Americans to remain technically out of the war only because they saw other services the alliance could extract from the United States in the form of the transfer of supplies in American ships, the arming of privateers in American ports, and the staging of invasions in

American territory. When these services were refused in the name of neutrality, the French then invoked the relationship of 1778. They were prepared to relieve the United States of the burden of defending West Indian islands only if the Americans would invoke and fulfill the articles of the Treaty of Amity and Commerce concerning freedom of the seas. For this occasion, France linked the two treaties.

Hamilton realized the sham of the alliance sooner than Jefferson. The Republicans erred first in thinking the proclamation would have been harmless if Hamilton had not perverted it. And they were mistaken later in emphasizing the unconstitutional action of the executive in taking the action, as if this was the source of the difficulties with the French. The secretary of state's stand on Genet's attempts to arm vessels in American ports exposed a position on the treaties that violated its spirit, if not its letter. Did Article 24 of the Treaty of Amity and Commerce imply that this privilege would be open to the French, since it was specifically denied to the enemies of both countries? Jefferson's negative answer appeared to be a mean-spirited literal interpretation of the treaty, worthy of the Hamiltonians.[32] The French construction was not unreasonable. But if compliance meant war with Britain, the Jeffersonians preferred embarrassment with France.

This does not mean that Madison, who led the Republicans from the Congress after Jefferson retired from the cabinet in 1793, would have taken the next step of a treaty with the British, which outraged France's sensibilities even further. Whether Jay's Treaty was the work of Hamilton's prudence or guile, it was a logical extension of the American neutrality in the war and of America's dependence upon British trade channels. While the terms stipulated that nothing in the document would affect obligations already binding on the signatory powers, the contents made a mockery of the Franco-American treaties. Article 24, forbidding foreign privateers from arming their ships in American ports, did not grant to the British what had been denied to the French in 1793; but it explicitly denied this privilege to the "ally." At the same time, the treaty gave Britain exactly the same concession that France had enjoyed since 1778 in bringing prizes captured from France into this country, directly in conflict with the French treaty. Combined with the failure to challenge Britain's interpretation of neutral rights and Britain's inclusion of provisions as contraband, it was hardly surprising that France read betrayal of the alliance into Jay's Treaty.

France was right. Its anti-American measures, in the face of the American position, were not inordinate. Abandoned by the United States in the one area the Americans could help the French, the mistreatment of American vessels that followed Jay's Treaty in French waters, and the undeclared war against the new undeclared ally of Britain, could be considered fitting retribution. Certainly, some of the Jeffersonian reaction followed this line.

91

FEDERALIST FOUNDATIONS

Unhappy though they were with France's descending to Britain's level in depredations against American commerce, they felt France to be the injured party provoked by the Federalists anxious to serve monarchism above republicanism. Washington's Farewell Address was simply a Hamiltonian ploy to divert the nation from the real entangling connection, that of England. They cheered French victories on the Continent and toasted impending French invasions of England in 1795 and in 1797.[33]

Yet visceral support for the French cause against Britain and the surrogate Britons among the High Federalists did not signify any surrender to France or to the French Revolution under the Directory. Jeffersonian distress over the damage to France in the Jay Treaty was based on the threat of war, initiated by either the Directory or the Federalists. The alliance was the touchstone of the relationship. In 1795 and 1796, when news of that treaty spread through Europe and discredited Monroe, the American minister to Paris, they feared the French government's denunciation of the alliance would be a prelude to full-scale war. Similarly in 1798, after France had humiliated the American commissioners sent by President Adams to Paris in the XYZ affair, they opposed the administration's unilateral abrogation of the alliance as a *casus belli*. Alliance in these circumstances was a symbol of the status quo, not of American loyalty or even of gratitude.

While no specific information was available about France's imperial intentions in America, the treatment of European satellite nations did not go unnoticed even among partisans of France. The Directory's ambitions in Louisiana may not have been fully clear, but Madison had no hesitation about speculating on an angry France conspiring with the Spanish to disturb navigation on the Mississippi River.[34] Jefferson gloomily predicted that there will be "new neighbors in Louisiana (probably the present French armies when disbanded)," which he equated with "a combination of enemies on that side where we are most vulnerable."[35] And Monroe added an apocalyptic note by suggesting that if war should come, the Federalists would link America to England "as a feeble contemptible satellite." And if France wins, "we are then to experience that fate which she will then prescribe. . . ."[36]

The Hamiltonians posed the most immediate danger of war by their exploitation of France's anger. Jefferson and his friends quickly saw that when Talleyrand, the French foreign minister, refused to deal with the American commissioners in 1798 until a suitable bribe had been offered, his mysterious emissaries, X, Y, and Z became a "dish cooked up" in such a way that the "swindlers are made to appear as the French government."[37] And even if the French foreign minister was a swindler, the insulting behavior was no cause of war. Madison railed against the "stupidity" rather than the depravity of Talleyrand. The Frenchman had lived a brief time in American exile, long enough in this country to know "the impossibility of secrecy."[38]

In the campaign for war against the Directory, the treaties of 1778 inevitably became the object of special attack. There was nothing new in this Hamiltonian assault. In 1792 the secretary of the treasury had proposed breaking off the alliance in return for British aid against the Spanish in New Orleans. A year later, after the Anglo-French war erupted, he urged the suspension of alliance on the grounds of its nullification by revolution.[39] But in 1793 he feared that the French connection would bring an American clash with Britain. In 1798 the severance had a different purpose; it was to launch a formal declaration of war against France, and with it, probably an alliance with England and suppression of Jeffersonian dissent.

Such was the scenario projected by the Jeffersonians in the summer of 1798. From the floor of the Congress, they worked against voiding the treaties. Albert Gallatin, a Jeffersonian leader from Pennsylvania in the House, admitted France's violations of the Treaty of Amity and Commerce, but claimed that the alliance was not affected by French measures. If the Federalists had asked for the voiding of the Treaty of Commerce, he could understand the argument, although he made it clear that Jay's Treaty with England would deserve denunciation along with the French treaty. Additionally, he protested the "novel" nature of the proceedings, since there was no precedent for legislatures to repeal treaties.[40] This theme was developed at great length in the Philadelphia *General Advertiser,* where it was coupled with the states' rights thesis of government found in the Kentucky and Virginia resolutions rejecting the Federalist Alien and Sedition laws of 1798. An editorial asked rhetorically: "Is not every officer of a State Government sworn to uphold the Constitution of the United States? If the Federal Government passes laws contravening the Constitution, is it not a breach of oath in a state officer to carry such laws into effect? . . . If Congress can annul a contract with a foreign country because of its violation, will not the same justice operate to modifying or annulling a contract between states which is no longer regarded?"[41]

The debate over the alliance was all the more spirited because the French treaties were mixed with suppression of states' rights, as well as with Hamiltonian ambitions for alliance with Britain. But how much specific meaning did it have beyond its function as a weapon of internecine political combat? Were the Jeffersonians willing to risk war with Britain for the sake of either of the treaties of 1778? The answers were negative. A preliminary examination of the press in 1798, in search of occasions which would celebrate the alliance—such as the twentieth anniversary of its signing or of Independence Day—yields no affirmative position on the treaties. In fact, the anniversary went almost unnoticed on 6 February; the cheers of the democratic societies had vanished along with the societies themselves. Where toasts were raised to the day, as in Norfolk, "may it ever be distinguished," the purpose was no more than to urge "speedy accommodation of all differences between the two republics."[42] The Fourth of July offered even less evidence of the commitment of 1778. Opposition to the annulment of the treaties was one thing; fulfillment of its obligation was quite another. When the word alliance was mentioned by the Rising Sun Militia Company of New York in its many toasts on Independence Day, it was against "all alliance with that almost ruined nation called Britain" and for friendship to all nations, "but in alliance with none."[43] No exception was made for the French alliance.

When it became apparent to Jeffersonians that the break between the Adams and the Hamiltonian Federalists was genuine and permanent and that the new mission to France intended seriously to reduce conflict and to repair the breach with the ally, none of the opposition leaders took this to mean a reinstatement of the alliance. Jefferson put it clearly to Gerry, just returned from France in January 1799: "I am for free commerce with all nations; political connection with none; & little or no diplomatic establishment. And I am not for linking ourselves by new treaties with the quarrels of Europe."[44] It is difficult to distinguish this sentiment from Washington's Farewell Address in 1796 or from President Jefferson's inaugural address in 1801.

Critics, over the years, have attributed such words of Jefferson, Madison, or Monroe to either a shrewd pitch for votes in the presidential campaign of 1800 or to the temporary shock over Napoleon Bonaparte's coup d'état of 9 November 1799. That Bonapartism affected the Jeffersonian judgment of France is not in question. Madison deplored France's defection from civil authority and felt it "left America as the only Theatre on which true liberty can have a fair trial."[45] Jefferson ruminated about men-on-horseback and made the connection between Bonaparte and Hamilton. If he could accept the former, and not the latter, it was only because France was fit for nothing better. The Consulate reflected the French lack of "the habit of self-government."[46]

But the Jeffersonian estrangement from France was deeper than Bonapartism and older than the most recent coup. Suspicions of French intentions in Louisiana and elsewhere, doubts of French reliability in commercial relations, fear of American entanglement in French imperial projects, or even in the republican struggles for survival—all had characterized Republican attitudes toward France from the beginnings of the Federal Union and indeed from the moment the alliance had been made. Such emotions as were felt for France or such calculations as were made on the basis of friendship with France were largely functions of domestic disarray and consequent fears of British designs on the United States. When those concerns were allayed, even temporarily, the familiar postures were restored. There were some differences in 1800. While British malevolence was to remain more dangerous than its French counterpart until the end of the war of 1812, the old dream of France replacing England as an economic partner died, never to revive. In its place was a vision of autarchy that was to become the American System a generation later.

When the Adams peace commissioners signed a new treaty with France in 1800 that terminated the alliance, there was not a single protest from Jefferson, his colleagues, or from the press which supported the new president. If Jefferson called it a "bungling" treaty, it was because it failed to win compensation for damages done to American shipping and because it might be regarded with hostility by the British.[47] President Jefferson was not much moved by such American friends in France as Joel Barlow or Paine who praised a new maritime convention the French were supporting in favor of the liberal maritime rulings, which both countries had subscribed to in 1778.[48] Neutral rights had lost their luster, if only because they had failed to affect British seapower. Jefferson pointedly agreed with George Logan, a devoted Pennsylvania peace seeker, that the United States ought to join no confederacies, even when they pursued laudable goals of freeing the seas for neutral trade: "It ought to be the very first object of our pursuits to have nothing to do with the European interests and politics."[49] This is American isolationism.

PART THREE:

REPUBLICAN SUCCESSES AND FAILURES

7

JEFFERSON'S FOREIGN POLICY AND NAPOLEON'S IDÉOLOGUES

Few qualities of Thomas Jefferson have been so noticed through the years as his attachment to France and everything French. Occasionally, it has won approbation. Vernon L. Parrington, for example, pointed out that the spirit of revolutionary France supported the program of social idealism that Jefferson put into effect as president.[1] On the other hand, Jefferson's enemies in every generation have traced many of his least desirable policies to the baleful influence of France. It is not surprising that his young contemporary William Cullen Bryant should have accepted his elders' judgments of Jefferson's Francophilia when in 1808 he identified him as "Napoleon's slave" and *"willing vassal* of imperious France."[2]

In the last two generations, however, there has been increasing recognition from scholars that Jefferson's philosophy was largely formed before he had been to France, and if it had any special origins, Locke or Kames must receive the credit, not Rousseau or Condorcet.[3] Instead of a wooly-minded devotee and enthusiast, the picture we now have is that of a tolerant and somewhat patronizing teacher of the French, encouraging them in their awkward groping toward democracy, but recognizing that France's lack of experience with freedom and responsibility would slow its advance. This is the Jefferson who resented Napoleon's violence and deplored the excesses of the French Revolution.

The friendly critic can even suggest without condescension that Jefferson's thought was closely related to that of the French idéologues, the liberal philosophers, scientists, and economists who had been criticized so vigorously in the nineteenth century.[4] His translations and support of the works of Destutt de Tracy and of Jean-Baptiste Say, and his intimacy with Pierre-Samuel Du Pont de Nemours and with Lafayette all reflect strong links with the leading figures of the French intelligentsia. Few honors pleased him more than his election to the National Institute, the center of Idéologie.[5] The idéologues were Americanists, believing that the exercise of man's reason would produce a better society, "where the principles of government are economy of blood and money, moderation in private and public expense, respect and love for justice. . . ."[6] Jefferson's equally strong faith in man's ability to reshape his environment and his conviction that Americans had accomplished precisely this objective mark him as a fellow idéologue.

What is less clear in this new evaluation of Jefferson is the answer to a concomitant charge of his enemies: namely, that his affinities for France, Frenchmen, and French ideas led him into the services of Napoleon, even if unwittingly. Particularly at the times of the embargo and of the War of 1812, it had been claimed, Jefferson pursued or urged a policy that served French interests.[7] Considering his long record of friendship with French philosophers, it is worth questioning whether they were consciously exploiting these ties for France's advancement, and whether their efforts were successful. Was Jefferson the dupe of the idéologues? Were they agents of Napoleon?

Jefferson's impressions of France were molded by his experiences there from 1784 to 1789, when as peace commissioner and minister to that country he was able to observe not only the delightful culture of the French but also the important counterbalance which France might provide against a hostile Britain. His identification with the popular Benjamin Franklin combined with his own reputation as the author of the Declaration of Independence assured him of the kind of social life he had dreamed of in Virginia a few years earlier. He enjoyed it immensely, particularly since the circle of intellectuals in which he moved included passionate admirers of America who were as anxious to lionize the new minister as they had been his illustrious predecessor.[8] Although few of these liberal aristocrats and middle-class reformers were republicans, and still fewer were democrats, all shared a hope of giving France a more satisfactory government that would provide some of the American liberties. Most of the later idéologues were to be found, as was Jefferson, enjoying the hospitality of Madame Helvétius's salon. The friendships he made in this circle endured a lifetime of trials.

Jefferson was always eager to send along the ideas of his French friends to American correspondents. Their conversation, however, seemed to stimulate him far more than their ideas. The latter found favor with him when they coincided with his own experiences or conceptions. In most respects their ideals and ambitions were different from his. Essentially they were dogmatists in their philosophy, while he was a pragmatist.[9] The difficulty in identifying Jefferson with any particular philosophical school is to find the mold into which his ideas fit. His efforts as a politician and statesman during most of his active life took precedence over his philosophical interests. The responsibilities of public life with its emphasis upon expediency strengthened his reluctance to pursue all the implications of formal doctrines. His association with physiocrats, for example, showed that he would accept only those portions of their doctrines which confirmed his American experiences. There was much in physiocracy that he approved— veneration of the farmer, dislike of excessive government interference in economic activity—but his chief bond with the physiocrats was their admiration for the United States.[10]

When Jefferson left for the United States in 1790, he could take satisfaction from the fact that one grave shortcoming of French society, its government, was being corrected by a revolution led by friends and admirers of the United States.[11] Although he had reservations about French abilities to govern themselves properly, these reservations were usually pushed into the background during his years in France.[12] The prospect of a liberal nation joined to America by ties of culture and mutual interest made a greater impression upon him than the widespread illiteracy, ideological rigidity, and political immaturity of many of the Frenchmen he had encountered in these years.

During the difficult decade between his assumption of the office of secretary of state in 1790 and his election to the presidency in 1800, Jefferson's correspondence reveals that he often thought about France, but usually in the context of his domestic problems in America. France as it underwent revolution was to be both a bastion of republicanism in a world of monarchy and a loyal foreign ally against the "monarchical" threat of Hamiltonianism.[13]

Actually, he had insufficient, often distorted, knowledge of what was happening in France in the 1790s. The Revolution seemed to have swallowed most of his friends. Much of the information he possessed in the middle of the decade came from James Monroe, his chief correspondent in France, who convinced Jefferson that the true heir of the early revolution was the Directory. But the men who had influenced Monroe were moderate republicans, veterans of exile and imprisonment under the Terror, who could be excused for welcoming a government that seemed to promise a degree of order.[14] As for the few French literary men he did meet during his vice-presidency, they enjoyed a measure of prosperity from the Directory. One of them, Constantin, count de Volney, even visited Monticello at this time and for two years enjoyed Jefferson's confidence as a fellow scholar and fellow republican while acting as an informal agent of Talleyrand and serving the cause of a new imperialism.[15] Absorbed in American politics, Jefferson did not see clearly either the differences among the revolutionary governments that succeeded each other in rapid order or the effects that Robespierre's Jacobinism might have for liberalism or the effects that the Directory's expansionism might have upon American sovereignty.[16]

The burden of presidential responsibilities after 1800 inevitably made France the focal point of his attention. As president he accepted gladly John Adams's Convention of Mortefontaine, which ended America's alliance with France. He also expatiated frequently upon the evils of Bonapartism and upon the immaturity of the French people who accepted this tyranny. Nevertheless, he remained a friend of France. Despite his intention of removing the United States from any participation in European affairs, his conception of the balance of power in Europe had not changed: Great Britain was still the major threat to America's security, and France's opposition to Britain was essentially a service to his country's interest.

Napoleon Bonaparte, however, was a far more dangerous enemy than the relatively inefficient body he had deposed. Like the Directory, he wanted to avoid arousing American suspicions while France completed negotiations with Spain for the retrocession of Louisiana. This was a major purpose of his reconciliation with the United States; but it was not enough for the ambitious first consul. He also wanted to exploit the Adams peace mission to further his war with Great Britain. American support for the principle of freedom of the seas would help him weld together the maritime powers of Europe into an anti-British League of Armed Neutrality.[17]

What he sought from the United States was a treaty that would uphold the liberal interpretation of neutral rights so that the small naval powers of northern Europe would have the necessary model for joining the League of Armed Neutrality against British sea power. By a generous treaty, France would show herself to be a true friend of the rights of nonbelligerents, and the United States would be an accessory to the league, an ally, at least in principle, in the eyes of the participating powers.[18] Thus the Franco-American Convention of Mortefontaine, signed on 30 September 1800, served a two-fold purpose for Bonaparte: the advancement of united action among the northern neutrals and the removal of the danger of American interference with French plans for the New World. As if to crown his triumph, his representatives in Spain signed the secret Treaty of San Ildefonso, whereby Spain ceded Louisiana to France, one day after the convention with the United States had been concluded.

Instead of worrying about Jefferson's discovery of his duplicity, Bonaparte sounded out the possibilities of inducing the president to bring the United States into the League of Armed Neutrality.[19] He suspected that Jefferson's well-known ties with France in general and with the philosophers in particular might serve his purpose. The delicate Louisiana issue did not inhibit him, since he had no intention of revealing news of its transfer until French troops had occupied the territory.[20] That day would come after Britain had been defeated and after the league had outlived its usefulness. In the meantime, Jefferson's reputation as an idéologue suggested that he might be receptive to the proposals of Thomas Paine and Joel Barlow, two prominent Americans in Paris who were intimates of the French intelligentsia. Either by coincidence or by direction of French officials, they had chosen the week in which the Convention of Mortefontaine was signed to suggest to their old friend that the United States join with the European powers in checking British aggression on the seas.[21] If men like Volney and Destutt de Tracy, Du Pont and Lafayette, as well as Barlow and Paine could succumb to Bonaparte's charms, their transatlantic colleague should be no more difficult to conquer. Jefferson's acceptance of nomination in November 1801 to the Class of Moral and Political Science of the National Institute appeared to bestow a presidential blessing upon France under the Consulate.

Bonaparte appeared to many of the French friends of America as one of themselves—a liberal in politics, a student of science, an advocate of revolution through reform. As evidence of his qualifications as a man of progressive ideas, he was a member of the National Institute and had frequently shown favor to scientists and men of letters during the years he had led armies in Italy and Egypt.[22] Consequently, it required little self-deception for these idéologues to regard his seizure of power as the rescue of liberty from the corrupt hands of the Directory at a moment when the country was in danger.

The general himself made no effort to disillusion them, for he needed the support of respectable republicans.[23] Nor did their illusions fade immediately. Even the most prominent liberals had become too closely identified with the constitution that legitimized Bonaparte's usurpations to make repudiation an easy matter. Volney, Destutt de Tracy, and Emmanuel-Joseph, Count Sieyès, representing the radical republican, limited monarchical, and moderate republican wings of the Revolution, respectively, had seats in Bonaparte's senate.[24] Even those who could not regard Bonaparte as a republican considered him the heir of the Revolution, remedying with his strength the evils of the Directory. Lafayette, who admitted that the first consul had overthrown the Republic, assured Jefferson of Bonaparte's good will towards the United States. He too was in debt to the dictator. The first consul gave him no office, but he did give him back his freedom after long years of prison and exile.[25]

Thus his French friends inadvertently did their part in keeping the president in ignorance of Bonaparte's plans for the United States. His enlightenment had to come from other sources. But despite their infatuation they meant no harm to America and engaged in no conscious conspiracy for reasons of personal profit, or even of patriotism. On the contrary, they sincerely rejoiced in Jefferson's election to the presidency and regarded it as a partial fulfillment of their own hopes for enlightened government.[26] Having shut their eyes to the dangers Bonaparte's regime held for French liberties, they naturally shut their eyes also to the dangers his ultimate success would hold for the United States.

Fortunately, when news of the Louisiana transfer from Spain to France was confirmed, Jefferson needed no outside information to arouse him to action against Bonaparte. The first consul was disappointed if he expected Jefferson's friendship for France or his membership in the National Institute to lull him into a false sense of security. The president not only regarded French possession of Louisiana as a potential threat to American security but actually expected his contacts with the French intelligentsia to serve American interests in blunting this danger. Jefferson and Napoleon each intended to use the same pawns for their respective national objectives.

Jefferson used strong language in dealing with France after 1802. If France prized America's friendship, she would have to cede to the United States New Orleans, the Floridas, all the territory that she received from Spain. If France refused his request, he predicted, she would lose the territory the moment the perennial troubles of Europe distracted its attention from the New World. France would be wiser to give up the land voluntarily and retain the good will of the United States. The alternative for Americans was an alliance with Britain. Jefferson warned that "the day that France takes possession of New Orleans, fixes the sentence which is to restrain her forever within her low-water mark. It seals the union of two nations, who, in conjunction, can maintain exclusive possession of the ocean. From that moment we must marry ourselves to the British fleet and nation."[27]

The president wrote these often quoted words in a letter to Robert R. Livingston, American minister to France, for the beneficial effect he hoped they would have upon its bearer, Du Pont de Nemours, a distinguished physiocrat and friend for almost twenty years. Although Du Pont was then a resident of the United States and was departing for France for what he thought would be only a brief stay, Jefferson saw an opportunity to exploit the economist's contacts with the French government by having him publicize the seriousness with which the United States regarded the Louisiana cession.[28] Lest the Livingston letter fail in its purpose, the president sent Du Pont a note asking him to impress upon his fellow countrymen the importance of ceding to the United States all French territory in America, not just New Orleans.[29]

The unofficial emissary served faithfully the task which Jefferson had chosen for him, but he did not accept it until his pride as a Frenchman had been appeased. The president's tactics, he thought, would antagonize rather than intimidate the French. It would be better for the United States to help the French win Canada in exchange for the surrender of Louisiana, for such a gesture would permit the arrangement to appear reciprocal. If this plan were impossible, he advised, Jefferson should offer a reasonable price for the territory at issue in language that would not offend Bonaparte.[30]

Du Pont's response reflects the ambivalence of the French intelligentsia: friendly concern for a country that was the hope of their youth, and yet a patriotic impatience with America's lack of appreciation for France's problems. In one sense, the result was unfortunate. The apparent importance of Du Pont's role in the Louisiana crisis led Jefferson to overlook pertinent factors influencing Napoleon's decision and to foster an illusion that his own diplomacy could bend the governments of Europe to his will.

Shortly after the Louisiana problem had been solved so satisfactorily, Monroe unwittingly gave the president an opportunity to express fully his motives in cultivating foreign friendships. While in France as special envoy Monroe noticed that Jefferson's correspondence with certain influential Frenchmen had produced a good effect during his mission. He suggested, therefore, that relations with literary and philosophic personages be continued and nourished, especially with those connected with the National

Institute. He was convinced that the National Institute was the most powerful organization in France outside the executive circle itself.[31]

If Jefferson's reply to these observations was somewhat didactic in tone, it was not because he thought that Monroe had misunderstood or overestimated the role of the intellectual in imperial France. He merely regarded the advice as gratuitous, since he had examined long before and put into operation just such a project with reference to British as well as French intellectuals. Indeed, he had consciously made use of his relations with Lafayette and Du Pont when he was minister to France. More recently, he pointed out to Monroe, he had been writing freely to men of the stature of Volney, Du Pont, and Pierre-Jean-George Cabanis "on subjects of literature, and to a certain degree on politics, respecting however their personal opinions, and their situation so as not to compromit them were a letter intercepted." Most of his suggestions were of the kind that "would do us good if known to their governments, and, as probably as not, are communicated to them." The president was confident that he was able to make "private friendships instrumental to the public good by inspiring a confidence which is denied to public, and official communications."[32] It is no coincidence that both Destutt de Tracy and Du Pont were elected members of the American Philosophical Society during Jefferson's presidency of that organization.

After the fall of the Directory, Jefferson's respect for the judgment of his French friends weakened. It was never without reservation. His comments about them and attitude toward them became even more patronizing than in the past. The fact that most of them had embraced Bonaparte upon his accession to power led him to wonder if their views and principles were sufficiently advanced to permit their understanding the free institutions of the United States.[33] Looking at the wreckage of the Revolution in 1800 and at the indecent eagerness with which the intelligentsia welcomed the young conqueror, the president showed his contempt for them by suggesting that the national character of the French was not suited to a republic and needed the ministrations of a dictator to prevent chaos.[34]

Aside from their putative influence in Paris, the French philosophers had little to offer Jefferson. He read only such samplings of their works as Say, Cabanis, and Du Pont periodically sent for his inspection. Even Destutt de Tracy, for whom Jefferson performed literary services without expectation of political compensation, did not plant any new ideas in the president's mind.[35] What he admired in these men, particularly in Destutt de Tracy, was their skill in expressing his own ideas, not their ability to teach him philosophical or political principles. Whenever their ideas corroborated his own thoughts about politics or economics or morality, he treated them with full respect. Should they omit points which he considered essential, however, or should they assert concepts which differed from his own, he would label their work too "metaphysical" or too "European."[36] Jefferson already had shown these prejudices when he was minister to France, but not until his presidency and retirement did he fully express his independence from European thought.

His own affection for and gratitude to his old comrades, however, remained undiminished. He sincerely urged Lafayette and Du Pont to return to the United States so that he might enjoy the pleasure of their company and benefit from their knowledge of scientific and philosophical matters. As inducements he considered offering Lafayette the governorship of Louisiana and wanted Du Pont to open an academy in New Orleans;[37] but these offers were not proofs of their influence over Jefferson—they were mere tokens of his friendship. President Jefferson accepted Du Pont's effusive congratulations over America's acquisition of fine French stock in Louisiana in the same spirit that an experienced teacher might listen to the ideas of a brilliant but callow student. Admitting these many fine qualities, he explained to Du Pont that the Creoles would not make good American citizens until they had learned the meaning of self-government.[38] All he would offer in the immediate future was as much liberty as the people could bear, a form of government which was not too different from that which he had advocated for the French themselves in 1789. Du Pont and Lafayette could be Jefferson's political advisers no more than the French people could be the political equals of Americans.

For all Jefferson's perceptiveness of the weaknesses of even the most distinguished French thinkers, his tactics with the intelligentsia bore no fruit. If anyone gained an advantage from his relationship with these correspondents it was Napoleon.

The French philosophical liberals did not enjoy special favors from him; rather they became objects of imperial persecution once the emperor no longer needed their services. He ridiculed them, deprived them of a free press and free speech, and drove many of them out of the country—all without losing the support of most of them.[39] The motives for their remarkable behavior were complex. They represented a belief among most liberals that Bonaparte's crimes, bad as they were, were preferable to the return of the Bourbons. At least he had brought to France liberal impulses, embodied in the equalization of taxes and the extension of education, and they hoped that in the long run these reforms would destroy his tyranny.[40] His greatest hold on them, however, was the power of patriotism. Whenever they became too disturbed about the shortcomings of the French government, they had only to look across the Channel and see the alternative of British conquest.[41]

That Bonaparte commanded the loyalty of these men even as he victimized them would not under ordinary circumstances have had a particularly adverse effect upon the United States. It would have meant merely that Jefferson's idea of using private friendships for public purposes did not succeed. But during Jefferson's second administration, at a time when he needed a clear understanding of the emperor's purposes, the silence of the liberals was at least in part responsible for Jefferson's failure to realize the significance of Napoleon's tyranny and helped to confirm the president's conviction that Britain was the primary threat to American security. Lafayette and Du Pont praised every project against Britain. When, earlier, the president had spoken of a possible connection with Britain prior to the purchase of Louisiana, Lafayette was more upset over such a possibility than he had been about the actuality of Bonaparte's tyranny. "Could I divest myself of my French feelings," he asserted, "I should still think it very dangerous for the United States to entangle themselves in any close connection with Great Britain."[42] Du Pont went even further with his advice. In his letters to Jefferson he made a point of urging him to seize Canada lest the British attack the United States from Canadian bases.[43] Although he never made specific mention of France's interest in America's relations with Canada, his repeated exhortations were in the interest of France's war effort. It was not surprising, therefore, that the steps leading to the embargo, which brought the United States into the service of Napoleon's Continental System, met with their heartiest approval, and few voices were raised warning the United States against entering the War of 1812.[44]

Responsibility for the president's actions in supporting the embargo and, after his retirement, in urging war rested in the final analysis upon his own judgment. Du Pont and Lafayette gave their opinions in good faith. They saw no conflict between the intentions of France and the interests of the United States. Lafayette, in particular, encouraged Jefferson to believe that Napoleon could be persuaded to understand the common interests of France and the United States and that men such as himself could push him along this path. On the problem of Napoleonic harassment of American commerce, Lafayette was convinced that the emperor was merely misinformed: "I had the other day a conversation on the subject with Minister Fouché who has the *interior* of the interior department. He promised to make an effort to enforce a truth of which every man of sense, about the Emperor, . . . seems to be convinced."[45] And again, two months later, he was still deploring the foolish mistreatment of the United States: "I every day hope his [Napoleon's] great powers of sagacity and calculation will at last discover that in his plan to bring about Great Britain he has taken the wrong end."[46]

Abused by the emperor, the idéologues looked all the more eagerly to Jefferson as their exemplar and to his administration as the embodiment of all their goals—limited government, equality before the law, free press. In short, the United States was the type of nation they had once hoped would emerge from the French Revolution or from Bonaparte's Consulate. Perhaps their continuing passion for America reflects their slim but still real hopes that close friendly ties between the two countries would result in the ultimate extension of some of the American virtues to France, even to a France under the emperor. As a testament to their faith, they accepted the judgment that a British victory in the war would be a greater disaster to France and to the United States than the realization of Napoleon's plans for world conquest.

Jefferson, for his part, was stimulated by their ardor and flattered by their attention. Besides, he shared their basic assumptions, even if he could see clearly their weaknesses. His error in his relations with them was in joining them in minimizing the evils of the empire and in overestimating their influence in Napoleon's government.

In his old age the ability of the philosopher-statesman to expunge unpleasant memories from his mind helped to protect him from the jibes of John Adams about his support of Napoleon and about his weakness for idéologues. "Pray explain to me this Neological Title! What does it mean? When Bonaparte used it, I was delighted with it, upon the Common Principle of delight in every Thing We cannot understand. Does it mean Idiotism? The Science of Non compos Menticism. The Science of Lunacy? The Theory of Delerium? Or does it mean the Science of Self Love? of Amour propre? or the Elements of Vanity?"[47]

Usually ignoring such rhetorical questions, Jefferson challenged Adams's thesis that democracy has no more inherent virtues than autocracy or oligarchy. Democratic government, in Jefferson's eyes, was a social instrument especially adapted for a country like America where every man could own property and thus acquire a stake in society. The people of the United States, trained by their environment and traditions, "may safely and advantageously reserve to themselves a wholsome controul [sic] over their public affairs."[48] Foreign nations were not to be excluded from these privileges once they had prepared themselves to assume the responsibilities of democracy. It did not matter that the French Revolution had failed, for in failing it had publicized the blessings of self-government, thereby preventing Europeans from being satisfied with the return of the old autocrats. Progress was inevitable.[49] Thus Jefferson could accept without question the assurances of Albert Gallatin and Lafayette that the seeds of liberty planted in France by the Revolution were sprouting even amidst the hostility of the restored Bourbons.[50]

In his last days Jefferson was again the schoolmaster showing his devoted pupils how they might acquire the knowledge of the teacher. Lafayette, Du Pont, and Destutt de Tracy were all encouraged to prepare themselves for a more liberal government. As long as they did not try to proceed too quickly, Europeans would eventually free themselves from their oppressors. The Revolution had given them a taste for freedom which they had lacked before; and more important, it had given them some experience in self-government. The old man, writing to his foreign friends in 1820, did not differ too much in his views on revolution from the diplomat of 1789. France was still his favorite foreign nation, and despite all the sins of her rulers and citizens, he still expected her to lead Europe along the path of liberty.[51]

Under these circumstances Jefferson could accept the temporary failure of the Revolution and rejoice in the downfall of Napoleon, "a cold-blooded, calculating unprincipled Usurper."[52] But there is nothing in the correspondence of his retirement to indicate his recognition that France under the dictatorship of Napoleon represented a greater potential threat to American sovereignty than he had attributed to her during his presidency. Perhaps the fixity of his assumptions about the malignity of Britain and the relative innocuousness of France in the Napoleonic Wars was his most legitimate claim to the name of idéologue.

8

JEFFERSON, THE NAPOLEONIC WARS, AND THE BALANCE OF POWER

The young American republic of 1800 has been compared by W. Stull Holt to a jackal living off the spoils it steals from more powerful animals diverted by fights among themselves.[1] And like the jackal the United States ran the risk of becoming involved in the struggles of others.

Thomas Jefferson would have appreciated this view of the Republic. Indeed, he had used a similar metaphor that placed even greater stress upon the precarious position of the United States in relation to the balance of power in Europe: "Tremendous times in Europe! How mighty this battle of lions and tigers! With what sensations should the common herd of cattle look on it? With no partialities, certainly. If they can so far worry one another as to destroy their power of tyrannizing, the one over the earth, the other the waters, the world may perhaps enjoy peace, till they recruit again."[2] Nevertheless, he expected that the United States would not only survive the strife but would "fatten on the follies of the old [nations]" by winning new territory and new concessions from their wars.[3]

As president of the United States and as unofficial adviser to his successor, James Madison, Jefferson was in a position not only to formulate a concept of the balance of power to be expressed in this kind of metaphor, but also to put into effect, or at least to influence, policy decisions based on his understanding of the balance of power. For him and for many of his colleagues that balance represented the equilibrium achieved by the distribution of economic and military strength of the world among the several great powers in such a way that no one of them was strong enough to destroy the others and thereby menace the security of the nonbelligerents. Even if the balance was never exact, the rapacious powers of Europe could check each other sufficiently to assure to smaller nations the maximum degree of peace and stability possible in a world governed by force. A further result of this deadlock was the possibility that a small neutral, such as the United States, might enhance its power and prestige by expanding its territories at the expense of the preoccupied nations of the Old World.

It is important, then, to understand exactly how Jefferson's idea of the national interest can be reconciled with his policy of aiding France by the embargo and by his vigorous espousal of the War of 1812. Did he see a change in the balance of power that favored the lion over the tiger, or did the "common herd" later acquire new strengths or talents that permitted foreign policy to be advanced by other methods? The difference between his often expressed suspicion of Europe and his equally firm support of French war aims has led twentieth-century critics as well as those of his own day to write off his ideas as inconsistent, unrealistic, and Francophile. He recognized the desirability of a deadlock in Europe, and yet, he appeared willing to work toward a French victory at a time when England was fighting a lonely battle to maintain the balance of power on the Continent. He indicated through his embargo program that he understood the risks a small power would run in entangling itself in European wars, and yet he was eager to abandon the path of moderation in 1812. No matter how offensive England's behavior toward the United States, England was fighting a defensive war against an aggressor bent on world conquest; Jefferson never accepted this fact.

The years 1805 to 1815 represent the period in Jefferson's life when his ideas about the balance of power can be fairly treated. Since his attitudes were no longer shaped by the gratitude he once felt for French support in the American Revolution or by sympathy extended to France in her struggle against monarchical invaders, he could look dispassionately at the struggle in Europe and at his country's stake in its outcome. By the time of the Napoleonic Wars, Jefferson realized fully that the United States was facing two powers, both powerful and both hostile to the interests of a small neutral. The course of battle after Britain's naval triumph at Trafalgar and after France's victory at Austerlitz in 1805 turned almost exclusively to economic warfare, which in turn affected the commerce of neutral nations. Britain, deprived of allies on the Continent, and France, lacking sea power, had no other means of coming to grips with each other. In this situation the United States would have been severely tried no matter what the policy of the president had been; but a clear understanding of the relative strength of the two belligerents might have enabled the United States to avoid, or at least to lighten, the burdens it had to suffer during these years.

As each British order in council and Napoleonic decree inflicted increasing damage upon American ships, commerce, and sovereignty, the state of public opinion in the United States made some kind of action necessary. It is clear that the measures Jefferson took deliberately favored France over Britain. From his point of view the contest in Europe was never really one between two titans of equal strength or of equal merit. France, after ceding Louisiana and after losing her fleet, looked less dangerous than Britain, who had the means, through American bases and control of the sea, to insult, plunder, or attack the United States, and who had the motive of revenge to feed her hostility. Jefferson's suspicions of British motives should not be underestimated. The deliberate insolence of her behavior was an important factor in inducing him to choose a weapon that accommodated the war aims of Bonaparte. After the death of Charles Fox, one of America's few friends in the British government, Jefferson's peace moves—the threat of a nonimportation act as well as the blandishment of a special treaty mission—were met with the same contempt by Britain. The crowning insult to American pride was Britain's handling of the impressment issue. One of Monroe's main objectives in seeking a treaty with Britain in 1806 was to end kidnapping of American sailors accused of being British deserters.[4] If Britain had acted with some sense of moderation in this issue, she might have calmed American feelings; Jefferson, even after strong rebuffs, was willing to continue negotiations.[5] Britain, however, abandoned all caution, and the *Chesapeake* incident was the result.

Jefferson was as shaken by this enormity as any of his countrymen. He immediately summoned his cabinet to consider measures of retaliation. But angry as the president was, his behavior was not that of a man carried away by emotional impulse, for an obvious reply to such an insult was war.

REPUBLICAN SUCCESSES AND FAILURES

Instead, he ordered all armed vessels of Great Britain to depart from American waters.[6] He talked about war in his correspondence with Du Pont and Lafayette, and even in conversations with the French minister, Turreau.[7] Nevertheless, Jefferson was more interested in "peaceful means of redressing injustice" than in war, and he eagerly listened to reports that Admiral Berkeley had disavowed the act of the *Leopard* and that the British in Norfolk had shown only peaceful dispositions toward the United States.[8] He declared that he wanted to give the offender an opportunity to make amends for the crime, to grant American merchants time to bring their ships and property back to American soil in the event of war, and, finally, to allow the question of war to be determined by the proper constitutional authority, the Congress.[9]

However, he did not avoid war with Britain at this time because of any belief that Britain was fighting America's battle against Napoleonic imperialism; in the president's mind, Britain's action in the *Chesapeake* affair was only an extreme example of the malice she had always borne the United States. He avoided war because he had a better instrument with which to strike Britain: an embargo cutting off American commerce nominally with all of Europe. It was actually directed against the British Isles, since the British navy had already effectively stifled trade with all countries under Bonaparte's control. This scheme was obviously more than just an answer to the *Chesapeake* affront. Jefferson might have had satisfaction from the British if he had been willing to accept an apology and amends for that crime, but in asking for amends he insisted as well upon the abolition of impressment itself.[10] The incident between the *Leopard* and the *Chesapeake* was merely the occasion that forced him to choose this particular weapon against the enemy, not the reason for his choice.

The embargo came at the time it did because America's position had degenerated so rapidly after the *Chesapeake* affair that an audacious action—war or its equivalent—was imperative. In the period from June to December 1807, when the act went into effect, Jefferson's meek reply to the British atrocity had encouraged the belligerents to continue their attacks on neutral rights. The result was the rejection of American demands for redress, the enforcement of the Berlin Decree, the promise of more rigorous impressment policies, and the Order in Council of 11 November 1807, forcing American ships into British ports to pay for permission to trade with the Continent.

The embargo was not altogether a new policy for Jefferson. To some degree it was the realization of an old dream that Jefferson shared with other Founding Fathers: the isolation of the United States from the evils of the Old World. As such, it was a measure that fitted easily into a pattern of behavior which he periodically had advocated for the "common herd" when endangered by the jungle world of international politics. Inasmuch as Britain and France had virtually banned American commerce from the seas, the embargo could be a face-saving means of giving their decrees the force of American law, and thus remove a source of conflict with the belligerents. This conception of the embargo was more in consonance with the ideal role of a small nation than were other considerations that motivated the president and the secretary of state at this time: namely, the territorial and pecuniary advantages that might be derived from Britain's vulnerability to commercial retaliation.[11] Instead of regarding the embargo as primarily a refuge, Jefferson envisioned it as a panacea which would protect American property, force the belligerents to revoke their decrees, strike a blow for neutral rights, and even help to win the Floridas.

In the embargo message, Jefferson made a point of emphasizing the new construction of the Berlin Decree, as if the embargo were directed against France.[12] This impression was deliberately misleading. Jefferson knew well that its first effect would be to give teeth to the Non-Importation Act against Britain that had gone into effect eight days before the embargo. The president believed that if Britain were deprived not only of her food imports but also of raw materials for her industry, powerful British manufacturers would force the government to yield to American demands.[13] One of Jefferson's aims was to strike a hard blow at Britain without committing his country to war and without bringing upon himself the charge of being a French agent.

It cannot be denied, however, that Jefferson was fully aware that the embargo constituted a service to Napoleon. He more than admitted knowledge that the embargo would not hurt France; he went out of his way to convince Turreau, who had charged him with placing France on the same footing with Britain, that the United States had no intention of treating both countries alike. "The Embargo which appears to hit France and Britain equally," the president told the French minister, "is for a fact more prejudicial to the latter than the other by reason of a greater number of colonies which England possesses and their inferiority in local resources."[14] France, unlike Britain, was reasonably self-sufficient; the supplies she needed from without could be obtained for the most part from her continental tributaries. While the Federalists saw through Jefferson's public pose of equal treatment of the belligerents and immediately sought political advantage from his aid to Bonaparte, they were mistaken in looking upon his actions as evidence of a belief that France was more friendly to the United States than was Britain, or that French violations of neutral rights were less hateful.[15]

Jefferson was aware of the deceit and malevolence of Bonaparte. He confessed that it was "mortifying that we should be forced to wish success

115

to Buonaparte, and to look to his victories as our salvation."[16] If Jefferson was willing to accept mortification, it was because the alternative seemed to be British domination and because France was unwittingly serving the cause of neutral rights. "I never expected to be under the necessity of wishing success to Buonaparte. But the English being equally tyrannical at sea as he is on land & that tyranny bearing on us in every point of either honor or interest, I say, 'down with England' and as for what Buonaparte is then to do with us, let us trust to the chapter of accidents. I cannot, with the Anglomen, prefer a certain present evil to a future hypothetical one."[17]

Because he was convinced that France was not an immediate threat to America's security, Jefferson saw the embargo as an offensive as well as a defensive weapon. Remembering Napoleon's pose as a champion of neutral rights, he pretended to offer the embargo as America's blow in behalf of maritime liberty[18] and also as America's equivalent of joining the Continental System.[19] In return, Jefferson hoped Napoleon would force Spain to cede the Floridas and rectify the western boundary—a hope based on the emperor's promise to Armstrong, the minister to France, that if the United States made an alliance with France against Britain, Jefferson would be free to intervene in Spanish America.[20] Thus the embargo would teach England that her crimes were costly, and it would inveigle France into working for America's territorial aggrandizement, all without the cost of one American life.[21] If a French victory resulted, the Atlantic Ocean would prevent Bonaparte from attacking the United States, if some other obstacle in the "chapter of accidents" did not stop him first.

Jefferson was outplayed in his dangerous diplomatic game with Bonaparte. The Embargo Act, intended as a fair exchange for the Floridas, in effect made America an ally in the Continental System without securing one square foot of Florida soil in return. Instead, the emperor's price kept rising: repeal of all restrictions against French commerce, the right to plunder American ships, and ultimate involvement in the war with Britain. In addition, he ordered the Bayonne Decree in April 1808, permitting confiscation of any American ship found in European harbors on the spurious grounds that he was aiding enforcement of the embargo. When Americans complained about the maritime restrictions or about France's procrastination over Florida, they were told that Jefferson himself had stated the embargo was aimed at France, and hence the emperor's measures represented a natural reprisal. In the same facetious manner French officials refused to listen to American designs on Florida, because Spanish law prevented the king from alienating any of his territory.[22]

Jefferson naturally and openly resented this cavalier treatment. But his retaliation seemed petty and inadequate in view of the provocations. He annoyed Turreau by his talks with British envoys in Washington, by his refusal to capture French deserters in the United States, and by the strict accountability to which he held any ship leaving an American port for France on a special mission.[23] Aside from these pinpricks, the president did little to assert America's independence of French foreign policy, certainly nothing to hurt France's war effort. To the very end of his administration he maintained that Britain's sea power made her the greater danger to the United States; the Spanish uprising against French domination in 1808 served only to convince him that France could never carry out a program of overseas aggression.[24] His deep-rooted fear of British power, combined with the temptations offered by cooperation with France, had induced him to throw over his official policy of encouraging a deadlock between the "lions and the tigers" and to risk instead final French victory.

Repeal of the Embargo Act coincided with the expiration of Jefferson's term as president of the United States. Britain, sure that the embargo would damage America more than herself, stubbornly persisted in executing her maritime policies and was rewarded by the opening of Spanish markets in time to offset loss of American trade. France, considering the United States as just another satellite, saw no reason for thanking Jefferson for the Embargo Act. In fact, Napoleon's minister in Washington welcomed the prospect of revocation in the expectation that the next American step would be war with Britain.[25] As for the United States, the embargo did severe damage to agriculture and commerce and brought unpopularity to Jefferson's administration. The loopholes in the act, widespread violations of its provisions, and the threat of secession in New England all contributed to the failure of the program.

Yet Jefferson's despair over the fate of the embargo and of his career was not justified by the facts. During his two terms in office he had assumed responsibility for doubling the territory of the United States and had succeeded in the even more formidable task of keeping his country out of Europe's wars. The embargo itself might have forced concessions from Britain, had it lasted longer.[26] The unhappiness of his last days as president was due in part to an overestimation of America's coercive powers and, in larger measure, to circumstances beyond his control. A major difficulty with the embargo was not in its composition or in its general purposes but in the special reasons Jefferson had for adopting it. Designed in part as an instrument to punish Britain, its failure portended a shift to less peaceful means of achieving this objective. In leading directly to the War of 1812, the embargo policy pointed up the flaws in Jefferson's understanding of the balance of power in Europe.

Jefferson's departure from Washington for his home at Monticello brought no change in his views concerning the international scene. As long as Bonaparte remained in power and at war with the British navy, he continued to aver that the "Leviathan of the Sea" was the chief threat to America's security. In the solitude of the Virginia piedmont he dwelt upon his prejudices against Britain and his hopes for a French victory. Instead of acting as a moderating influence upon President Madison, Jefferson helped to stimulate his old friend's wrath against Britain.[27] The weaknesses in Madison's leadership that resulted in a declaration of war received no check from his former chief. In fact, the War of 1812 appeared to Jefferson to be the logical extension of the embargo program, and the results he had expected from the embargo were just those he hoped war would bring in 1812.

Reflecting carefully on the plight of his country, Jefferson weighed the virtues and faults of each belligerent and found the British to be more dangerous than ever before. Aside from the fact that Napoleon, without a navy, could not easily disturb the United States, he noted particularly that the French Empire lacked the stability and permanency of Britain. The emperor's personality was as distasteful to him as ever, and his regime was admittedly the most violent and most ruthless of Europe. But it was also the most ephemeral. When the dictator died, the flimsy structure he had erected would collapse with him. British power, on the other hand, was all the more intimidating because it could survive the death of its chief of state.[28] The implications of this unpleasant reflection were so inimical to American interests in 1810 and 1811 that Jefferson appeared more disposed to accept a complete French victory over Britain than he had been at the time of the embargo; "a *republican* Emperor" would at least reserve the United States for the last step in his march to world domination.[29] While Jefferson may have felt no more liking for the emperor as an individual or any more trust in his promises than before, he was not awed by France. Britain, on the other hand, both frightened and angered him.

His disquisitions on the sins of foreign nations, on the mortal sins of Britain in particular, were not made on the sole basis of past experience. He considered them in the light of new actions which the warring powers took against neutral America. Britain once again was the chief offender. The British foreign minister, George Canning, repudiated in 1809 a newly made agreement with the United States whereby each country would repeal punitive laws directed against the other. Canning's recall of Erskine from the post of British minister to the United States was technically justified because Erskine had not followed his instructions, but the tactless way of handling the matter added fuel to the fire of Anglophobia in America. Jefferson was all the more upset by this new evidence of British perfidy, because he had hoped that a real truce with Britain would permit the United States to deal more resolutely with Napoleon.[30]

Seeking revenge for this blow, the United States fell into the next snare of the wily French emperor by scrapping the nonintercourse system, which had replaced the embargo, in favor of Macon's Bill Number 2 of 1810. Knowing that restoration of American trade with the belligerents would serve the British cause, Napoleon induced Madison to accept a purposely ambiguous announcement of the revocation of the Berlin and Milan decrees as meeting all the requirements of the Macon Bill.[31] Jefferson was no less willing to accept these French professions, even if they were not made in good faith.[32]

To trust Napoleon's statements in the face of new hostile actions against American ships and sailors and in the absence of any official document canceling the Berlin and Milan decrees requried the president to shut his eyes to reality. Actually, Madison placed no more faith in Napoleon's pledges than did Jefferson; he frankly expressed his skepticism about France's promises and pondered dolefully over the advisability of declaring war on both countries.[33] He shut his eyes to reality not by trusting the French but by allowing the crimes of the British and the desire for American expansion to push Napoleon's rapacity into the background.[34]

The explosive issues of neutral rights and impressment were not the only ones that brought the United States into war with Britain. America's desire for continental expansion inflamed passions in the West and South, and not the least articulate voice among the expansionists was Jefferson's, urging his countrymen to observe that America had more to gain from a war with Britain than from a war with France. He applauded Madison's decision to send occupation troops into Spanish Florida to protect American interests and advised him to take over East Florida as well as West Florida lest Britain, as Spain's ally, seize it first on the pretext of helping the Spanish against Napoleon.[35]

Florida, however, was small pickings compared with the vast territory to the north which Britain could cede to the United States. Control of Canada would not only give new riches and power to the young republic but also bring security to the pioneers whose lives were constantly being menaced by British-led Indians. "The possession of that country," Jefferson wrote, "secures our women and children forever from the tomahawk and scalping knife, by removing those who excite them."[36] The acquisition of Canada had long been in his mind, although obscured by other problems that had diverted his energies when he was president. His only objection to Madison's declaration of war was its timing; war should have been declared when the weather first permitted entrance of American troops into Canada.[37]

Jefferson made no move to halt the course of the conflict; rather he anticipated it and welcomed it. He did not prefer war to diplomacy; in his view diplomacy had failed with the downfall of the embargo, and the only method of handling the British thenceforth was war. Having stoically accepted the ultimate necessity of war, he could afford to brush aside the malice and greed of Napoleon as minor problems.[38] Jefferson's pacifism, which had been a dominant factor in his policies as a statesman, had always had a limit. When it was reached, he sought America's advantage from her own war just as in the past he had sought advantage from wars of other powers.

The calmness with which the former president accepted the news of war with Britain was increased by his complacent expectation that American soldiers would have little difficulty in occupying Canada. Britain did not have many men in Canada; she was too absorbed in her European ventures to man her American possessions adequately. "The acquisition of Canada this year, as far as the neighborhood of Quebec, will be a mere matter of marching, and will give us experience for the attack of Halifax the next, and the final expulsion of England from the American continent."[39] To be sure, Jefferson anticipated some hardships, such as the burning of New York and other seaport towns, but he had hopes that incendiaries, recruited from the starving workers of Britain who would be deprived of gainful employment by the lack of markets, would amply compensate for such a catastrophe with retaliatory attacks on London.[40] As for probable British victories on the high seas, American privateers would counterbalance their damage with destruction of Britain's merchant marine. So confident was the squire of Monticello of America's ability to defeat Britain that he was not at all sorry that Congress had learned too late about the revocation of the orders in council which should have removed the immediate cause of hostilities. If the British wanted to have peace now, they should surrender Canada as indemnification for the ships and men seized during the past twenty years and as security against further attacks by them or by their Indian allies.[41] "The British government seem to be doing late, what done earlier might have prevented war; to wit: repealing the orders in Council. But it should take more to make peace than to prevent war. The sword once drawn, full justice must be done."[42]

For the United States to win her objectives—new territory in America, destruction of British commerce, and the humbling of British sea power—complete cooperation with the French Empire should have been the logical result of her entry into the war. The United States and France were fighting a common enemy, and Jefferson counted heavily upon Napoleon's support for success. Only by being assured that British forces would be tied down in Europe could Americans expect free rein in America; only the Continental System could shake the financial structure of Britain. The former president showed his understanding of America's dependence on France by approving Napoleon's invasion of Russia, which coincided with America's initial war moves. "The exclusion of their [British] commerce from the United

States, and the closing of the Baltic against it, which the present campaign in Europe will effect, will accomplish the catastrophe already so far advanced on them."[43]

The United States government, nevertheless, maintained the fiction of fighting its own separate war and saw no occasion of making this an excuse to fraternize with the emperor. Jefferson heartily concurred in this attitude. It was, first of all, good politics to disassociate America's action from France's war against Europe. Claims for spoliations and amends for imprisonment of American seamen remained a sore point in Franco-American relations.[44] Any talk of open alliance with the French would have invoked the wrath not only of the Federalists and the Francophobes, but also of those Republicans who detested the Napoleonic dictatorship.[45] Moreover, there was no need for a change of status between the two countries; France, it was felt, would perform the service of tying up the British in Europe no matter what course the United States pursued.

Jefferson's attitude toward the two major adversaries during the War of 1812 was probably more confused than subtle. Clinging to his old theme that Britain was America's principal enemy, he seemed early in the war to look favorably upon a thorough defeat of Britain. The next step was to be war with France if necessary.[46] Singlehandedly, it seemed, the American David could take on the two Goliaths of Europe and defeat them each in turn!

As the war progressed and the invasion of Canada proved more troublesome, Jefferson reflected further upon this scheme and found it wanting. It finally occurred to him that despite all the obstacles Providence might throw in the way of Napoleon's conquest of the United States, a victorious emperor might easily possess the British fleet and all the resources of the British Empire, combining therewith the power of the Leviathan of the Sea with that of the Mammoth of the Land.[47] "The success of Bonaparte in the battle of Dresden," he observed, "and the repair of the checks given by Bernadotte and Blücher, which I have no doubt he will soon effect, added to the loss of Canada, will produce a melancholy meeting between the Executive of England and its parliament. And should it overset the ministry it might give us peace with England, and consequently war with all those arrayed against her in Europe, which will hardly mend our situation."[48]

Therefore, the United States would do better to let the two powers battle themselves to mutual exhaustion so that neither would have strength left to hurt smaller countries. He decided that it was wise for the United States to send grain to British troops in Spain where they were locked in combat with the French, because the British were fighting America's battles in the Iberian peninsula. Should the British be starved out of Spain, he feared they would be sent to the American theater of operations. On the other hand, the United States should do nothing to interfere with the French campaign in the Baltic, for there France was serving our cause by shutting off Britain's manufactures from that sea and hence from the Continent, thereby "assisting us in her reduction to extremity."[49] So difficult was the choice that "we know not what to fear, and, only standing to our helm, must abide, with folded arms, the issue of the storm."[50]

While the devious course of Jefferson's opinion on foreign policy pointed toward a stalemate in Europe as the desirable result for America, the logic of his country's position in Europe's war indicated service to French interests. Understandably, his followers were never so mystified about his views as they were at this time. If a French conquest of Europe was inimical to the United States, why make a common cause in war? How was he to explain a policy that advocated a French victory, but not too much of a victory? And Jefferson was forced to make explanations, for even in retirement he was considered the fountainhead of all wisdom in the Republican party and as such was expected to exert considerable influence upon the Madison administration.[51] The issue of friendship with France divided Republicans into two groups: those whose contempt for Bonaparte as a destroyer of liberty made them as anxious for his defeat as for Britain's, and those whose hatred for Britain transformed Bonaparte into an agent of republicanism. Since Jefferson's ideas on America's relations with France were susceptible to both interpretations, it was not surprising that both groups claimed him for their patron.

The consequence of a misunderstanding arising from the intraparty confusion of war aims could have been political embarrassment to the country's war effort as well as personal grief for Jefferson. For the most part he was successful in reconciling the two factions without bringing the issues into the public eye, but in one instance he was forced to admit to hostility toward both major belligerents so openly that he feared the French minister would lodge a protest claiming his statements were lending comfort to the enemy.[52] The cause of this storm was the controversial figure, George Logan, an ardent supporter of the French Revolution until the rise of Bonaparte. He was the idealistic and perhaps naive Pennsylvania Quaker who had made a visit to Europe in the summer of 1798 to find out for himself whether the French government intended to make war upon the United States. Although the Federalists had reprimanded him by passage of the Logan Act penalizing private citizens undertaking such missions to foreign governments, Logan's report of the friendliness of the Directory influenced many Americans, including Thomas Jefferson. Fifteen years later, Logan's missionary zeal was no less strong, except that his love for France had been converted into hatred for the dictator. Making another trip to Europe, this time to England, he found in 1810 confirmation for his prejudices, just as he had in 1798. England was free and powerful and much less under the control of the sordid commercial class than most Americans imagined.[53] Hence, when the Anglo-American war broke out, Logan considered it his duty to inform Jefferson that an honorable treaty could be made with the British if the former president asserted his influence on Madison.[54]

Jefferson had standard answers for Republican critics who opposed America's fighting alongside France. He would usually marshal his old arguments admitting the villainies of Napoleon and France's animosity toward the United States, while at the same time claiming that British enmity was more immediate and more threatening to national security. Possibly in deference to Logan's emotional state, his reply in this instance emphasized more forcefully than was customary his own horror of the imperial regime: "No man on earth has stronger detestation than myself of the unprincipled tyrant who is deluging the continent of Europe with blood." The letter also contained the usual qualifying remarks about his hope of "seeing England forced to just terms of peace with us," a hope that could be realized only through the agency of Napoleon.[55] Whether Logan misunderstood the qualification or purposely misconstrued the letter is not clear. What is clear was his release to the press of an excerpt that presented the former president as an enemy of France and an apparent opponent of the war.[56]

Publication of Jefferson's condemnation of Napoleon immediately antagonized Republicans, like Thomas Leiper of Philadelphia, who considered the French to be performing a noble service, if unwittingly, in fighting Britain and forces of monarchical reaction. Leiper wrote Jefferson a letter of rebuke, lecturing him on the consequences of a British victory. The triumphant British, he foresaw, "would not suffer a Cockboat of any other nation to swim the Ocean." The only consolation he could find in the old statesman's apparent Anglophilia was the possibility that the letter was a forgery.[57] Jefferson did not fail him. Shocked "by the infidelity of one with whom I was formerly intimate, but who has abandoned the American principles out of which that intimacy grew, and become the bigoted partisan of England," he explained the details of Logan's "infidelity" to Leiper.[58] Despite the unpleasantness that this contretemps caused him,[59] the incident made it perfectly clear that when he was forced to choose between Britain and France, his choice fell to the latter.

The fact that the Treaty of Ghent in December 1814 ended the War of 1812 without entailing the loss of any American territory testified to the essential truth of one of Jefferson's favorite theses: Europe's troubles were America's opportunity. With Napoleon brought to heel and banished to the island of Elba, Britain was master of Europe as well as of the high seas and hence was in a position to impose her will upon the hapless United

REPUBLICAN SUCCESSES AND FAILURES

States whose campaigns against British America had failed even while the French emperor was still ruler of the Continent. If Britain did not complete her reconquest of America, a prominent deterrent was the difficulties facing her in the redivision of Europe. Worn out by long years of warfare, Britain envisaged sufficient obstacles at the Vienna peace tables—potential squabbles among the victorious allies and the possible return of Napoleon—to dampen her ardor for revenge upon the Americans.

The retired statesman of Monticello saw none of this at first. When the emperor departed for Elba in the spring of 1814, Jefferson expected that his country would be exposed to the unchecked wrath of the British, to their lust for reconquest.[60] Contemplation of this frightening prospect made him regard Bonaparte in an almost favorable light. He remembered that "he gave employment to much of the force of the nation who was our common enemy" and that "diabolical as they paint that enemy, he burnt neither public edifices nor private dwellings. It was reserved for England to show that Bonaparte, in atrocity, was an infant to their ministers and their generals."[61]

But while Jefferson mourned the loss of French power and expressed his fear of the anger of Britain, he observed Britain's disposition to talk peace and urged Americans to meet her efforts at least halfway. The invasion of Canada having ended in ignominious failure, Jefferson made little mention of territorial ambitions as being obstacles in the way of American reconciliation with Britain. As for the issues of neutral rights and impressment, he hoped that the conclusion of the European war would make them academic. He personally was happy to do his part in calming British passions by letting it be known that he had never really been hostile to the British people; he merely disliked some of the principles, such as their interpretation of neutral rights, and even those principles would be acceptable if the United States might thereby escape from the war.[62] He approved of the work of the peace negotiators, although the posthumous victory of American arms at New Orleans gave him back some of his old boldness: "I presume that, having spared to the pride of England her formal acknowledgment of the atrocity of impressment in an article of the treaty, she will concur in a convention for relinquishing it."[63] The last was only face-saving bluster.

As soon as the United States was released from war with Britain, Jefferson's attitude toward France gradually became more hostile. Not that he admitted his mistake in having supported the imperial regime in the past. On the contrary, his disgust for the stupidity of the restored Bourbons made him welcome for a moment the return of Napoleon from Elba as a defender of "the cause of his nation, and that of all mankind, the rights of every people to independence and self-government."[64] But with the British

124

threat removed, these thoughts were no more than an expression of anger at the greed of the coalition and its Bourbon puppet; he knew that France could never enjoy lasting peace under a Bonaparte. No matter how democratic his guise, the result would be military despotism for France and renewal of conflict for the world. Jefferson did not regret Waterloo for long.[65]

It is obvious that Jefferson understood the importance to American security of an equilibrium in Europe. As he had asserted many times, the objective of the United States in any European struggle should be ultimate stalemate, leaving the belligerents too weak to affect to any important degree the sovereignty of small neutrals. Nevertheless, his confidence in America's powers of coercion and his preoccupation with the British menace led him to adopt a foreign policy that misread the scales of power. The freedom of action which he enjoyed in dealing with embattled Europe stemmed from an assumption that the balance was fundamentally in favor of the British. Thus he could risk supporting France's ambitions, secure in the knowledge that the services he was rendering Napoleon would not affect the desired stalemate. While he recognized the evils of the dictator's regime, he saw an imbalance in the comparative positions of France and Britain which allowed diplomatic maneuvers that would not have been ventured had he been dealing with two countries equally dangerous to the United States.

He was not without his doubts about his balance-of-power policy. Periodically, he expressed fear concerning the consequences of a victory for either belligerent, but even in his darkest moods he would still take his chances with a victorious France, if such a choice had to be made. Those rare occasions when he spoke out in favor of an alliance with Britain or on the benignity of British sea power were prior to the intensification of the European wars and reflected either a devious gambit designed to extract concessions from the French or an errant faith in the friendliness of the short-lived Fox ministry.[66]

Jefferson's activities on behalf of Napoleon are difficult to explain on the basis of national interest. Granting the material and psychological damage done by British maritime practices and granting also the threat to American's sovereignty inherent in their actions, one may still claim that Britain's war was essentially a defense against the continuous pressure of Napoleonic imperialism, and the policies which disturbed or injured Americans were essentially by-products of Britain's response to that pressure. To illustrate the difference between the two nations, one need only speculate as to what Jefferson's foreign policy might have been if France and not Britain had been a neighbor in Canada during this ten-year period. His behavior in the Louisiana crisis suggests that he would have been far more disturbed over potential French aggression than he actually had been over a British attack in 1812. Britain's war with the United States was fought reluctantly—despite the malevolence of Canning—and her war aims were limited. As to Napoleon's plans in event of victory, Jefferson had no illusions, whatever he might have felt about the emperor's ability to carry them out.

Even if the United States had been buttressing the weaker power, the idea of competing so vigorously in the international arena was exceedingly dangerous when all adversaries were so much more powerful than herself. But Jefferson's policies, centering as they did on retaliation against Britain and on using France to win new Louisianas, pushed the country inexorably into the European maelstrom. Only by keeping out of Europe's wars could the plan of playing one country against the other be executed with any real success; by engaging in the war as a cobelligerent if not as an open ally, the country deprived itself of the advantages Jefferson had anticipated. Once involved, the danger of being either overwhelmed by the superior force of the enemy or treated as a satellite by the powerful ally was far greater than the opportunity for making gains at the expense of Europe.

Ironically, the isolationism for which he has been criticized—specifically, abstention from European quarrels—best suited the national interest at this time. Isolationism was not necessarily opposed to realism in foreign policy and, in Jefferson's case, was not in practice equated with ideological rigidity. His greatest successes as a statesman were characterized by an appreciation for the importance of the European balance of power to America's fortunes, the need for freedom from foreign entanglements, and the value of a cautious diplomacy in advancing westward expansion. His rationalizations for the embargo and for American participation in the Napoleonic Wars represent a departure from this policy.

9

FRANCE AND MADISON'S DECISION FOR WAR, 1812

One of the few incontrovertible issues in Franco-American relations in the War of 1812 is the fact of cobelligerency. This circumstance should have made the role of France a major one in the United States' decision for war, particularly when the implicit premise of Macon's Bill Number 2 was that American power would swing behind France should Great Britain fail to correct its behavior toward the United States. Yet the idea and even the very name of "alliance" was studiously avoided by Republicans and emerged only as one of many epithets hurled at the administration by Federalist and Quid opponents of the war. Except in the most elliptical terms, no war leader appeared willing to regard military or political collaboration as a necessary measure for victory. Perhaps fear of the stigma of Francophilia inhibited serious thought of recreating the alliance of 1778 in any form; or perhaps a genuine isolationism, founded on disillusionment with the French Revolution and Napoleon, was responsible for Republican insistence that no connection existed between the war efforts of two nations fighting a common enemy.

The administration's aversion to an entangling relationship with France did not preclude its looking upon the military power of that country as a useful instrument of American foreign policy. The success of Federalist propaganda about the menace of Napoleon combined with the military disasters that befell both countries in the subsequent years have buried the sound tactical reasons behind Madison's apparent pro-French policy. Nevertheless, they deserve more respectful attention than either War Hawks or Federalists paid them at the time. That the administration did give consideration to the French factor in its war plans made the decision for war more comprehensible.

Federalist rhetoric on the eve of the War of 1812 centered on the charge that France had a willing tool in its American supporters, who, having followed every directive of their master, were merely forging the last link in a long chain of subservience to that country. This argument was by that time almost twenty years old. It had been applied against the continuation of the French alliance in the 1790s and against the embargo in 1808. One Federalist newspaper, *Poulson's American Daily Advertiser* of Philadelphia, noted that "as early as 1780 France had its partisans in our councils; of these Mr. Madison was one. He was willing that the terms of a peace treaty be dictated by the ministers at Versailles."[1]

For Federalists the phrase, "alliance with France," summed up the meaning of the declaration of war against England in 1812. It remained for them only to assess its significance and to assign reasons why Napoleon wished for the action at that particular time. Some Federalists professed to see no problem in explaining the war. One New England minister asked his congregation rhetorically, "Has not the French emperor told us that he will have no neutrals, and that in fact we were at war with Great-Britain, long before the formal declaration of it? Have not our restrictive measures been in perfect agreement with his wishes and expectations?"[2]

Others found the war issue more complicated than this. Timothy Pickering, formerly secretary of state and senator from Massachusetts, was accustomed to condemn all Republicans in extravagant terms, but he was perplexed over the special circumstances behind such a calamitous action as a declaration of war. He could understand how the demagogic Republican representative Henry Clay of Kentucky might seek war with Britain as an excuse for a Canadian adventure, but he wondered if "party prejudice" could have rendered "absolutely blind" other more sensible colleagues such as William Lowndes, John C. Calhoun, and Langdon Cheves. Pickering was amazed that anyone might be under the illusion that the United States could survive a French victory. Six months before the United States' declaration of war he had conjured up a vision of what would happen if war came and Canada were won by American arms: he was convinced that a victorious France would sail up the Hudson and reclaim "its ancient possession" just as it reclaimed Louisiana from Spain a dozen years before.[3]

While admitting that it was difficult to trace all the motives that led Jefferson and Madison into the service of Napoleon, Pickering felt he grasped the essential elements of their behavior—a combination of weakness and guile. He vigorously rejected the relatively indulgent view of Federalist representative Samuel Taggart of Massachusetts, who had suggested that since Jefferson believed Britain would inevitably succumb to the power of her rival, it was of the "utmost consequence that the United States be on good terms with France." Such a view, according to Pickering, did the Republicans too much justice. Most men "do not well consider the peculiar character of the administration of Jefferson & Madison, and that these are not to be judged by the rules which in other men would lead to correct conclusions. . . . They have been advancing with some caution. But temporizing will no longer answer their own purposes, or satisfy their French master: they are therefore bent on war, which they expect will smother a full investigation into their conduct, & silence complaints." To avoid "personal disgrace, they plunge the country into war," and thus escape from the consequences of the economic depression and other embarrassments produced by the incompetence of the administration.[4]

The Federalist minority in Congress, explaining its position on the war, couched this theme in somewhat more restrained language. The crimes of France against American shipping, the importance of the survival of Great Britain as a bulwark of American liberties, and the ignominy of subservience to Napoleon were all fully presented, but—the Federalists maintained—"it cannot be concealed, that to engage in the present war against England is to place ourselves on the side of France, and exposes us to the vassalage of States serving under the banner of the French Emperor." Considering "on land, robberies, seizures, imprisonments, by French authority; at sea, pillage, sinkings, burnings, under French orders," should the United States aid the French cause by fighting France's enemy, particularly "at a crisis of the world such as the present"? The answer of the thirty-four congressmen was that war was unnecessary and the French relationship deplorable.[5]

REPUBLICAN SUCCESSES AND FAILURES

Madison's own reaction to such charges was always one of outrage. In 1836 in an interview with historian George Bancroft, the former president claimed to have wanted peace, but "that the British left no option . . . that under the circumstances of the negotiations with England war was inevitable." Nine years earlier he disposed of the issue of subservience to France by suggesting merely that America's national interest coincided with the interest of the "enemy of Great Britain."[6]

John Quincy Adams was even more direct and vigorous in his defense of the administration against the accusations of French influence. He dismissed them as Pickering's "old fable of a compact between Mr. Jefferson and Napoleon that the United States should go to war with England. . . . Pickering is cunning enough to see that war with England may be unavoidable, and *then* he thinks to batter down the administration with this foolish tale of its having been concerted with France beforehand."[7]

It was left to War Hawks Clay and Calhoun to heap a full measure of scorn upon Federalists and Quids who raised the French issue in 1812. Calhoun attacked the impudence of John Randolph, anti-administration representative from Virginia, for asking "how can we without partiality resist the aggressions of England," when France had not dealt justly with the United States. He regarded this view as a "novel doctrine, and no where to be found out of this House, that you cannot select your antagonist without being guilty of partiality."[8] Pursuing England's claim to be the bulwark of civilization against the French menace, Henry Clay noted complaints about the danger of America weakening Great Britain's exertions: "If indeed the aim of the French Emperor be universal dominion, what a noble cause is presented to British valor." But British behavior is hardly that of a champion of virtue, he asserted; their arrogance and malevolence are not worth accepting as the price of "a chimerical French subjugation."[9]

Jefferson echoed these sentiments in more magisterial terms: "We resist the enterprises of England first, because they first come vitally home to us, and our feelings repel the logic of bearing the lash of George III for fear of that of Bonaparte at some future day."[10] But perhaps the bluntest Madisonian expression of Anglophobia with its attendant effect upon the French danger was that of William Jones of Pennsylvania, later secretary of the navy: "Some tender hearted politicians who still amuse themselves with chimerican [*sic*] notions about the balance of power, say we must not strike Britain *too hard* least [*sic*] she should sink and leave no barrier between us and the insatiable ambitions of Napoleon. Now I say if Britain can only be kept afloat by the maintenance of her nefarious pretensions, and the consequent prostration of our dearest rights and interests, *then let her sink.*"[11]

Republicans and Federalists were obviously unable to communicate with each other when they spoke of France. It was almost as if two separate languages shared the same term but invested it with different meanings. To Republicans the real enemy was Great Britain, and if France seemed a "friend," it was only because she represented a lesser threat than her rival. That this outlook on France should be equated with an alliance was absurd to the men who wanted war with Britain in 1812. In fact, the general Madisonian disposition toward France in the year before war was one of impatience and annoyance with the country for failing to fulfill its promised revocation of the discriminatory decrees against American commerce. In a letter to Jefferson, Madison expressed his puzzlement as well as his disturbance at France's behavior:

> It is as, you remark difficult to understand the meaning of Bonaparte towards us. There is little doubt, that his want of money, and his ignorance of commerce have had a material influence. He has also distrusted the stability & efficacy of our pledge to renew the nonintercourse agst G. B. and has wished to execute his in a manner that would keep pace only with the execution of ours; and at the same time leave no interval for the operation of the British orders; without a counter operation in either his or our measures. In all this, his folly is obvious. Distrust on one side produces & authorizes it on the other; and must defeat every arrangement between parties at a distance from each other or which is to have a future or a continued execution.[12]

Almost from the moment of his arrival in February 1811, the new French minister, Louis Sérurier, was the recipient of continuous harassment over the revocation of the decrees. He reported that the president pretended that this issue occupied him more than anything else. When news of fresh outrages against American commerce arrived in the late spring of 1811, Monroe upbraided Sérurier for France's apparent willingness to abandon the United States to the attacks of the common enemy. On the other hand, the secretary of state hinted that if the decrees were genuinely repealed, the United States would ship goods to France no matter what the risks might be.[13]

In France, the American minister received from Sérurier's superiors no more satisfaction than Monroe enjoyed in Washington. Joel Barlow pleaded for a specific statement, an "authentic act" on the part of Napoleon that would silence all doubts in the United States about French sincerity. None was forthcoming. On the contrary, as war with Britain grew closer in 1812, the administration had to cope with the depressing new information that a French squadron under orders was burning and sinking American ships on the high seas.[14]

Sérurier bore the brunt of American anger. Monroe claimed that the Federalists would be within their rights to ask why the United States should

131

be at the point of war with England over the orders in council when it was apparent that France not only had not repealed her decrees but had actually expanded her scope of depredations. He warned the French minister that if the administration were abandoned by France, it would be forced to declare war against both belligerents. And one week before the declaration of war, Sérurier took note of Monroe's comment "that he was among his friends obliged to admit that they had been too weak toward France, and that perhaps they had been too quick in regard to England."[15]

No action of France between March and June of 1812 suggested for a moment that Napoleon had acceded to America's importuning; the St. Cloud Decree, as presented in May, was a complete forgery. Nevertheless, the demands of Barlow combined with the warnings of Sérurier finally convinced France's councilor of state, Emmerich Joseph de Dalberg, that American complaints no longer could be overlooked except at the risk of losing all influence over that country. In May 1812 he urged Bassano to reach a détente with the United States. It was by then obvious that America's intention to wage war with Britain was genuine and deserved reward for its valuable services to France's struggle. An American declaration of war would not only engage British forces in America and on the high seas but would also imperil Britain's principal source of supplies. Hence it would be good policy to free American ships, provide indemnities for damages inflicted since 1810, and make a treaty of commerce that would include provisions for naval cooperation as well as for the support of the principles of neutral rights. The result, assured Dalberg, would be a "more intimate alliance" between the two countries. Failure to act in this way would risk the loss of influence in America or would minimize the extent of America's war operations if it should declare against Great Britain.[16]

Napoleon might not have felt the same urgency about the peripheral problems of America even if he could have spared the time now devoted to preparations for an invasion of Russia. It is questionable whether the advantages outlined by Sérurier would appear necessary to the emperor, considering his customary unflattering opinions of Americans. He was interested in bringing the United States into war, but only on his own terms. Official action on the decrees would be suspended until the Americans had won from Britain the right to carry French goods or had canceled all trade with the British. Until the Americans were formally at war, he felt it valuable to let the issue remain "a little obscure." But to keep up America's hopes he dangled the prospect of French support of the United States in the Floridas and suddenly issued a St. Cloud Decree, officially revoking the earlier decrees, and even brightened Barlow's harried life in Paris with his willingness to discuss the possibilities of a commercial treaty with the United States.[17]

The record revealed Napoleon to have been more accurate than Sérurier in his diagnosis of the American situation. At very little cost and with only minor changes in plans he was able to continue the seizure of ships trading the Great Britain or supplying the British in Spain while continuing to assure Americans that the Berlin and Milan decrees no longer applied to them. At the same time he was able to count on Great Britain's refusal to withdraw its measures against the United States on the obvious grounds that France's declarations were not supported by its actions. His tactics appeared successful. The United States declared war on Great Britain on 18 June 1812.

Federalists have cast doubts upon the sincerity of the administration's willingness to declare war against both belligerent powers. Looking back a year later, Federalist representative Joseph Pearson of North Carolina implied that if the Madisonians had talked about coupling France with England in 1812, they had done so merely to divert national attention from their partisanship for Napoleon. "Had we not been told," he asked "that the return of France to a sense of justice demanded our resistance to Great Britain?" In other words, war with Britain was to be the agency for securing full cooperation from France. If this were so, the inclusion of France as an enemy would have been both unnecessary and harmful to American interests.[18]

The voting behavior of Republicans in Congress on the eve of war appeared to confirm Federalist doubts about the genuineness of their Francophobia. On 12 June, by seventeen to fifteen, and again on 15 June the Senate defeated attempts of Republicans John Pope of Kentucky and Michael Leib of Pennsylvania to punish France and England equally with maritime reprisals unless the former furnished convincing proof of repeal of the Berlin and Milan decrees. Even more suspicious was the fate of the amendment of Republican William Giles of Virginia on 17 June which would have attached to the war measure a provision specifically authorizing the United States Navy not only to recapture ships seized by France but also to seize the "capturing vessel." It was defeated by a vote of eighteen to fourteen. With the exception of Federalist Jeremiah Howell of Rhode Island, the very senators who had refused to couple France with Britain on 17 June voted for war against England the same day. They were joined by the two maverick Republicans, Giles and Andrew Gregg of Pennsylvania. The House had already taken a war stand on 4 June with the more impressive vote of seventy-nine to forty-nine.[19]

One may accept the sincerity of the Madisonian revulsion against French behavior and still ask why so little was done by the government and its supporters to express it. A mitigating factor in favor of France, and a natural one considering the special role of Great Britain in Republican thought,

133

was the fear that somehow perfidious Albion would take advantage of the United States if it fought both Britain and France. Republican representative Jonathan Roberts of Pennsylvania said a month before the war, "I should be sorry to see our policy toward Britain affected at this moment by French aggression—If Britain could get us embroiled with France she would offer such terms of peace as we could not refuse & the next moment go on with her aggression with more impunity than ever." Before fighting France, he hoped the United States would extract a pledge from Britain "that will give some security that she shall not play the fool with us."[20] Secretary of State Monroe also was convinced that in waging war against the two offenders the United States would serve British purposes and increase American difficulties: "I believe that a declaration of war against France, at the same time" would have increased Britain's determination to push "the war against us with the utmost decision in her power." British malevolence, after all, was at the root of America's troubles. Had Britain repealed her orders in council in the first place, "is it not probable that none of these acts would have been committed by France?"[21]

There were, in addition, less subtle motives in excluding France from the punishment of war. Self-interest dictated a special treatment of France. William Jones offered a blunt explanation for distinguishing between England and France. If the latter were included in the declaration of war, "we greatly impair our means of annoying G. Britain by excluding our flag and our prizes of commerce from the continent of Europe from whence we could more effectually annoy her commerce & coasting trade than all the maratime [*sic*] forces of combined Europe."[22] Since the United States needed a continental base to fight Britain effectively, France would become a vital cog in the machinery of war. Obversely, if the United States had included both countries in the declaration of war, a major weapon of victory against one of them would be immediately removed. Such considerations were clearly understood by President Madison who observed to Jefferson in May that "To go to war ag[st] both, presents a thousand difficulties, above all, that of shutting all the ports of the continent of Europe ag[st] our Cruisers who can do little without the use of them."[23]

Following this line of reasoning, one may understand how the apparent unpreparedness of the United States becomes a matter of little significance. France, one of the belligerents which caused America so much misery in peacetime, could be the instrument of the United States in redressing the score in wartime. The French diplomatic counterweight, French bases on the Channel and on the Atlantic, French armies in Spain and in Russia were all part of Republican military calculations in 1812. France would thus facilitate the waging of a successful offensive against Britain, with the prospects of a quick and painless victory. In the words of William Jones,

"War with Britain is the short and direct road to an honorable and durable peace. . . . With France it can only be a defensive war."[24]

The French minister in Washington was aware of the use to which the administration intended to place his country in the common war with Britain. But he felt that the Americans deceived themselves in thinking that the emperor would create a diversion in their favor. It was more likely that Britain would use the American war as an excuse to disengage itself from Napoleon's forces, desert Spain and Portugal, and transfer its forces to the more favorable regions of Canada. Should this eventuality occur, French assistance to the United States would be imperative, but not for the purposes that the Americans were anticipating.[25]

Although there was little likelihood that Sérurier had communicated these thoughts to Monroe, the secretary of state shortly before war began rejected the idea that the British could supply their forces in Spain and Portugal without American aid, let alone reinforce their troops in Canada. He was equally positive that the British would raise the blockade of the United States before they would withdraw their armies from the Iberian peninsula.[26] By the very nature of the European struggle France would have to serve America, thereby compensating for whatever military deficiencies the American military establishment might bring to the war. With a note of smugness the *National Intelligencer,* organ of the administration, could trumpet to Great Britain a warning that drew its strength from the power of France:

> But it is said that we are not prepared for war, and ought therefore not to declare it. This is an idle objection, which can have weight with the timid and pusilla-nimous only. The fact is otherwise. Our preparations are adequate to every essential object. Do we apprehend danger to ourselves? From what quarter will it assail us? From England, and by invasion? The idea is too absurd to merit a moment's consideration. Where are her troops? But lately, she dreaded an invasion of her own dominions, from her powerful and menacing neighbor. That danger, it is true, has diminished, but it is not entirely, and forever, disappeared. . . . The war in the peninsula lingers, requires strong armies to support it. She maintains an army in Sicily; another in India, and a strong force in Ireland, and along her own coast and in the West Indies. Can anyone believe that under such circumstances, the British government could be so infatuated, or rather mad, as to send troops here for the purpose of invasion?[27]

Secretary of State Monroe attempted to impress this message upon Britain in the hope that a fresh look at the implications of Franco-American collaboration would win for the United States the concessions which other methods had hitherto failed to secure. As early as the fall of 1811, Monroe had reproached Britain for not estimating correctly the resources the

REPUBLICAN SUCCESSES AND FAILURES

United States had to disturb Britain in the event of war. "Reflect that the U[nited] States are, as it were, in your rear, and that while your face is turned toward your enemy on the Continent, & every nerve exerted, it may exceed your utmost means to repel an attack made from this quarter on your commerce, in the East, the West Indies, & with South America." He was still hopeful a week before war that reflections about America's diplomatic power "will at an early day rid the British nation of its present ministry, and that an accommodation will soon follow the change."[28]

France's service, moreover, was not to be confined to the Spanish arena. The prospect of a French invasion of Russia provided another weapon for America's war with Britain. Knowledge of the break between the two emperors was widespread in the United States by spring of 1812. Every vessel arriving in New York, Philadelphia, and Baltimore brought fresh news of Napoleon's ambitious invasion plans. Westerners in the Ohio Valley knew that one hundred thousand men were taking positions at the Oder and the Vistula. This was not mere rumor; the information came directly from the *Journal de Paris* of 10 April and was reproduced in the Cincinnati *Spy* of 6 June.[29]

A Franco-Russian conflict appeared to guarantee the success of America's venture. According to one Madisonian, the result of the conflict "will be a completion of Napolion's [sic] continental system in every port on the continent, and if continued must inevitably work the destruction of G. B., for how can she exist without naval stores and materials for shipbuilding."[30] While there is the temptation to suggest that the declaration of war was timed to coincide with the attack of Russia,[31] no evidence supports any explicit link between the two events. Madison in later years denied such a connection, but at the same time he acknowledged the potential benefits of the invasion to the United States and the hopes he cherished for America's fortunes as a consequence of the extended war. In fact, he regretted the failure of Napoleon in Russia, tying it to America's own disasters in the summer of 1812:

> Had the French emperor not been broken down as he was, to a degree at variance with all probability, and which no human sagacity could anticipate, can it be doubted that G. B. would have been constrained by her own situation and the demands of her allies, to listen to our reasonable terms of reconciliation. The moment chosen for war would therefore have been well chosen if chosen with a reference to the French expedition agst Russia; and although not so chosen, the coincidence between the war & the expedition promised at the time to be so favorable as it was fortuitous.[32]

The retired president, writing from the distance of 1827, came close to asserting that if the United States suffered defeats at the hands of Great Britain in 1812, the blame for failure rested in good measure upon France's inability to play its proper role in Europe, most notably in Russia.

In the light of its great expectations, the remarkable tolerance of the administration toward French aggression was at least understandable. Its anger against France, while genuine enough, would most certainly be checked before it boiled over into open conflict. If France had to be punished by war, this measure would be applied only after that country had been exploited for the important chastisement of Britain. As the Madisonians pointed out repeatedly, the British were more vulnerable than the French, but their vulnerability was dependent in part upon American cooperation with Napoleon. Once Britain had been successfully called to account, there would be opportunity to deal with France. Or at least when they turned their thoughts to the nature of Franco-American relations. For the most part, they paid little attention to the future. Their concern was with the recent past, and, above all, the absorbing present.

When one considers the vital role France was expected to play, it is not surprising to find a certain ritualistic flavor in even the most violent Republican denunciations of France or of Napoleon. The very fact that self-interest led to support of some Napoleonic activities, such as his involvements in Spain and in Russia, inevitably produced a softening of the image of Napoleon himself. It might appear obliquely in the form of admiration for the swiftness of his operations rather than as a re-evaluation of his character. "It is by the promptitude of his legions and the rapidity of his movements that Napoleon has been able to plant his standard, and extend his influence to the northern shores of the Baltic," noted the Cincinnati *Liberty Hall.* "With a similar or a proper organization of our yeomanry, we may defy the injustice of the world, and deal out destruction to those who with hostile attitude dare transcend the limits of our country."[33] Conceivably, this western admonition to Americans had Napoleon for its object, but more reasonably the unnamed foes would be Napoleon's own enemy.

The very shrewdness and amorality of Napoleon, although much deplored, had their beneficial, even titillating aspects. Without expecting justice from Napoleon, "attributes unknown to despots," William Jones calculated that his own selfish concerns should induce the wily emperor to modify his aggressions, since this would be a policy "which a profound and subtle statesman like him may be supposed to cherish."[34] While such views were by no means universally shared by the administration or its friends,[35] their subordination of Napoleon's crimes to those of Britain allowed everyone to take a certain pride in the power of this man who could wreak such damage on the common enemy.

It was only a short step from appreciation of Napoleon's glory to recognition that he was a lesser villain than his enemy. Reviewing the causes of the war, William Cobbett, America's occasional friend in London, asserted that it was not surprising to him that Americans liked "Napoleon better than Messrs. Perceval and Ross, and Lords Liverpool and Wellesley. It may be bad taste in the American government and people to entertain such a liking; it may be great stupidity, and almost wilful blindness, that prevents them from perceiving how much more the latter are the friends of freedom than the former."[36] But it should have been perfectly understandable. It certainly was to the influential Hezekiah Niles, publisher and editor of the *Niles' Weekly Register,* who was "astounded with the cries of 'French tyranny,' and the lust of *Bonaparte* for universal dominion. Granted that the French government is a tyranny, and that *Bonaparte* is ambitious, but what has he done to merit the exclusive reprehension of *these* friends of humanity? His tyranny is far more tolerable than that of *Great Britain,* over conquered countries, or even over *Ireland.*"[37]

One consequence of these backhanded apologies for Napoleon was an unwarranted respect shown by some congressional supporters of the administration for the emperor's unofficial revocation of the Berlin and Milan decrees on 1 August 1810. Through the Macon Bill they felt the United States had contracted a species of treaty with France to which the French and Americans had mutually bound themselves. Even so resolute a War Hawk as William Lowndes was astounded to encounter Republican argument in the House of Representatives in April 1812, against any admission of goods and wares from Britain which would modify the nonintercourse provisions or the embargo, even if such a change were to the nation's advantage. The reason, according to Republican Robert Wright of Maryland, was simply that the United States had made a contract with France which should be deemed valid until the president had announced that France had not fulfilled its part of the bargain. Not only was there no contract or obligation, claimed Lowndes, but the French themselves continued to accept and to encourage the importation of English goods in the midst of war. "If we had become parties to what is called the Continental system by a formal treaty, should we consider ourselves as bound more strongly than France herself to exclude English productions?"[38]

Although the administration leaders had recognized the falsity of Napoleon's promises, their decision to accept publicly the fiction of France's compliance with the terms of the Macon Bill inevitably created a special status for France and promoted unwittingly the confusion in Republican ranks over the proper treatment of this "ally." Aroused citizen's committees and state legislatures around the country sent letters strongly supporting war against Britain on the simplistic grounds that France had promised redress for its crimes whereas Britain had not. According to the preamble of a resolution passed by the Virginia General Assembly on 25 January

1812, "France has paused in her career of hostility, and thereby afforded to her rival, England an opportunity of performing her solemn promises without a compromitment of her pride." Similarly, the Ohio General Assembly on 1 January 1812, after condemning the wrongs of both powers recorded that the "conduct of the government of France in rescinding the Berlin and Milan decrees, has, as it respects the United States, manifested a disposition to return to the path of justice."[39] For those unable to see that France was in fact following the proper path, there were at least great expectations that it would soon be moving in that direction as a result of the negotiations for indemnities and new commercial accommodations then taking place between the French foreign minister and Barlow in Paris. Only after an unsuccessful conclusion of these negotiations should the United States "in due season, mete out the same measure to France, which they are about to mete out to Great Britain."[40]

The prevalence of this spirit in the ranks of Madisonians helps to explain the unusual faith that was placed in Barlow's powers of persuasion. How could the mission fail when an intelligent if tyrannical emperor appreciates his own interests? Besides, he had begun to retreat from his earlier position; all Barlow had to do was to complete the process begun in 1810. This wishful thinking played a role in fostering wildly optimistic rumors about Barlow's success in the spring of 1812. The journalistic supporters of the administration were probably the worst offenders. From the Philadelphia *Aurora* western newspapers learned that all matters of dispute between the United States had been settled and that a favorable commercial treaty had been signed. This story had been circulating in Philadelphia since March. The Richmond *Enquirer* was even more specific in its presentation of gossip. It reported that Postmaster General Gideon Granger had received a letter from his friend Barlow, in which the minister told of completing arrangements for a commercial treaty. And after Barlow had sealed the letter, he wrote on the back of it that the treaty had been signed. According to the Richmond paper, the mailship *Hornet* would have full details upon its arrival in the United States.[41]

The *Hornet* arrived in May without any news of a treaty or indemnities. Although the government leaders had as few illusions about Barlow's prospects as they had about Napoleon's character, the imperatives of the impending war permitted them to exploit the fact that if the *Hornet* brought no good news, at least it did not bring bad news. There was still hope for future improvement of Franco-American relations while nothing comparable appeared to mitigate Anglo-American hostility. Both the president in his war message to Congress on 1 June and the responding report of the House Foreign Relations Committee on the reasons for declaring war made a clear distinction, though frequently by indirection, between the crimes of the two countries. Only in the last paragraph of the message did the president give more than passing mention to France. "I abstain at this time, from recommending to the consideration of Congress definitive measures with respect to that nation, in the expectation that the result of unclosed discussions between our Minister Plenipotentiary at Paris and the French Government will speedily enable Congress to decide with greater advantage on the course due to the rights, the interests, and the honor of our country."[42] While the Foreign Relations Committee spelled out the iniquities of France more fully, it suggested that the United States could take care of the problems arising from them in due time and should not be distracted from dealing with the principal enemy, Great Britain. The committee made a special point of exposing Great Britain's assertion that its orders in council had been retaliation against French decrees by noting that British aggression had antedated French action. "The facts prove incontestably, that the measures of France, however unjustifiable in themselves, were nothing more than a pretext for those of England."[43] By implication at least, France's actions were less criminal, its government more reasonable than Britain's, and its assigned role too important for America's immediate future to be bracketed with Britain.

The question still remains: did some form of alliance exist when the president led his country into war against Napoleon's enemy in 1812? If an alliance consists of a formal agreement for mutual objectives, or if an alliance symbolizes a client relationship with a Napoleonic master, as Madison's enemies insisted, the term cannot properly apply. The administration's frequent outbursts of anger over Napoleon's deceits were too sharp to be simulated. Certainly the French minister, Sérurier, was convinced of their reality. Only five days before the declaration of war, he reported his fears that the United States would combine its war measure with the reopening of trade with the enemy. The nation's need for revenue to fight Britain could be provided by trade with the enemy, which in turn would damage the Continental System and Napoleon's scheme of bankrupting Britain through commercial warfare. Sérurier had in mind the bill, supported by leading War Hawks, to modify the nonimportation provisions against England as a substitute for a heavier tax burden. Although it failed to pass, at that time there was no spirit of alliance in the actions of such men as Calhoun.[44]

But the idea of alliance was more than a Federalist nightmare. Some attributes of alliance were to be found in the uses which the administration hoped to make of France in the conduct of the war. Just as Napoleon attempted with some success to manipulate American reactions to Europe's war to his own ends, so Madison and his colleagues consigned to France a prominent if not always acknowledged role in their war against

Britain. Should their measures of coercion fail, they could always comfort themselves with the knowledge that the awesome military power of France would be available to them for chastising the enemy. The downgrading of the Napoleonic menace and the professed hopes in the Barlow mission did not reflect French mesmerization of the Madisonians; they pointed rather to a purposeful acceptance of penalties for dealing with France as the price of the important benefits that France was expected to confer upon the United States.

This evaluation of Madison's approach to France should not recast him in a Machiavellian image. In employing the wiles of the Old World to serve the New, he revealed less of the Old World diplomat than he did of the New World innocent. His wish to exploit France coexisted with a horror at the idea of an alliance and its responsibilities. The president's behavior at this point was strongly reminiscent of that of the Founding Fathers during the Revolution, but with a significant difference: they had a more realistic estimate of the costs of France's cooperation, as evidenced in the Treaty of Alliance they signed in 1778. Even if fear of domestic consequences of an alliance was partly responsible for the intensity of Madison's or Monroe's distaste for the idea of an alliance, their reactions were considerably more emotional than rational.

More than tactical demands of politics determined Republican aversion to any "kinship" with Napoleon. America's moral superiority among the nations of the world would be sullied by even the suggestion of a tie. As George Harrison, navy agent in Philadelphia, expressed it, "I would rather have no arrangement with her at present, if thereby we may be drawn into something in the nature of an alliance, it is more meritorious, and honorable to stand alone in a just cause; I would rather fight both than have an entangling alliance with either." While France might be used to good advantage by the United States, Jefferson himself earnestly urged that "no compact of common cause with the other belligerent" be made. France had different, less honorable, and certainly less desirable war objectives than the United States; the New World republic should not be identified in any way with those aims.[45]

Thus, when Secretary of State Monroe informed Joel Barlow and Jonathan Russell, United States agents in France and England, respectively, of the administration's position toward Europe, a rigid isolationism was presented as the basis for all relations with France in the event the United States also went to war against Britain. "The French Government must not suppose," Barlow learned, "that the attitude now taken by the United States toward Great Britain has changed their sentiments or their expectations of redress, for the various injuries received from French Decrees enumerated in your instructions. . . . Nor will the pressure on France be diminished by any change which may take place in our relations with England to whatever extent it may be carried." When the change was war itself, Monroe fulfilled his promise by observing to Russell that "the United States are under no engagement of any kind to the French Government. With that Government our affairs are as yet in many important circumstances unsettled. It is not wished to connect ourselves with France, nor shall we if to be avoided." Although Monroe admitted that possible disaster in future campaigns against Britain might require undesirable connections, this development would be consistent with the views the administration had always held toward France, namely, that of an agent of the American war effort and nothing more.[46]

What emerges from the welter of charges and countercharges about the Madisonians and France in 1812 is certainly an informal link, unacknowledged by the United States and unaccepted by France. Yet, Republicans could deny it with good conscience. Despite the services the French might provide in the crisis of 1812, Napoleonic France was unquestionably a hostile and alien force in the eyes of the administration, as it was to the administration's enemies. Indeed, a far better case may be made for an Anglo-Federalist alliance than for a Franco-Republican alliance in 1812. Federalists were concerned for reasons beyond immediate partisan advantages about the survival of Great Britain as the defender of civilization against Napoleonic barbarism. No such equivalent consideration affected Madisonian thinking about France. The administration leaders brushed aside as chimerical the possible consequences of a French victory; their interest was confined to the here and now. They fought a separate war for entirely different objectives, and aside from the immediate utility of French strength they had no concern for the fortunes of the "cobelligerent."

The name of isolationist belongs not to the opponents of war, but to the war party itself. When Alexander Dallas, secretary of state of Pennsylvania, challenged Great Britain in 1815 to "produce, from the recess of its secret, or of its, [sic] public archives, a single instance of unworthy concessions, or of political alliance and combination," he was on safe grounds.[47] There was none to be found.

10

FRANCE AND THE WAR OF 1812

There are many reasons to discourage a student of diplomatic history from reexamining the diplomacy of the War of 1812. The recent contributions of Bradford Perkins, Harry Coles, Patrick White, and Reginald Horsman implied that a new look into the statecraft of this period would not yield a verdict substantially different from those of past observers.[1] It may be enough to view with Henry Adams the tragicomical plight of James Madison and James Monroe in a situation beyond their talents to manage, or to recount with Fred L. Engelman the redemptive exploits of the commissioners at Ghent.[2] But there is an area of diplomacy which has been almost wholly ignored in recent considerations of the War of 1812, despite the fact that it concerned many contemporaries: namely, the role of France in American foreign policy during the war.

Although every account of the war gives France attention as a causal factor, France seemingly disappears once war has begun. This is even true of Henry Adams's version, except for his chapter on the romantic fate of Joel Barlow, the exemplar of the American ideologue abroad. (Compare Henry Adams's full treatment of Barlow's mission to France with his scant notice of William Crawford, Barlow's successor.) When France is mentioned at all in newspapers and magazines or in congressional debates and administration white papers, it is as the center of the debate over the origins of the war. Did Napoleon trick Madison into war? Did the United States intend to ally itself with France? These, of course, were the persistent allegations of Federalists throughout the war.[3] With equal persistence, the administration provided thorough, if repetitious, answers to Federalist charges of collaboration with the French by its professions of independence of French influence and its periodic public rebukes to Napoleon for his misconduct toward America before and during the war.[4]

Although the administration's caution in publicizing its relations with France is understandable, was caution carried to the point where the administration failed to consider, let alone to utilize, the benefits the French might have conferred on the American war effort? If not, perhaps French aid in any form was unnecessary; indeed, it should have been, had the conquest of Canada been a "mere matter of marching," as Thomas Jefferson said in early August of 1812.[5] But what was the administration's view of France after the defeat of William Hull, after Britain's dallying over peace negotiations, or after the defeat of Napoleon's armies in 1814? Certainly, France's impact on the struggle with Britain had a place in American calculations about the conduct of the war.

In fact, on the eve of war, this place is clearly evident in Madison's thinking. He consciously linked Napoleon's impending invasion of Russia with the assumption that Britain would be unable to supply its meager forces in Canada. He thought that French cobelligerence would permit the United States to exploit French bases for maritime warfare against Britain.[6] Moreover, he believed that Americans had every reason to expect that many of the problems which had bedevilled Franco-American relations—depredations on commerce, imprisonment of sailors, settlement of indemnities, and the final arrangement of a mutually beneficial commercial treaty— would automatically be resolved.

Americans did not indulge in these hopes with any spirit of humility; they owed nothing to France; on the contrary, France had amends to make for its treatment of the United States. Republicans wished for Napoleon's success in Russia, but not for overwhelming success, at least not to the point where a French victory would lay the continent and England at Napoleon's feet, freeing the British armies in Spain for a Canadian adventure.[7] Such reflections permitted Monroe to rationalize the continued illegal American trade with the British in the Iberian peninsula that did not cease with the coming of war. Louis Sérurier, the French minister to the United States, was shocked to discover that the secretary of state did not even deplore these "unpatriotic expeditions" which prolonged the war with Britain. Instead, Monroe pointed out that Spain and Portugal were neutral powers; and, even if the British were the ultimate consumers of American produce, the trade was in essence no different from the Anglo-French wartime traffic in Bordeaux wines.[8] Although the French minister understood that the pressures of a presidential election required the appeasement of Republican wheat farmers who had a stake in the Iberian trade, he also recognized that appropriate French action on indemnities might produce a bill against that trade or, at least, bring some zeal to the administration's efforts on France's behalf.[9]

Monroe's behavior was not that of an ally, client, or dupe of France. It recalls John Adams's mood in 1776, when he contemplated the role that Europe in general and France in particular would play in the war for independence.[10] In 1776 as in 1812 American policymakers, even partisan newspaper editors who supported the war, held few illusions about France. America's policy was independent of Europe. Europeans, it was assumed, provided assistance to the United States for reasons of self-interest and without expectation of reciprocal commitments. The "active sympathies" with Napoleon, which Henry Adams found in the Republican press, need close examination.[11] If Napoleon was freely praised it was usually in the context of his function as an American agent punishing the British enemy; and, if Americans expressed a desire for a French victory, it was usually stated when Napoleon was on the brink of defeat, and it reflected the more serious fear of an American disaster which might result from French weakness.[12]

Expressions of anger over France's continuing disregard for American property in Europe and of annoyance over French unwillingness to recognize the existence of a contribution against the common enemy were far more customary. Even so staunch a friend of France as Barlow distrusted French intentions toward the United States which, given the opportunity, might be as hostile as England's. As late as September 1812, the American minister warned the president that he should not discount the danger of an Anglo-French plot to make peace and carve the United States into dependent territories of the two superpowers. Shades of John Jay in 1782, and from no less an authority than Barlow! He was relieved that the United States had not declared war against both countries, since such an act could calm "the violence of their animosity against each other and smooth the way to a speedy peace between themselves."[13] Here is a *realpolitiker,* examining the balance of power and finding neither a friend nor an ally in the cobelligerent, but rather a useful if dangerous collaborator.

In light of these sentiments the professions of distaste for France, underscored so forcefully in the *National Intelligencer*—the unofficial voice of the administration—and in the addresses of Madison and Monroe, assume a meaning beyond a simple reaction to Federalist attacks. The government's posture toward France was both genuine and guileful. It was also unsuccessful, since France failed to perform even the minimal functions assigned to it. The seizure and destruction of American ships bound for Lisbon continued, American sailors remained in French prisons, indemnities for past depredations went undiscussed, and new damages were committed under color of the repealed Berlin and Milan decrees. Neither threats nor blandishments of American ministers to France served in 1812 and in 1813 to change the treatment of American commerce. Even worse, the role of France as the great antagonist of England collapsed, as Napoleon in 1813 reeled from a succession of reverses, and then in 1814 toppled to defeat, leaving the United States exposed to the full wrath of a powerful and revengeful England.

Obviously, one of the reasons for American disappointment was the churlishness of Napoleon's response to the nature of America's participation in the war, which was as gratuitous as it was ungrateful. Considering France's long campaign to bring the United States into the Continental System if not into the war itself, an attempt to redress grievances would have been the appropriate token of Napoleon's recognition of services the United States might supply to France. In fact, Sérurier urged the emperor to concede commercial advantages to the Americans in order to detach their commerce from England as well as to reward them for sharing a "common enemy." Or, Sérurier warned, at the first opportunity Americans would seek an accommodation with England.[14] Throughout 1812 and most of 1813 French policy remained unchanged, and the only hopes for concessions were those raised through Barlow's optimism about a prospective commercial treaty. After the death of the American minister, Sérurier gloomily foresaw an American backlash in the form of increased receptivity to Russian mediation and the repeal of the nonintercourse act.[15]

Napoleon's attitudes toward America had frequently been expressed in casual terms, as if the country and its people were unworthy of more than a fraction of his time and energy. In the abstract he envisaged a powerful

146

America emerging in the future to challenge British commercial hegemony and saw that France would profit from this friction.[16] But for the moment American power was too weak to warrant much attention: its military contribution was too small for his present needs; and its political intelligence, as reflected in reactions to his decrees, was too sluggish to make concessions necessary. In addition to these considerations the French had their own grievances against the Madison administration. No other country had the privilege of bringing their prizes into French ports and selling them there, but in place of gratitude the United States only pressed harder for indemnities and refused to suppress the grain trade to Iberia.[17] As late as November 1812, Napoleon had to warn Americans that his favor required them to defend their flag against the British.[18]

But more than Napoleonic malevolence and resentment were responsible for French disregard for American interests and sensibilities. Napoleon did not have much time for peripheral problems when he was fighting for the survival of his empire. Given the personal control of the government that he had exercised for fifteen years, his ministers were in no position to satisfy American demands when he was away from Paris. Even if he occasionally felt generous toward the United States, as Crawford reported after one of his few meetings with Napoleon, it is hardly surprising that this fleeting benevolence would not seep down to the Ministry of Foreign Affairs, let alone to the Ministry of Marine, unless it was specifically translated into a decree.[19]

Moreover, even in areas requiring no sacrifice of French interests, the American war made little impact on France. When war was declared, French newspaper attention centered on Russia not Washington. The official *Moniteur* reprinted the Madison war message without comment. The *Journal de Paris* applauded America for drawing "from the scabbard, Washington's sword," but it was a tepid cheer.[20] An appreciation of a common bond was hard to find, and when it was present in 1812 it was used to exhort the Americans to do their duty toward the French "ally."[21]

Perhaps Sérurier went to the heart of the matter when he warned the foreign minister to follow the advice that Giulio Cardinal Mazarin once gave his sovereign: "In order to serve the purposes of His Majesty in Switzerland, it is necessary to serve the purposes of the Swiss."[22] A large part of Franco-American friction in the War of 1812 was the product of the inability as much as the unwillingness of Napoleon and his harassed government to respond to this advice. If in the dead of night Napoleon's coach swept past the Polish town where Barlow was lodged on 6 December 1812, it was not because Napoleon was trying to avoid the reproaches of the American minister; and if Crawford had to wait from July to November 1813 to meet

Napoleon, it was affairs in Germany, notably at Leipzig, that had much to do with the delay. Although the evidence is inconclusive, it indicates that the French were guilty of neglect rather than of malice.

The French responded to the long and heated American demands for indemnities and a commercial treaty only at the very end of the Napoleonic regime, and the response contained more elements of charade than of reality. As France's fortune declined, Crawford's importunities assumed a more querulous note and focused increasingly on the issue of neutral rights—the very issue that would lose practical meaning as the European war ended. It was also an issue that ultimately disappeared from America's own negotiations with the British. The purpose of the war, Crawford admonished the French, was the vindication of the rights of nations on the high seas.[23] In falling before the onslaughts of the allies in the winter of 1814, the French should take solace in supporting the one country that was willing to carry on the battle for principle. Hence, the simple act of justice in paying indemnities to Americans might give heart to all peoples who oppose British tyranny.[24]

For what it was worth, the French capitulated to the demands of the Americans. The foreign ministry at long last acknowledged that America had been fighting alongside the French against the common enemy and appeared to agree that something more than sale of prizes in French ports should be granted to Americans. Indemnities should be paid, lest the Americans turn to reconciliation with England.[25] This advice had made sense when it was first urged on the government by Sérurier two years before, but in 1814 it was too late to serve any but a rhetorical purpose. There was something ludicrous about French officials fearing Anglo-American reconciliation at the time that Napoleon's imminent defeat would create instant Anglo-French reconciliation. Whether Napoleon would have acceded to his ministry's urgent recommendations is wholly academic. The allies had invaded France early in the month in which the recommendations were made. Three months later, Napoleon was on Elba.

The fall of Napoleon and the triumph of England awakened in Americans a sense of general despair over the future of their war, but it was never deeply rooted or long lasting. The Richmond *Enquirer*, one of the leading Republican newspapers, found it difficult to accept the reality of Napoleon's defeat, and it was convinced to the end that he would confound his enemies once more. The *National Intelligencer* speculated that not even the fall of Paris would doom Napoleon; after all, he had occupied Moscow less than two years before.[26] In the unlikely event of a British-dictated peace in Europe, Americans asked, "what then? We shall not shrink from the issue. Our countrymen are brave; they are numerous, rich and devoted to our cause."[27] Invaders would be repulsed as they had been in the Revolution. It is true that the implications of France's departure from the war ultimately registered even with the editors of the *Enquirer*. In May and June 1814, Americans anxiously awaited news of British arrogance, of new armies dispatched to America, and of peace hopes dashed at Gothenburg; but their fears seemed superficial, ready to be displaced by new hopes.[28]

In Paris, Crawford, the American closest to the French scene, shared this mood. Like the Richmond *Enquirer* before and immediately after Napoleon's defeat, he did not reflect a sense of special danger to the United States. If anything, he seemed more surprised than he should have been when the monarchy refused to continue the permission for American ships to arm in French ports and to sell their prizes on French territory.[29] It may have been unsporting of the French to admit British letters of marque into French ports and to exclude American privateers,[30] but Crawford's posture toward a French government that owed its existence to England might have been less aggressive if he had recognized the full significance of America's isolation in the war with England. Periodically, when he thought about Britain encouraging Spain to reclaim Louisiana or the war prolonged until it would be bequeathed "as a legacy to our sons," his observations and prognostications were as gloomy as the *Enquirer*'s.[31] But these worries were not persistent, and they were alleviated by hopes or illusions which informed Americans everywhere.

The key to American optimism in 1814 was the quiet confidence that the government of Bourbon France was probably more sincerely pro-American than Napoleon's government had ever been. The king, Crawford led Monroe to believe, really liked Americans and might even provide the indemnities that Napoleon had avoided giving during the years he had "usurped executive authority."[32] As late as December 1814, Crawford was still trying to collect compensation for Napoleon's spoliations in addition to new damages committed under Louis XVIII; and he thought he had a slightly better chance to collect than he had had a year before.[33]

The American observers were not wholly mistaken. There was an undercurrent of sympathy in France for the American cause, and it extended to circles more influential than those of such incurable Americanophiles as the marquis de Lafayette and the marquis de Barbé-Marbois. Not surprisingly, Frenchmen, unhappy over their defeat, took pleasure in the American victory at Plattsburgh—a fact that the duke of Wellington noted with anger during his stay in Paris.[34] He also upbraided Arnail-François de Jaucourt, Charles-Maurice de Talleyrand's deputy in the foreign ministry, for continuing to permit American ships to bring their prizes into French harbors in violation of new royal ordinances against American vessels.[35] But if the French held any pro-American sentiment, the British presence in Paris and the Bourbon's special dependence on British favor inhibited an official expression of it. As foreign minister, Talleyrand's plans to restore French prestige required a close working relationship with England at the Congress of Vienna.[36] Even if a neutral France had been willing to risk British displeasure by making quixotic gestures in support of America, the regime of Louis XVIII would never have jeopardized its precarious existence by elevating them to state policy. No matter how eloquently Crawford appealed to past friendship, to a common interest in maritime rights, or to impartiality in the treatment of belligerents, he was never able to win satisfaction on the issues of indemnities or prizes.

His failure to win concessions in this area did not limit American optimism. The knowledge that old friends, such as Lafayette, were free and active once again to use their influence on behalf of the United States, was more important than any vague royal good will. Indeed Lafayette's attempt to win Emperor Alexander to the American cause and to the side of neutral rights was impressive confirmation of these hopes.[37] Crawford reported rumors of an "army of French officers" that was ready to fight for the United States, and Levett Harris, the United States chargé d'affaires at St. Petersburg, heard it "whispered" that France would be among the countries that would raise the issue of maritime rights if England became too overbearing at the Congress of Vienna.[38]

Freedom of the seas, a cause of war, might be the issue to force England to end the war, and a new France might be an instrument in mobilizing Europe against the Leviathan. There was obvious substance to this hope since, early in the war, Russia had proposed its negotiations for peace. It was unimportant that England was able to dismiss Alexander's friendly intervention and to intimidate the Russians along with other Europeans.[39] With France removed as a threat, Europe was expected to turn its wrath against the usurper of maritime liberties and give proper recognition to the one country that resisted England's outrages on the high seas. At one time or another in 1814, other members of the former leagues of armed neutrals were seen as aides to America. In September, British negotiator Henry Goulburn speculated that American hopes of Dutch opposition to the British blockade might explain why the American commissioners at Ghent had rejected the British terms for peace.[40]

France's particular function was to serve as the makeweight in the reshuffling of the European power structure at Vienna and to assert traditional French leadership against British influence in Europe.[41] Pennsylvania's Alexander Dallas, later secretary of the treasury, speculated that Bourbon France would sign a favorable treaty of commerce and amity, which might force England either to make peace with the United States or else to forfeit its monopoly over the valuable American market.[42] Whatever elements of fantasy there may have been in these views of France—and they are considerable, since neither Crawford in Paris nor the American commissioners at Ghent could find meaningful evidence that France was anything more than a dependent of England in the six months before the Peace of Christmas Eve—they point to the truth of the persistent Jeffersonian claim that no attachment beyond his use to America ever tied them to Napoleon. Their transfer of interest from emperor to king was desirable and natural, especially if the Bourbons might serve to diminish British power and support the American fight for neutral rights.

The Treaty of Ghent omitted the maritime issue, but no matter how deep the silence of the document, the symbol of freedom of the seas remained a basis for American optimism in the difficult days of 1814. Years later, when he arranged his letters, which spanned almost forty years of diplomacy, Sérurier offered his personal evaluation of America's contribution to the great wars of the early nineteenth century. The United States, he felt, had battled a great power for a great principle and it had done so with insufficient appreciation from France or other European maritime nations. His case for American idealism was exaggerated; the cause was more an instrument than a goal; and France was less culpable than he implies. Yet Sérurier's commentary corresponds to America's ultimate self-image in the War of 1812.[43]

In conclusion, it seems reasonable to assert that the French factor in the War of 1812 was significant. In one sense, too much has already been said over the years, mostly by the wrong people and on the wrong issues. Federalist charges, refined by Henry Adams and regularly rebutted by Jeffersonians of every generation, are as irrelevant as they are inaccurate. The administration made no alliance with France, received no special benefits from the cobelligerent, and conferred none in return. But France did affect American calculations in 1812, and if Napoleon failed to perform as expected, it was more the result of his failing fortunes than of his refusal to provide indemnities or to sign a new commercial treaty.

The defeat of France protected the United States from facing the potentially tragic consequences of a Napoleonic world. And the confused state of Europe in 1814 protected the United States from the consequences of British victory. Indeed, it allowed American statesmen to hope that Bourbon France would be a better agent than Napoleonic France in bringing about a successful peace with Great Britain. While American policy toward France in the war reveals serious deficiencies in statecraft, it also suggests justification for America's faith in its ability to profit from Europe's troubles.

11

THE PARIS MISSION OF WILLIAM HARRIS CRAWFORD, 1813-1815

In the latter eighteenth and early nineteenth centuries the diplomacy of the United States, according to Samuel Flagg Bemis, profited greatly from the distresses of Europe,[1] and in none of America's confrontations with the powers of Europe was this fact so apparent as in the War of 1812 against Great Britain. The Americans entered the war with almost no thought about coordinating America's efforts at belligerency with the government of Napoleon Bonaparte, whose regime in previous years had proved almost as costly to American commerce as had the several ministries of Great

PARIS MISSION OF WILLIAM HARRIS CRAWFORD

Britain. One of the most curious missions in American diplomatic history was thus that of the Georgia senator, William H. Crawford, whom President James Madison in 1813 sent to France, presumably (so Europeans might have thought) to help bring the American war effort into line with French efforts against Britain, but actually to push for reparations from the French government because of its bad behavior toward American commerce. Crawford unctuously advised the French as to what a good example they might set by being kind to the Americans. The mission of Crawford constituted a piece of American nationalism of the first rank, exhibited in the midst of what might well—for the United States—have been a disastrous war.

It is difficult to conceive of greater contrast in personalities than that of Joel Barlow and William Crawford, the American ministers to France in the critical years of the War of 1812. Diplomatic dealing with Napoleon Bonaparte required the maximum employment of statecraft at all times; when both the United States and France were fighting Britain, the diplomat's weaknesses as well as strengths would be particularly exposed. Barlow, a resident of France for many years, was a devoted Republican who shared the Jeffersonian vision of a liberal France that would serve as a counterweight to England and as a republican bastion in a monarchical world. His disillusionment led to a futile pursuit of Napoleon which ended in frustration and death on the frozen plains of Poland in 1812. His successor was a shrewd popular politician from Georgia whose republicanism contained no sentimental ties with revolutionary France and who before arrival in France in 1813 was not burdened by a speaking knowledge of the language. If Barlow belongs to the category of the sensitive intellectual amateur in diplomacy, Senator Crawford, later secretary of the treasury and presidential candidate, is part of an even stronger tradition in American diplomacy: that of the successful politician willing to display talents in a wider arena.

What sort of man was the new minister? It was clear that he was no ordinary appointee. He was a symbol of the importance the United States attached to relations with France during the War of 1812.[2] Blunt and domineering, he enjoyed a reputation for courage and intelligence which had earned him leadership of the Senate as president pro tempore and an offer of the secretaryship of war before his acceptance of the mission to Paris. In later years these qualities were to take the senator from Georgia into Madison's and Monroe's cabinets as secretary of the treasury and to presidential candidacies in 1816 and 1824. The historian Henry Adams observed in Crawford "the faults of a strong nature—he was overbearing, hightempered, and his ambition did not spurn what his enemies called intrigue; but he possessed the courage of Henry Clay, with more than Clay's intelligence though far less than his charm."[3] Whether or not his temperament provided the best background for a diplomat, Crawford's entry into the field of diplomacy represented an important American tradition, that of the political leader moving from domestic into foreign affairs.

Crawford's republicanism, unlike that of his predecessor Joel Barlow, contained no sentimental ties with revolutionary France. Crawford never had to fear the accusation of French sympathies which had dogged Barlow's diplomatic career.[4]

Neither emotional loyalties nor philosophical speculation complicated his attitude toward France, Britain, or war in general. While his senatorial record reflected deviation from some of the policies of the administration, notably opposition to the embargo in 1807, none of his attitude showed the mistrust, fear, or partisan maneuvering that characterized the Federalist opposition. His view on the embargo was that it did not go far enough in retaliation against British provocation. After the *Chesapeake* incident of 1807 he had preferred war. "He was no half-way man," claimed an admiring nineteenth-century biographer, Joseph Cobb.[5]

The declaration of war in June 1812 had appeared reasonable to Crawford, not only because of Britain's disregard for American rights but because of the opportunities that any alert Georgian would anticipate in the British-ruled Floridas.[6] He was a leading member of Clay's congressional committee which declared in 1811 that the United States "could not see with indifference the said territory pass into the hands of any other foreign power, and that they feel themselves called upon by the peculiar circumstances of the existing crisis, to provide under certain contingencies for the temporary occupation of the said territory."[7] The Georgia senator had every right to consider himself a member in good standing of that group of patriots known as the War Hawks.

There was much that was appealing in the clarity and force and even in the naiveté of Crawford's role in the senate during the period immediately preceding the war. The interests of his nation and state seemed to require a strong policy in peace and war, and he had had little patience with those fellow Americans who wished to temporize or employ subtleties in national policy. The increasing proximity of war seemed to improve Crawford's mood, although the refusal of the Congress to prepare for it annoyed him. A month before the declaration he predicted complacently to a fellow Georgian: "We are going on here, pretty steadily, and will unless a change takes place in the Sentiments of the Representatives to the Eastward of this place, be engaged in hostilities before the middle of June."[8]

But then the war's first year was marked by a series of military blunders which evoked from Crawford a wholesale denunciation of the War De-

154

partment and even higher authority. Generals William Hull and James Wilkinson were objects of his attention. Even the hero of Tippecanoe, William Henry Harrison, appeared to him overrated. The president did not escape Crawford's wrath. "If Mr. Madison finds it impossible to bring his feelings to consent to the dismission of unfaithful or incompetent officers, he must be content with defeat and disgrace in all his efforts during the war. So far as he may suffer from this course he deserves no commiseration, but his accountability to the nation will be great indeed!"[9]

Crawford's political influence, abilities, and integrity nonetheless induced the president to offer him first the secretaryship of war and then the ministry to France.

In the latter assignment he soon would show that he did not consider France an ally of the United States. He was indignant over Federalist charges that the administration was subservient to France. The Federalists, he was convinced, knew perfectly well that the charges were false. "Our political course is a clear one," he asserted a few months after arrival in France.

> We can feel no interest in the wars of the old world, only as they affect our right of neutrality. The empires of the East and of the West, and the intermediate states, together with our oppressive mother country, are alike indifferent to us. In other words, we feel no partiality or prejudice toward any of them. Whatever sentiment of partiality or friendship is felt can be traced distinctly to the conduct of the nation for whom it is manifested.[10]

Crawford's instructions, like Barlow's, took no account of the diplomatic possibilities attending cobelligerency. They remained the demands of a neutral power anxious to settle the "multiplied wrongs committed upon American commerce."[11] The urgent orders to the new American minister were to win compensation from France and prevent recurrence of illegal seizures of American ships at sea, spoliations of American commerce in French harbors, and imprisonment of sailors captured under the infamous decrees of the imperial government, decrees which Napoleon putatively had repealed before American entry into the war. Only after these terms had been met would the minister negotiate a new commercial treaty.

Minister Crawford followed these instructions closely, if with varying tactics. At first he tried the artfulness of a courtier. Upon arriving in Paris he postponed demands for indemnities for depredations upon American commerce, and awaited the emperor's return from the Russian campaign. He feared that without accreditation his remonstrances might offend the government and provide an excuse for delay. "There is a greater danger of this," he wrote Monroe, "as I am informed that I have been represented as an impetuous and unaccommodating man, who will be disposed to say and do harsh things."[12] The reward for this restraint was the kind of rebuff that every American minister to France had encountered since the Louisiana Purchase of 1803. The French Foreign Ministry appeared determined to put off Crawford's importunings into an indefinite future. Crawford was not received by the emperor until November 1813. He explained his mission to the duke of Bassano in September, only to have to repeat it to Bassano's successor as minister of Foreign Affairs, the duke of Vicence, in December. The minister's store of patience, apparently well stocked and on display in summer of 1813, was close to exhaustion by winter. He angrily began to demand of Vicence an explanation of circumstances attending the St. Cloud Decree of 28 April 1811, which had repealed the Berlin and Milan decrees interdicting neutral commerce, insofar as they had applied to the United States. Crawford made clear that he considered the St. Cloud Decree fraudulent, that American shipping was still suffering.[13]

As for the bond that the presence of a common enemy produces, or is supposed to produce, Crawford's awareness of it was reflected only in his efforts to extract reparations from the French for prewar depredations upon American commerce. The most he did about the issue of a joint war effort was to make cryptic allusions in a manner that had little meaning for the French. He did not argue that a French payment of indemnity would be reasonable recompense for services the United States was rendering France in a de facto alliance. Neither he nor his superiors wished to view the war this way. The minister presented a case for reparations to Bassano in 1813 on assumption that "the long and destructive war in which he (Napoleon) had been engaged for the last ten years" was to "establish the rights of neutral states, upon a just, enlightened and permanent basis."[14]

Bassano accepted Crawford's sentiments without comment. The French hardly conceived their major objective in the war to be the securing of rights of neutrals. They certainly did not regard the American prosecution of the war as vigorous. Nor did they believe that the United States had an alternative to war at that moment.

Crawford tried the same approach the next year, in 1814. The American minister invited Napoleon's government to support neutral rights—and, of course, American pecuniary claims for French violations of American neutral rights. He proudly suggested to Vicence that by the end of that disastrous year in the emperor's European fortunes the United States and Britain would probably be the only two belligerents left, which would mean that America alone would be fighting "for the vindication those rights which vitally affect the interest of every civilized state."[15] The other European nations, because of their commercial ties with Britain, could not help themselves, and so if America failed, maritime law would be an empty idea. If France should fulfill its obligations to the United States, the consequences would not only strengthen international law, but

> may even have a strong influence on the conduct of the continental powers, whose measures now appear to be directed by England—it may have a tendency to shorten the connection which at the present moment exists between them—it may even have a good effect upon France herself—suffering from the defection of allies and indignant at the flagrant breach of treaties which so strongly characterize the present epoch—the nation will rejoice to see itself by this act of justice placed beyond the reach of complaint.[16]

It is doubtful that Crawford ever had serious hopes for a favorable response to such a bald plea. Not far beneath the level of diplomatic language was a rebuke to France for past behavior toward the United States. He appeared to be using France's plight in 1814 to strike back at the regime which had treated America with contumely for so long. Obliquely he was pointing out that France had brought its own downfall; if the French had acted differently, perhaps those countries which now supported Britain would have rallied to the emperor in his time of trouble.

Bitterness did not, of course, cause Crawford to question the prudence of America's declaration of war on Britain or soften his feelings about the British enemy. His resentment against Britain increased during the course of his tenure in Paris, especially after the new Bourbon government in 1814 under Louis XVIII revealed itself to be a ward of England's prince regent.

Although the independent-minded minister continued his attempts to win indemnity from the royal government, as he had from the imperial, his major worry in 1814 concerned royal pronouncements rescinding the permission for America to arm ships in French ports. The new decrees also suspended, at least temporarily, the sale of prizes brought in by American armed vessels, and even prevented the departure from French ports of American warships which had entered those harbors at the time of Napoleon's abdication.[17] When he complained to the royal government that British ships carrying letters of marque had been admitted to French ports when American privateers were being excluded, the new government first professed unawareness and then shrugged off his complaint with a specious distinction between a letter of marque and a privateer.[18] American position was not so bleak as Crawford pictured it; he recognized a concealed sympathy of the weak royal government for the American cause.[19]

It was only at this time, in 1814, that Crawford began to appreciate some of the consequences of the defeat of Napoleon. He worried over the twenty thousand troops Britain was sending to America, and wondered whether

157

on this occasion the chronic distresses would operate in America's favor. Bourbon France was weak; Spain was hostile; all Europe appeared ready to accept the usurpations of England on the seas. There was no reason to expect Britain to give up the hated practice of impressment "unless we are disposed to bequeath this war as a legacy to our sons."[20]

As he had feared, the British triumph in Europe did not make it easy for Americans to conclude peace with the enemy. British newspapers in 1814 were suggesting that Spain would attempt to regain Louisiana and would receive British support.[21] Crawford was convinced that the British would attempt to humiliate the American peace commissioners then treating with British envoys at the little Flemish town of Ghent.[22] With few exceptions the Englishmen he met in Paris behaved arrogantly.

Despite increasing frustrations Crawford was not a person to retire from the fray; he was a man of action, and so in the summer and autumn of 1814 a stream of advice went forth from Paris to the commissioners in Ghent, who indeed needed all the advice available.[23] The minister sought to point out to them an issue which he had raised during the last days of the Napoleonic regime, namely, recognition on the part of Europe that America's continuing war served the interests of all maritime powers.[24] This issue eventually might assure the United States of a favorable settlement with Great Britain. The Americans were defending the freedom of the seas, a principle dear to the maritime hopes of all the European nations including, of course, France. Crawford trusted that there would be an implicit European support of the Americans, and that the British, contemplating a restive continent, would conclude a favorable American peace. If Europeans only could be shown that Britain was the real enemy of all. Such a sly diplomatic course seemed to offer more hope for the deliberations at Ghent than merely to wait for the squabbles of the victors at the peace conference in Vienna to distract Britain from the war with the United States. Crawford felt that even if a new war broke out over the spoils, it would not have any permanent effect upon America's position except to "postpone the moment when the maritime states of Europe will have leisure to attend to their marine, and feel the practical effect of British usurpation on the Ocean."[25]

For a time, he had some expectation that the Russian tsar, Alexander I, would lead the way to neutral rights. A former member of the League of Armed Neutrality and victim of British seapower, Russia as an ally of Britain against Napoleon had displayed friendly concern as early as the summer of 1812 by offering to mediate between Britain and the United States. Although Britain at first rejected the tsar's offer, and then after reconsidering it moved the scene of negotiations from St. Petersburg to Gothenburg and finally to Ghent, Crawford hoped that the Russians would notice the service the United States was rendering by opposing British pretensions through defense of maritime law. Unfortunately the hostility of the Russian foreign minister, Count Nesselrode, prevented Crawford from meeting or even communicating with the tsar when the latter was in Paris in 1814.[26] To circumvent Nesselrode, Crawford applied to one of the United States' oldest friends, Lafayette, who responded by presenting to the Russian ambassador a statement on neutral rights drawn up by Crawford and then speaking with Alexander at the house of Madame de Staël, but not much more seemed to happen.[27]

Crawford persisted in his attempts to arouse Europe to an appreciation of the danger in not contesting Britain's control of the seas. On one occasion he did manage to disturb the composure of the British Foreign Office, for in a letter to the major nations of the Continent, he indicated at great length the many British violations of maritime law, especially the extravagant abuse of blockade, and contrasted these actions with American sensitivity to the rights of neutrals.[28] Only two months earlier Admiral Sir Alexander Cochrane's proclamation of a blockade of the American coast, he said, had represented a paper blockade in its most outrageous form, in the opinion of neutrals as well as of Americans.[29] Crawford's letter became the subject of a special memorandum by one of the British commissioners at Ghent, Admiral Sir Henry Goulburn.[30] Sadly, the American minister never knew that one of his shafts had found its target.

The conclusion of the Treaty of Ghent led rapidly to the denouement of the Crawford mission to France. The president had promised him relief from this office once the negotiations at Ghent had ended, and the minister was anxious to redeem his pledge.[31] He had accomplished as much as he could expect in the year and a half of his tenure, and he saw little prospect for diplomatic victories that might be won by his presence in Paris. Even the return of Napoleon from exile failed to change his mind on this subject. Wise in the ways of Europe at last, he was willing enough to exploit the interesting frame of the "new" Napoleon, and even to continue his search for a solution to the indemnity problems.[32] He listened to repeated protestations of France's friendship for the United States. No matter how incredible such statements may have sounded he was inclined to give credit to revelations concerning Bourbon orders favoring Britain in every way possible in dealings with the United States. As for the French interest in cultivating America, he was convinced that such sentiments would coexist with a refusal to touch the indemnity problem. While France might not place obstacles in the way of American trade in the future, the life of the regime in his opinion would not last long enough for such a policy to bear fruit.[33]

The bright future of Franco-American trade rather than the dubious future of indemnities or of the imperial regime was occasion for a lengthy and thoughtful discussion with Louis-Guillaume Otto, an American expert and an Americanophile in the imperial service, shortly before his departure from France. In a memorandum to the minister of foreign affairs, Otto reported Crawford's informal suggestions for improvement of Franco-American relations, and they are strongly reminiscent of the Jeffersonian arguments of a generation earlier. Thus Americans would buy French goods because they can be made more cheaply than British equivalents and were of better quality. The results would lead not only to the establishment of close commercial ties with France but also the ending of American dependence upon British products, the key to British influence in the past. Crawford did not neglect, however to make this happy future conditional upon France's removal of all arbitrary regulations against American commerce.[34]

This Jeffersonian note in Crawford's correspondence became increasingly evident during his last days in France, and was expressed in matters of political philosophy as well as of economics. It might have been the Jefferson of the 1780s writing in the following passage of his patronizing concern for the way in which Frenchmen were groping for liberties which Americans had enjoyed as a birthright. Homeward bound from London, Crawford analyzed carefully for Otto the virtues and shortcomings of the new constitution that Napoleon had introduced after Elba. "Your new constitution, altho' better than the royal ordinance of last June, has not answered the expectations of the friends of civil liberty in France." It was still too paternalistic. "I believe mankind capable of being governed by reason," he asserted.

> When the government addresses itself to the understanding and to the interest of the people, it will not do it in vain, if this is its habitual conduct. But if it habitually addresses itself to their fears— if it relies upon force, or fraud, then an appeal to the good sense, to the patriotism of the people, will be made in vain. France has just passed thro' a revolution—it has in its bosom an immense mass of intelligence, good sense, and patriotism. Let a manly and frank appeal be made to the people—let the legislative bodies be assembled—let them give an impulse to the nation which will rouse it from its lethargy; and then the resentments, the pride, and ambition and the army of the congregated monarchs of Europe will be humbled in the dust.[35]

These sententious words suggest a detachment from the scene of battle and imply a faith in the superiority of the American system of government that is strengthened by his observations of the follies of other nations.

Such were the thoughts which seem to have filled Crawford's mind as he set sail for home in June 1815. Dwelling as they did upon differences between Europe and America, they legitimized the path of American isolationism which had been followed implicitly in Franco-American relations, and insulated him perhaps from any serious reflections upon his own or his country's mistakes in dealing with the enemy of their enemy in the recent war. If the gulf between European and American political systems was still unbridgeable, then the idea of regarding France as a genuine ally in the struggle with England would be unthinkable, a subject to be pushed from one's mind. Undoubtedly the unpleasant memories of the formal French alliance of 1778, the violent attacks upon the Jeffersonians for their putative Francophilia, and personal preoccupation with French insults and injustice help explain this state of mind. Yet it cannot explain away a commitment to war with Britain whose outcome depended in large measure upon the actions of France. For example, a French victory in Russia in 1812 would have changed the course of the Anglo-American war, for the better or for the worse. Crawford must share responsibility with his colleagues for refusing to consider seriously the effects of a Napoleonic defeat upon American interests. Would a successful Franco-American war have served the cause of maritime law for which both parties presumably were fighting? Which country was the more dangerous to the national interest as master of the world—Britain or France? If France was as dangerous as Britain, was the war directed against the proper enemy? These questions never came to the fore during Crawford's ministry to France.

Despite these observations the verdict of failure through errors of omission and through inability to achieve his mission's stated objectives is not realistic. Crawford, first of all, proved himself a stubborn and resourceful diplomatist, maintaining the interest of his country as well as any minister might have under the circumstances.[36] Handicapped by limited acquaintance with the French language, he was a nonetheless shrewd observer of the French scene, placing his insights at the service of the secretary of state and the American commissioners at Ghent. Although emerging from a political background strikingly different from that of his predecessor in Paris, his thoughts and actions about France and America often appeared indistinguishable from those of Joel Barlow. The practical politician betrayed qualities of the American ideologue, while the poet-philosopher revealed a grasp of *realpolitik*. The differences among Americans abroad became slight compared with the differences which they identify between Americans and Europeans.

In this light, Crawford's rejection of France as an "ally" is part of a larger American rejection of Europe, a rejection with roots deep in the American past, strengthened by the experience of history since the Revolution. The judgment of posterity supports this position. The security and prosperity of the United States in the nineteenth century were consequences of the Treaty of Ghent. The Founding Fathers of the Revolution had warned of the dangers of alliances, and the next generation heeded the admonition.

PART FOUR
TO THE MONROE DOCTRINE

12

THE INDEPENDENCE OF LATIN AMERICA:

NORTH AMERICAN AMBIVALENCE, 1800-1820

It is hardly surprising that the romantic qualities in the American war for independence should have inspired responses from libertarians everywhere. That Kosciusko the Pole or Lafayette the Frenchman would have Spanish-American counterparts was a natural consequence of a vision of a new society in which liberty triumphed over tyranny and in which the New World triumphed over the Old. While Latin American revolutions were deferred until the Napoleonic conquest of Spain and were not won until British sea power asserted itself, the American model was always present in the minds of revolutionary leaders. Such dynamic figures as the Venezuelan Francisco de Miranda and the Chilean José Miguel Carrera were deeply affected by the example of the United States. The former's service with the Spanish forces in Florida during the American Revolution inspired his efforts to reproduce the experience for his own country. Carrera dramatically chose 4 July 1812, to dedicate the symbols of Chilean independence. The American Bill of Rights, the state constitutions, and even Washington's Farewell Address were translated into Spanish and acclaimed in Latin America as goals of the liberation movements against the mother country.

The spectacle of the ferment among the Spanish colonies understandably stirred Americans. Even without expectations of material advantages from revolution, the imitation of the American example was a powerful form of flattery. It evoked sentiments as high flown as those expressed by Latin admirers. Among leaders succumbing to the attractions of revolution were Speaker of the House Henry Clay, whose presidential ambitions were linked to his embrace of the revolutionary cause. Although he was not unwilling to exploit a popular issue for his own advancement, his response to Latin American calls for assistance rings true: "We were their great example. Of us they constantly spoke as of brothers, having a similar origin. They adopted our principles, copied our institutions, and in some instances, employed the very language and sentiments of our revolutionary papers."[1] His rhetoric suggested that it would have been unnatural for Americans, of all people, not to offer full support to this fraternal revolution.

Given the enthusiasm of the American public, the recognition of five new Latin American nations in 1822, when no other power would grant recognition, could be interpreted as a logical corollary of hemispheric solidarity. Such is a traditional reading of the Monroe Doctrine, which not only supports Latin American independence but also speaks out in defense of the hemisphere's rejection of monarchical Europe. A new chapter in American history seemed ready to open in 1823.

To advance this relationship in the United States, a score of ship captains, commercial agents, and adventurers, such as William Shaler of Connecticut and Joel Poinsett of South Carolina, carried copies of the Constitution with them on mercantile ventures and saw in Latin American fraternity an opportunity of striking down the British as well as the Spanish enemy. At any event, a well-placed Anglophobe like Poinsett and an enterprising shipmaster like Shaler shared the excitement of participating in the building of a free world in the Southern Hemisphere. Their counterparts from Latin America, who moved in large numbers to Washington and Philadelphia after 1810 to enlist American aid and recognition, exulted over the response they encountered at the grass-roots level in the United States.

166

The *Gazeta de Caracas* in August 1810 told its readers about the treatment accorded Venezuelan agents Juan Vicente Bolivar and Teleforo de Orea: "Although we have not received any official statement, we have the satisfaction of announcing to the public that English America is very much in agreement with the sentiments of the Venezuelans. Our memorable resolution has filled the sons of Washington and Franklin with enthusiasm, and the subjects of Ferdinand the VIIth in Caracas, have succeeded in having the illustrious and liberal pray to heaven for a fortunate conclusion to their patriotic efforts."[2]

This ideological kinship was promoted among Americans for reasons other than a fraternal or even self-protective interest in striking a blow at the Old World. Economic advantages in the Caribbean and Latin America beckoned to American traders. The trade which had been fueled by Spain's periodic opening of its West Indian ports under the stress of war in Europe at the end of the century could be expanded indefinitely if independence was achieved. The facts seemed to support such expectations. American entrepreneurs such as Stephen Girard had already built a trade, licit and illicit, in the Caribbean, had moved as far as the west coast of Latin America before the revolution, and saw possibilities in Chile as an entrepôt for the China market. Between 1795 and 1810 commerce with the Spanish empire quadrupled. By 1808 it was one-fifth of the nation's total foreign trade.

With so many incentives for assistance linking the United States to the new republics, a hemispheric system, economic and political, of the order envisaged from time to time by Henry Clay, seemed realizable. Even if the official reaction to importunities of provisional governments was cautious, it did not preclude support along the lines of France's in the American Revolution. When Joel Poinsett was appointed consul general at Buenos Aires in 1811, Secretary of State Monroe observed: "The disposition shown by most of the Spanish provinces to separate from Europe and to erect themselves into independent States excites great interest here. As Inhabitants of the same Hemisphere, as Neighbors, the United States cannot be unfeeling Spectators of so important a moment. The destiny of those provinces must depend on themselves. Should such a revolution however take place, it cannot be doubted that our relation with them will be more intimate, and our friendship stronger than it can be while they are colonies of any European power."[3] While the tone of this communication hardly places the government in the role of an enthusiast, it might have opened the way for an active role in the liberation of the American continent.

If the United States did not emerge as the liberator of Latin America or even as the assistant of revolution in the manner of France a generation before, much of the credit—or blame—fell upon Secretary of State John Quincy Adams, whose influence governed American policy for a decade after 1817. His doubts and suspicions about Latin America extended from dislike of the Anglophilia of many of the new states to scorn for Clay's extravagant idea of a pan-American counterpoise to Europe. They were well summed up in his harsh judgment of the Latin revolutionaries: "As to an American system, we have it; we constitute the whole of it; there is no community of interests or of principles between North and South America. Mr. Torres and Bolivar and O'Higgins talk about an American system as much as the Abbé Corea, but there is no basis for such a system."[4] His recognition of Latin America would be forthcoming only when the governments of the area had proved their vitality, and his defense of their territories would only follow a genuine danger of invasion of the American continent.

Adams's views prevailed. Official assistance to the Latin American cause never materialized; recognition came over a dozen years after the revolution had begun; and a division between the Americas developed in the nineteenth century that ranged from mutual indifference to mutual hostility. How much of this record can be attributed to the power of Adams? How was he able to stem the tide of American sentiment, which appeared ready to extend a fraternal embrace to the new nations to the south?

The answers lie not in the personality of Adams, formidable though it was, but in the men and circumstances that governed Latin American relations from the stirrings of independence to formal recognition. Among them was the coincidence of the Latin American uprising of 1810 with the increasing entanglement of the United States in the same Napoleonic conflict which had bred revolution in the Spanish colonies. Such temptations as there were to give official blessings to the revolutionary cause were counteracted by the exigencies of war with England. And when that war ended in 1814, the reduced fortunes of the Latin rebels and the necessity of maintaining a minimal level of amicability with Spain combined to divert the Monroe administration until the acquisition of the Floridas had been secured in 1821. These practical deterrents to recognition were reinforced by doubts of many kinds which assailed even the best disposed of Americans. Some were disturbed about the reality of a revolution limited to wealthy aristocratic Creoles, others were concerned by the special favors consistently granted to Great Britain by the revolutionary governments, and still others questioned whether either commercial or ideological ties would result from new republican governments in Latin America.

To resolve these doubts and to quicken the pace of American support, American and Latin American agents of all sorts used their considerable energies and influence. Despite American vulnerability to the claims of revolutionary fraternity displayed by Clay and Monroe, the lobbyists failed to budge the government into overt support of the new states. Despite interest in Latin American economic opportunities, entrepreneurs such as Stephen Girard and John Jacob Astor failed to pursue them. What emerges from the propaganda and pressure are fundamental flaws in the arguments and the personalities of the lobbyists. Long before Adams presented his blocks against major aid, disillusionment had set in among Americans in Latin America and Latin Americans in the United States. If the secretary of state succeeded in frustrating demands for recognition or alliance, he was able to exploit the underlying weaknesses among the agents on both sides, of which the most noticeable was the absence of a permanent community of interest.

The romance of the Latin revolution notwithstanding, its impact on the administrations of the United States was shaped from the beginning by advantage, not sentiment. Opportunity to be derived from Spain's troubles took two forms. One was the expansion of trade with the new republics willing to free American commerce from the restrictions of Spain's mercantilism. During its troubles in the 1790s, Spain had temporarily opened Caribbean ports to the United States, and the consuls it had permitted to reside at Santiago in Cuba and at La Guaira in Venezuela continued to operate illegally but successfully even after Spain had rescinded privileges to American shipping. Freed from Spain, the former colonies could open a new era in commercial relations. The second consideration inspiring American action was the ambiguous prospect of a revolution that might bring European monarchism down upon all the Americas or might alternatively leave areas of the Spanish Empire open to American acquisition. The former would have to be resisted with military force; the latter should be accepted as a happy fortune. As long as Louisiana or Florida or Cuba was the object of Spanish territorial expansion, the United States would not fail to display a lively concern for the fate of the Spanish Empire in America.

The case of the Venezuelan adventurer, Franciso de Miranda, is instructive not only because he was the first of many revolutionary figures to come before the American public but because his experience—enormous initial private support from the highest public figures degenerating into failure and disavowal—were to be shared in the future by other hopeful supplicants in the United States. As early as the 1790s Miranda appeared in London and Philadelphia to intrigue Federalist leaders with his ambitions. The prospect of a free Latin America was all the more attractive to such men as Alexander Hamilton and Rufus King because the realization of this project would invoke a close military collaboration with Great Britain on the basis of Anglo-American equality. Hamilton dreamed of the personal glory and power to be gained from a war against Spain in the Americas. The wonder of Miranda's long campaign for American help is not that he failed for so long, but that his visions could appeal to a Paine and a Jefferson as well as to the Federalist Anglophiles.

The climax of Miranda's activities in the United States occurred under Republican auspices. Having failed for the moment with his British connections, he was in New York in 1805 at a time when Spain's relations with the United States were at a low ebb. Benjamin Rush, the Philadelphia physician and a leading Jeffersonian, gained an interview for him with Madison and a dinner engagement with Jefferson himself. The latter, in his customarily gracious way, extended his blessings to the cause of Spanish American freedom, regretting that he was born too soon to see the New World achieve its full measure of splendor. Madison was less elliptical in his comments, coupling permission for American citizens to assist the revolution with a barrier against direct governmental support that might compromise the position of the United States. American relations with Spain required, according to Madison, that "nothing would be done in the least inconsistent with that of a sincere and honorable regard to the rule imposed by their situation." Whether this conversation should be interpreted as the administration's "tacit approval" for Miranda's ventures, as the Venezuelan represented it to his British friends, is doubtful, but his reception helped him to secure vessels from New York merchant Samuel Ogden as well as an advance of twenty thousand dollars for arming and provisioning three troopships.[5]

Despite the American ships and supplies and some clandestine help from the British navy, Miranda's Venezuelan expedition ended in a fiasco in 1806. The American role did not go unnoticed by the angry Spanish minister to the United States. Spurred on by Spain's protests, the United States indicted Ogden for arming Miranda's ships, along with Colonel W. S. Smith, a customs official in New York and son-in-law of John Adams, on the charge of collusion. The administration's position was that Ogden and Smith had acted illegally without its knowledge in assisting the Miranda expedition. Madison disavowed Miranda's letter in which the secretary of state was thanked for his good offices, which would be kept secret until the "delicate affair" was accomplished.[6] But Smith and Ogden protested that they had acted with the consent of the president and secretary of state. In a strong memorial to the Congress, they claimed that federal officials not only knew of the plan but did nothing to stop the departure of the expeditionary force. Both men were acquitted, to the acclaim of most of the public and to the satisfaction of most newspapers. As for the administration's reaction, the president explained its role as delicately as he could: "To know as much of it as we could was our duty, but not to encourage it."[7]

As more successful revolutions unfolded after 1806, the official positions of Jefferson, and later of Madison, remained unchanged. They recognized popular interest in the insurrections, they saw opportunities for expanded trade, and they explored possibilities of territorial acquisitions in Cuba and Mexico; but they weighed these potential assets against the lack of preparation for self-government among the new juntas, the losses in antagonizing Spain, and the gains Britain or France, rather than the United States, might win from autonomous governments in Latin America. It was the latter concern that governed Jefferson's dispatch of General James Wilkinson to New Orleans in 1808 to talk with Cubans and Mexicans about America's unwillingness to have those territories fall into the hands of the two great European belligerents. Wilkinson urged American intervention to steal a march on Britain. While Jefferson was not prepared to extend recognition immediately, his cabinet agreed in October 1808 to "sentiments which should be unauthoritatively expressed by our agents to influential persons in Cuba and Mexico, to wit, 'if you remain under the dominion of the kingdom and family of Spain, we are contented; but we should be extremely unwilling to see you pass under the dominion or ascendancy of France or England. In the latter cases should you choose to declare independence, we cannot now commit ourselves by saying we would make common cause with you but must reserve ourselves to act according to the then existing circumstances.' "[8]

The ambivalence felt by Americans is obvious, as is their regret that Latin America was unable to sweep it away by succeeding in a clean break with all of Europe. But rather than a muddled or aborted revolution that would invite British or French intervention, the United States preferred to keep the status quo. If insurrection did come, the government would have no choice but to encourage it and seek profit from it discreetly. In all the deliberations of the cabinets of Jefferson and Madison, there was recognition that a formidable combination of merchants looking for new commercial outlets and libertarians envisaging republican fraternity would demand a strong anticolonial policy from the government. It is against this background that the United States in 1810, following the first major upheavals in Buenos Aires, Mexico, and Venezuela, appointed "agents for seamen and commerce" to those centers to serve as political observers and, even less officially, as adventurers and entrepreneurs in the thickets of Latin American revolutionary politics.

The line between official and unofficial American agents was always thin and sometimes invisible. Since the United States recognized neither Ferdinand's government in exile nor Bonaparte's monarchy, agents had considerable leeway in their handling of provisional governments which professed nominal allegiance to Ferdinand but in practice governed themselves. Their vague title, "agents for seamen and commerce," enhanced the informal character of the missions, since no Senate confirmation was necessary. Their functions included the gathering of intelligence.

It required no leap of imagination for a libertarian of Poinsett's disposition in Buenos Aires and Chile or a merchant navigator of William Shaler's interests in Cuba to place the broadest of interpretations upon their instruction. Most of the agents were republican zealots, like Poinsett, whose revolutionary passions had been stoked by residence in Europe, or merchants and ship captains, like Shaler, with a buccaneer's temperament and an eye to the advantages independence in Latin America might have for the shrewd investor. Poinsett had learned from experience to regard the United States as a "country which Liberty, leaving the nations of Europe to mourn her light in the gloom of despotism and corruption, has chosen as her favorite asylum."[9] Having found in Great Britain the enemy of America as well as the enemy of liberty, Poinsett's concern was less with the spread of American commerce than with the blocking of British imperialism in Latin America. He never lost his obsession with the issue. When he left Buenos Aires for Chile in 1811, he departed with the conviction that the concerted opposition of British merchants had frustrated the intentions of the governing junta to liberalize commercial arrangements for American shippers. His subsequent experiences in Chile reinforced his disillusionment with Latin revolutionaries.

But he never failed for lack of personal initiative. Indeed, Chile at first seemed to be an ideal place for American influence to work to mutual advantage. Poinsett took up the cause of the Carrera family and became a close friend of youthful José Miguel Carrera, who rose to power under the spell of the American and French revolutions. As president of the junta in Valparaiso, Carrera turned to Poinsett for advice, drawing both on his knowledge of constitutions and on his official connections with sources of arms and munitions. The American consul, enjoying his intimacy with the new government's leader, went far beyond his instructions. He urged full independence, advised on suitable tariff legislation, offered a draft of a bill of rights, and finally joined the Chilean revolutionary forces as a participant in the battle against the royalist government in Peru. What better augury for close continental relations than in these acts of revolutionary camaraderie?

In the end, the excitement of combat and political involvement subsided into bitterness on all sides, raising doubts about the wisdom of Poinsett's particular militia diplomacy. His influence inevitably declined when his friend and client Carrera first split with his family and then was ousted from power and from the country in 1814. The triumphant factions of O'Higgins and San Martín as well as Spanish royalists identified Poinsett with the discredited Carreras and blamed the United States for the troubles of Chile. The winner in the confused struggle for power in Chile was Poinsett's bête noir, Great Britain.

In the future, Poinsett was not to keep his back turned fully against independence, but his guard was up; he remained suspicious of Latin ties with Britain, the Latins' lack of democratic experience, and their domination by an authoritarian church. In one form or another, Americans encountering opposition or failure in their enterprise in South America would invoke memories of the "Black Legend," the brutal behavior of Spanish conquistadors of the sixteenth century, to explain the unfitness of their descendants in the nineteenth century.

Latin American agents who went north in search of money, men, and arms as well as official American recognition of their governments experienced equal disillusionment before they returned home. Most of them initially received such warm welcomes on triumphal marches to Washington that they were encouraged to expect much more than Madison or Monroe was prepared to give. Even a figure like José Bernardo Gutierrez de Lara, a Mexican bourgeois with very questionable credentials—his junta chiefs were captured and executed within a week of his departure— was enchanted with the people he met as he traveled toward the capital in 1811. He appreciated, as did Miranda before him, the freedoms the people enjoyed, although he would not advocate them for the average man in his country. He was so touched by the public rejoicing in the insurgents' victory at Vera Cruz that he reported his impressions with hyperbolic effect:

> . . . I am delighted with the desire of everyone to see the insurgents win. They say that these are defending the most righteous (*justa*) cause that has ever been defended in all the ages. I have noted also the great desire which many of them have to go to Mexico, and many of them have put themselves to school to a teacher whom they have paid to teach them the Spanish language. I am of the opinion that if a free passage were given to these people, there would be more than a million inhabitants who would go in a short time.[10]

Inevitably, this euphoria dissipated when Gutierrez finally met officials and placed his requests. Monroe expressed a cool and tentative interest, which was hardly unreasonable in light of the envoy's vanishing constituency. Gutierrez at least had the consolation of having his travel expenses paid by the United States government. According to the Mexican agent, however, he was promised ten thousand muskets if a provisional government was formed, a generous offer if it was actually made. Lending the color of truth to the claim, however, are conditions attached to this generosity which all Mexicans would have found offensive.

Offers of American assistance to Mexico were clearly linked to an American annexation of Texas, or at least to an extensive revision of the Louisiana border. The most that Gutierrez would concede with respect to the Texas issue was creation of a neutral territory, presumably to be carved out of the Mexican claim, that would separate the two countries and obviate "the many discords which commonly result from the close contact of two powers."[11] A further clash between Mexican nationalism and American expansionism was averted by the unwillingness of the United States in wartime to do more than talk about its interest in the territory.

Because of its absorption in other affairs, the Madison administration refused to give any assistance to Gutierrez's venture. The agent did better with the American private sector. In 1812 he was able to return to Mexico with four hundred volunteers whom he had recruited openly and easily in New Orleans. Emboldened by this success, he made a proclamation of rebellion from American territory and set up a provisional government in Texas. Plots and counterplots, including those of American conspirators, soon pushed him out of his own "government" and doomed the whole revolutionary enterprise for a time. Before Gutierrez terminated his operations, he alienated most of his American friends and collaborators, including such influential men as William Shaler, the United States agent to Vera Cruz.

Most Latin American visitors had similar experiences to relate, and many of them indeed did relate them in books and pamphlets. The pattern usually entailed enormous initial optimism stemming from a warm American reception, then a cooling of relations as the caution of government officials became evident, and then suspicion and resentment if they left empty-handed or felt, as in the case of Mexico, that assistance from the administration would be only a prelude to American occupation. From private citizens, particularly businessmen and soldiers, responses were more positive. Guns, ammunition, volunteers, and money did find their way out of American ports to the various insurrectionary forces. But even here the aid was never massive, the strings frequently oppressive, and the prudence of the entrepreneur annoying or demeaning to the revolutionary cause. Such were the impressions brought back to Latin America by agents as diverse as Gutierrez, Aguirre of Buenos Aires, and Telefore de Orea of Colombia, each of whom between 1810 and 1822 spoke for governments in being or in the process of formation.

Of all the agents from Latin America, the most successful and persuasive was Manuel Torres, the first accredited minister from Latin America when recognition was granted. Torres had lived in the United States since 1796 and knew the ways of the country. Like many other revolutionaries, he looked upon the American Revolution as his inspiration. Like other agents, he found friends in influential places. Where he differed was in his patience, persistence, and ability to flatter his adversaries, which won him a wide range of admirers. He even won the grudging respect of John Quincy Adams, who thought it fitting that this representative of Gran Colombia be granted the honor of inaugurating a new era in international relations in the Americas in 1822.

Torres was the exception. If his sensibilities were ruffled by American presumptions, indifference, or hostility, he managed to conceal his anger or recognized that assets outweighed debts in the American connection with revolution. Despite the official reserve reflected in two neutrality acts in 1817 and 1819, the United States government never placed any serious obstacles in the way of mounting filibusters or the shipment of men, munitions, and supplies. Even during the most delicate periods of Spanish-American relations, the South American delegates lobbied openly in Philadelphia and Washington. They had friends in high places who patronized and reproduced their arguments in the newspapers of a William Duane or the speeches of a Henry Clay.

When José Miguel Carrera arrived in the United States in 1816, an exile from Chile and an opponent of the insurrectionary regimes on both sides of the Andes, his cause was neither friendless nor hopeless. A close companion of both Poinsett and navy captain David Porter, he anticipated the recouping of his fortunes and his country's independence. Carrera's American connections paid almost immediate returns. Porter presented him to Madison and Monroe. He was patronized by the owner of the ship that took him to the United States, Henry Didier, a leading Baltimore merchant with a stake in the outfitting of privateers. Through Didier he met John Skinner, postmaster of Baltimore and dabbler in Latin American ventures, who made a personal loan of four thousand dollars. When he returned to Latin America in November 1816, it was with two ships, paid for by Baltimore businessmen, which were scheduled for an invasion of Chile and filled with American recruits.

But Carrera was dissatisfied with American assistance. It could have been much greater. He accused Poinsett of timidity and implied disloyalty when no official recognition was given to his cause. Perhaps this petulance was a consequence of failure. By the time his expedition had reached Buenos Aires, he learned that San Martín had libertated Chile without him, and his enemy O'Higgins was in command of the country. Carrera's army joined the victors, and Carrera himself was left with frustration and imprisonment at the hands of the Argentines. He went to his death by execution in 1821 convinced that America could have done more.

But how much more for him, or for others? The unofficial aid offered Carrera by Baltimore entrepreneurs was made possible by official America's looking the other way. For a time Carrera attracted great merchants, such as John Jacob Astor and Stephen Girard, as well as men on the make. Astor's interest was a natural by-product of his involvement in the fur trade of the Pacific Northwest and in the China market. Carrera carried with him to the United States letters to Astor from the merchant's commercial agent in Buenos Aires, David DeForest, aide of the revolution in that area. And Astor himself was indirectly involved in insurrections, whether or not he wished it. The mariner Richard Cleveland, a close friend and former partner of Shaler, had Astor's goods on board his ship when he stopped in Valparaiso in 1818, ostensibly to facilitate a shipment of wheat to Lima, but primarily to negotiate for an armed ship of the East India Company on behalf of the patriot government. This activity was fully known to the New York merchant prince through Cleveland's detailed correspondence.[12] If Astor did not pursue the channels, political and economic, which were afforded him in Latin America, it was largely because the debits of enterprise there appeared greater than the assets. His correspondents made it clear to him that the factional quarrels among revolutionaries, the excessive duties imposed by their regimes, and the omnipresent rivalry of Great Britain would combine to limit success of any venture.

Girard was even more explicit in his evaluation of opportunities in Latin America. The Philadelphia merchant was looking for new trading outlets after the Napoleonic conflict blocked his European markets. His commission house sent its super cargoes to Valparaiso and Canton instead of more familiar ports. Noting the meaning of this change, Venezuelan agents in 1810 approached him to serve as broker in obtaining help for their revolution. But he was cautious, requiring first that his service as a private citizen not be "unlawful or disagreeable to the President" and secondly that "the Government will facilitate me the means of obtaining said muskets &c, either by selling or lending them to me under such terms and conditions as will be judged reasonable."[13] Legality and propriety aside, Girard wanted guarantees from the State Department before making any commitment. When Monroe failed to respond to his questions, Girard dropped the matter completely. Since his republican sympathies were deeper than those of most of his peers, his unwillingness to continue negotiations with the Latin Americans may have derived from the advice of his own agents, such as the captain of the *Rousseau* who observed from Valparaiso that the revolution had caused "stagnation of business very prejudicial to your affairs for in such times as these it is dangerous giving credit and the scarcity of money is such that few sales can be effected without it."[14]

The evidence all suggests that the reluctance of merchants to invest seriously in South American revolutions was not the product of fear of Madison's or Monroe's disapproval. They shared many of the misgivings which disturbed the government and acted accordingly. But they wished the revolutions well and, like the government, did nothing to injure their prospects. There were other entrepreneurs, too, who expected profit from the revolution and entered into the game with zeal. Many of them were shipbuilders and privateers with headquarters in Baltimore who made fortunes out of the troubles of Spanish America. If they were ultimately curbed, it was only when their operations became too blatant and their privateering took a toll of American shipping as well as Spanish.

Unlike Astor and Girard, the Baltimore shipping magnates whose rise coincided with the fast "Baltimore Clipper" in the War of 1812 had no compunctions about using their influence in the Congress or in the administration to help their friends and partners in Latin America. Foremost among individual leaders was Skinner, the postmaster, his father-in-law Theodorick Bland, and General William Winder. Their intimacy with Carrera and DeForest brought Baltimore close to Buenos Aires and Valparaiso after 1815. DeForest and Manuel Aguirre, both agents of La Plata, were as much the spokesmen of the "American concern," Didier and Darcy, the most active privateering operation in Latin America, as they were of their provisional government for which they sought recognition in Washington.

The wrath of the Baltimoreans and the unhappiness of Latin Americans were particularly keen in 1817 and 1818 when the election of James Monroe, reputed to be sympathetic to revolution, led instead to neutrality laws and to the appointment of the unsympathetic John Quincy Adams as secretary of state. Under Adams's sponsorship, privateering was an object of government hostility, which moved lobbyists for business interests to mobilize sympathizers in the country and in Congress.

The opposition to Adams was formidable and by no means from Baltimore or privateering interests alone. Libertarians and Anglophobes could now find a more active response from a Congress freed from the burdens of war, as America's own increased pride in nationalism found a natural expression in the call for the independence of Latin America. The most sensitive note played, and one which could win attention from Adams as well as Monroe, was always the British threat.

One of the first blasts came from the pen of William D. Robinson in *A Cursory View of Spanish America,* published one month after the Battle of New Orleans had been won in 1815. Robinson was a veteran of filibusters along the Texas border who had been in as many scrapes with Mexican leaders as he had been with Spanish authorities. But his primary passions were directed against Great Britain. While recognition of independence was necessary to keep the mines of Mexico out of Spanish control, it was only because Britain controlled Spain. Robinson was convinced that Britain intended to use Mexico as a stepping-stone in the detachment of Louisiana from the United States. What it had failed to achieve by force of arms in open combat it would gain by temptations offered from its Mexican base. Robinson's proposed counteraction was simply American recognition of the new governments. "The *independence of this new world will alone arrest the ambition and influence of Great Britain.—*This event would give birth to a new and auspicious order of things not only over the Western Hemisphere, but throughout the whole world."[15]

The appeal of the Latin American revolution was not confined to paranoids or romantics. William Duane, the powerful editor of the Philadelphia *Aurora,* repeatedly underscored the economic benefits recognition would bring. In 1817 his journal publicized the important speech of Isaac Briggs, chairman of the House Committee of Commerce and Manufactures, on the necessity of a country embarking on a protective tariff to find markets in the Americas for cotton and woollen manufactures. In their emphasis upon the economy, both Duane and Henry Clay borrowed heavily from Manuel Torres's pamphlet, *An Exposition of the Commerce of Spanish America,* published in 1816, which employed circumspect flattery and an invitation to American self-interest to make its point. Observing that Spanish America annually consumed "the value of one hundred millions of dollars in articles of foreign manufacturing industry," Torres proposed that the United States be the country to sell these articles. Once Latin America has won freedom, "we cannot doubt that the spirit of enterprize, which has hitherto distinguished the American merchant in so remarkable a manner, will be conspicuous in that part of the new world, under the aid and protection of the best of governments."[16] Torres's case, called by Clay a "valuable little work," gave the Kentuckian the facts and figures he needed to win over his audiences.[17]

Under the impact of emotions arising from so many sources during his first year in office, President Monroe felt the need to take some positive measure on behalf of the revolutionaries. "An instinctive apostle of the rights of man," as Samuel Flagg Bemis has called him, Monroe inclined toward recognition when he appointed a commission to report whether conditions in Latin America were suitable for recognizing any of the provisional governments.[18] Such a step might have been a prelude to a new relationship with Latin America that reflected the wishes of the Latin American agents, the Baltimore businessmen, and the congressional friends of the revolution. The fact that one of the three commissioners was Theodorick Bland gave substance to expectations of a major change in official policy.

Despite all the favorable portents, no change developed out of the commission's activity. It is tempting to ascribe its failure to the return of John Quincy Adams from London to take up his duties as secretary of state. Adams was not in Washington when the commission was conceived or when the commissioners were chosen, and his opposition to recognizing the United Provinces of La Plata or any other aspiring government was widely known. But if he checked the belligerent Clay and the complaisant Monroe, he did it with considerable assistance from men who ordinarily would have been the leaders in the revolutionary cause. In 1817 Joel Poinsett, who had been asked to join the mission, refused to accept the assignment out of disillusionment over his experiences in Chile and disappointment with the leadership of the revolutions. Bland, whose interest in going to Latin America, according to Adams, was solely to collect the 100 percent interest on his son-in-law's loan, divided the commission with a negative judgment on the question of recognition.[19] His friends were on the losing side of the factional strife in La Plata and Chile, and hence the change was unworthy of assistance.

Commissioner Bland's attack diluted the very favorable reports of Buenos Aires's revolution which Commissioner Caesar Rodney offered and which were fervently reiterated in the observations of Secretary Henry M. Brackenridge. While Bland foresaw no prospect for reconquest by Spain, he was certain that "unless present civil dissensions are healed, and the warring provinces are pacified and reconciled with each other, a very great proportion, if not all, the benefits and advantages of the revolution which would accrue immediately as well to themselves as to foreign nations, will be totally destroyed, or at least, very much diminished and delayed."[20] Rodney's distinction as former congressman from Delaware and attorney general under Jefferson and Madison did not counterbalance the strictures of Bland. In fact, Rodney's praise was so overblown that the third commissioner, John Graham, chief clerk of the Department of State, was moved to submit a separate report since he felt that Rodney had exaggerated his account of the stability of the Latin American regimes.

The disarray of the divided commission in the fall of 1818 further dampened American enthusiasm for the Latin American cause. The Latin American lobbyists were not content to wait for the results of the investigating commission. Spurred on by the Neutrality Act of 1817, which was aimed against arming privateers in American ports, they used the arrival of Manuel de Aguirre from Buenos Aires as the official representative of the United Provinces as an occasion for a test of Adams's power. Under the benevolent eyes of Clay, Aguirre rebuked the secretary of state for the unfairness of the Neutrality Act and the hardship it created for the young states seeking freedom from the Old World. Secondly, he accused the United States of violating the territory of Latin America when it seized Amelia Island, a haven for smugglers and privateers between Georgia and Florida. And finally, he warned that if the government did not act to recognize the regime at Buenos Aires, and if it did not provide arms and ships for

San Martín's campaign in Peru, the United Provinces would cut off trade with the United States. Perhaps Aguirre's stridency was the result of special frustrations over Acting Secretary of State Rush's disavowal of unauthorized agreements between American agents in Buenos Aires and the provisional government whereby loans had been assured to Aguirre for the purchase of arms and ships. Whether his temper was contrived or genuine, it was orchestrated in early 1818 with a congressional campaign to force the president to send to the House all correspondence with the revolutionary governments.

Aguirre went beyond the bounds of common sense as well as of propriety, and Adams cut him down to size. When the secretary asked if his request for recognition developed from a new set of instructions, since his original instructions made no mention of it, Aguirre confessed that he was influenced by congressional suggestions to him on this subject. On Aguirre's threat to revoke the temporary privileges given to American commerce on the La Plata, Adams threatened to close the ports of the United States to his government. But it was over Amelia Island that Aguirre lost the sympathy of much of his American audience. Even when he admitted that Buenos Aires was not assuming a "superintendency" over all Spanish territories in the Americas, his protest invoked a question about the sovereignty of Florida, an issue which united all factions against Latin Americans as well as against Spaniards.[21]

Aguirre's retreat in the face of Adams's counterattack did not stop the momentum for recognition of the new republics developed by his friends in the Congress. Although Clay succeeded in having the documents connected with the occupation of Amelia Island opened to the inspection of the House, he failed in his major test of strength with Adams. He had expected that the administration's unpopular repression of privateering activities, combined with the secretary of state's surliness toward Aguirre, would arouse Congress to force recognition upon Monroe, thus winning new prestige for himself. Clay's device to tap these sentiments was to attach an amendment to a bill defraying expenses for the Rodney commission which would appropriate eighteen thousand dollars as annual salary for a ministry and legation in the United Provinces of the Rio de la Plata. The Speaker employed all his great oratorical skills to force the administration into a backdoor acceptance of at least one of the revolutionary governments. He failed by a margin of 115 to 45 on 28 March 1818, and had to settle for an amendment to the Neutrality Act that deleted mention of vessels armed outside the limits of United States sovereignty. This concession was undone the next year in a new neutrality act that permitted American naval vessels to retake ships unlawfully seized on the high seas.

Even the charming Manuel Torres found his way blocked by the stubborn resistance of the United States government to pressures for official assistance to the provisional regimes. Despite his impressive connections, Torres was unable in 1819 to win the massive private aid he had counted upon from American investors. Bolivar's triumphs over Spain on behalf of the new Gran Colombia, as Venezuela and New Granada were now called, had to be weighed against the effects of the Panic of 1819 upon the American economy. In desperation, the agent turned again to the administration for surplus arms for Bolivar's army and won the votes of Secretary of War John C. Calhoun and Secretary of the Navy Smith Thompson. But once again Adams's negative prevailed. The secretary of state had the last word: "To supply the arms professedly for the purpose set forth in the memorial of Torres would be a direct departure from neutrality, an act of absolute hostility to Spain."[22]

What stayed America's hand from 1817 to 1822? Concern for Spanish reaction was certainly one factor, as suggested above. The Spanish Minister Louis de Onis was convinced that the Latin American agents were in close collaboration with the Monroe administration, and he looked upon the Neutrality Act of 1817 as prejudicial to Spain's attempts to curb rebel spoliations of its commerce. In fact, Aguirre was jailed for four days for illegally outfitting ships, and the action which exposed his lack of diplomatic immunity was done in deference to the anger of Onis. As long as Florida was a subject of negotiations, the secretary of state was unprepared to allow either pressure for recognition or blatant violations of neutrality to block the acquisition of the Floridas.

But it was not fear of Spanish power that moved Adams. He was not above using Spain's own fears to nudge negotiations along. The occupation of Amelia Island was not only an affront to Latin Americans; it was a warning to Spain that Florida itself could be as easily taken if the Spanish position remained obdurate. And after the treaties had been concluded, Adams successfully resisted the potential blackmail in Spain's attempts to link the matter of recognition of Buenos Aires with ratification of the cession of Florida. The United States refused to comply. The most that would be conceded was a statement that the United States "probably would not precipitately recognize the independence of the South Americans."[23] Before the end of 1820 Spain ratified the treaty, well aware of the success of Clay's relatively mild resolution of 10 May of that year in which the House had agreed to the outfitting of ministers for service in Latin America when the president, "by and with the advice and consent of the Senate," saw fit to send them.[24]

The possibility that the Old World might mobilize its power to force the rebellious states back into subordination to Spain represented another inhibition against recognition. In 1818, the same year in which Clay attempt-ed to force the president's hand, the European powers met at Aix-la-Chapelle where the French delegate, the duc de Richelieu, recommended a general plan of pacification to thwart American recognition of La Plata. The idea had originally been circulated by Pozzo di Borgia, the Russian ambassador to France, and was no secret from the United States. But it inspired no special caution in the secretary of state, who advised Albert Gallatin, the American minister in Paris, to "take occasion, not by formal official communication, but verbally as the opportunity may present itself, to let the Duke de Richelieu understand that . . . we can neither accede to nor approve of any interference to restore any part of the Spanish suprem-acy of any of the South American provinces."[25] The threat of military coun-teraction notwithstanding, Adams was well aware that British coolness to-ward a European invasion had rendered the conference a failure before it had adjourned.

It was the British position that created the major distress for Adams. Not that its position was unclear or even hostile toward the ultimate aims of American foreign policy. The British gambit in this period went back to the Napoleonic period for its source. Castlereagh wanted preservation of a nominal Spanish sovereignty in the interest of monarchical legitimacy, and at the same time he intended to keep the fruits of a profitable trading rela-tionship which had grown out of the revolution in Spanish America. Popu-lar opinion and a ministerial sense of reality informed Britain of the impos-sibility of restoration. Richard Rush, the American minister in London, perceived the heart of British policy to lie in the aborted mediation pro-posal whereby Great Britain would assist in the return of the colonies if their ports would remain open to British ships. The nuances of the cabinet position were clear enough for Adams to exploit Castlereagh's dilemma and deflate Clay's demands in 1819 by having Rush suggest Anglo-American cooperation in completing the emancipation of the Americas. Castlereagh politely declined the invitation, and Adams continued his resistance to the Congress.

Adams's concern about Britain, then, was not over a potential clash with the old enemy. It rested in the special relationship between the rebellious governments and Great Britain, and it took the forms of both ideology and commerce. The new republics seemed to Adams to lack the political framework, the popular infrastructure, or the historical traditions to make a democracy that would have a political or philosophical kinship with the United States. The provisional governments represented a Creole elite, an aristocracy whose sympathies would incline them to ties with France and Great Britain, even if they remained republics. The likelihood of their re-turning to monarchy seemed reasonable when ideas of a Bourbon princeling's assumption of control over La Plata were not dismissed as absurd by the juntas. A genuine libertarian like Simon Bolivar, the liberator of much of Latin America, was far more in tune with the society of Great Britain than he was with that of the United States, although he spoke with reverence of George Washington and with appreciation of the American freedoms. Bolivar knew that his people would not become North Americans and that they needed a dictatorship to maintain the republic. While those Latin American leaders and agents who looked to American state constitutions, the Bill of Rights, or the Declaration of Independence for inspiration were men of talent and integrity, they were not the men who completed the revolution. Furthermore, their North American visits left them disaffected with the United States—fearful of American imperialist ambitions, doubtful of future trade relations, and resentful over the self-interest which governed American attitudes. Adams recognized all these symptoms in his analysis of relations with Latin America.

As for commerce as a binding tie for the future, the subtle propaganda of Torres or the blunt assertion of Duane that vast fortunes were to be made in Guatamalan trade in indigo had to be countered by the facts that trade with Latin America had been declining over the years and the beneficiary replacing the United States was Great Britain. The record of trade with the United Provinces of Rio de la Plata tells the story: in 1825 United States commerce there was valued at a little over one million dollars, while Great Britain's approached six million dollars. For all of Latin America, from 1808 to 1830 American commerce declined from thirty million dollars to twenty million at a time when the British trade climbed from twenty-five to thirty million. The United States appeared as a competitor in the production of raw materials in many areas of Latin America, Great Britain as a supplier of finished goods. As Adams expressed it in 1822, "Do what we can, the commerce of South America will be much more important to Great Britain than to us, . . . for the simple reason that she has the power of supplying their wants by her manufactures."[26]

In light of these realities, Adams intended to defer recognition of revolutionary governments until the time was ripe. When that time came in 1822, the United States was the first nation to recognize their independence, and both Adams and Poinsett gave the act their blessings. What made the time appropriate was that the Floridas had been secured and the revolution, after new victories by Bolivar and San Martin, seemed irreversible. With reasonable grace, although with continued wariness, the secretary of state appeared to acquiesce in the triumph of Henry Clay. The latter had never accepted defeat in 1818. Each succeeding year, congressional resolutions were offered to no effect, until Monroe finally responded. In March 1822 a willing president called for recognition from the Congress and received it in the form of an appropriation of one hundred thousand dollars to defray the cost of diplomatic missions to Mexico, Gran Colombia, and the United Provinces of La Plata, Peru, and Chile. It was especially fitting that Manuel Torres was received as the first minister of the Latin American republics shortly before his death.

What should have resulted was the realization of Clay's dream of an American-led continental association as a counterpoise to European influence or, at least, a series of separate alliances with the United States along the lines of Torres's recommendations. The Monroe Doctrine which followed closely upon these acts a year and a half later symbolized the linking of the Western Hemisphere. Instead, the common destiny, whether political, economic, or ideological, turned out to be the illusion Adams always feared it was.

The record of American involvement with the revolution of Spanish America reveals that America contributed eager partisans, intrepid adventurers, speculating businessmen, and considerable quantities of arms and ammunition. Yet, the interests that divided the Americas were deeper than those that linked them. It may have been unfair for Great Britain to receive the credit for and benefits of revolution, but given the differences between Anglo-Americans and Latin Americans, their ultimate mutual indifference, if not hostility, should not have been surprising to leaders on both sides. It was not to John Quincy Adams or to Simon Bolivar.

The vital differences were also apparent to those who had most at stake in the future collaboration of the Americas: the propagandists and lobbyists, the agents and missionaries—both North and South American—who wanted to exploit the common revolution against the Old World to the advantage of their country or their faction or their private enterprises. The biases on both sides that emerged from the experiences each had in the other's society laid the groundwork for the mistrust that was to characterize future relations. For a brief time in the first quarter of the nineteenth century, circumstances permitted a commingling of the destinies of the Americas based on common sentiments. Although this harmony turned out to be fleeting and insubstantial, it remained the source of the rhetoric of a pan-Americanism that was to revive in the next century.

PART FIVE:

JEFFERSONIAN HISTORIOGRAPHY

13

FOUNDING FATHERS ON THE FOUNDING FATHERS:

REFLECTIONS ON THREE GENERATIONS OF AMERICAN DIPLOMATIC HISTORIANS

There was once a time when diplomatic history was a young and virile branch of American history. While that time is not distant chronologically—scarcely half a century—the subject in recent years has shown signs of arteriosclerosis. Although the diagnosis may not be accurate, it is widely held within the profession. Even the fact that the founding fathers of the field lived long lives, or indeed are still living, is an occasion for reproach on the part of critics. What may have been youth in the 1920s is undeniably age in the 1970s, and was even so in the 1950s and 1960s.

JEFFERSONIAN HISTORIOGRAPHY

Such excitement as the pioneer diplomatic historians, Samuel F. Bemis and Thomas A. Bailey, Julius W. Pratt and Dexter Perkins, Richard W. Van Alstyne and Arthur P. Whitaker yielded from their studies had implications outside the historical profession. Woodrow Wilson had been a historian as well as a president of the United States, and was a bearer of a world outlook that made American diplomacy important. Theodore Roosevelt, president before him, was also a historian as well as a strenuous actor on the world stage. And before him Henry Adams, sometime public figure, had made his history of the United States during the administrations of Thomas Jefferson and James Madison an exercise in diplomatic history. Even Frederick Jackson Turner, perhaps the most renowned American historian in the first quarter of the twentieth century, had a share in the beginnings of diplomatic history. Among his many contributions were essays in Franco-American diplomacy concerning the Mississippi Valley.[1]

The rise of diplomatic history coincided with an awareness of America as a world power, as a maker and shaker in an arena larger than the American continent. The seminal years in the education of the first generation of professional historians ranged from the Spanish-American War to the First World War when the power of the United States manifested itself in Latin America, in the Far East, and ultimately in Europe itself. It was a success story that called for explanation. Bemis's explorations in the Federalist era, Pratt's in the origins of the War of 1812, and Perkins's authoritative studies of the Monroe Doctrine were all testaments to a pride in American values and American strength which were exhibited in a successful foreign policy in the early national years.[2] Their objectives were the sources of American power, and they were achieved to the satisfaction of the seekers.

Disillusionment with the League of Nations and the fall of Wilson as a cult figure had a particularly negative impact upon historians: Never again would historians occupy quite the seats of prominence they had occupied when Theodore Roosevelt or Woodrow Wilson was president; lawyers, economists, and political scientists would take their place from the academic community in the next two generations. But diplomatic history did not suffer diminution of status as a consequence of Versailles. Historians were leaders in both the defense of and in the assault upon Wilson. Despite the rise of neo-isolationism in the interbella period, the continued vigor of diplomatic historians may have stemmed from the self-confidence of the historians themselves in their assumptions about what was good for America. Their lessons were drawn from the foreign policy of the postrevolutionary period. If Wilson went astray it was because he had failed to adhere to the advice of the Founding Fathers. Statesmen had failed to extract an

American advantage from Europe's distress, as Bemis had identified in the Pinckney Treaty in 1795. They lost sight of the meaning of the two hemispheres which Perkins had set forth in the Monroe Doctrine.

But if diplomatic history as a discipline blossomed in this age of disillusionment it was also because its practitioners were impeccable scholars. They went beyond Henry Adams in multiarchival research, uncovering in the archives of England, France, and Spain a fuller record than had been known before and analyzing it with wit and learning. While the results of their labors proved to be flattering to Americans, they made no attempt to alter or to shy away from the materials they discovered. Whether they asked the appropriate questions of their materials is another matter. Most of their findings remain definitive conclusions, no matter what glosses subsequent generations may place on them. The decades from Bemis's *Jay's Treaty* (1923) to his first volume on John Quincy Adams (1949) constituted a golden age for diplomatic historians.

The coming of the Second World War did not check the outpouring of studies in diplomatic history. Many of the leading diplomatic historians may have been isolationists in the 1930s, but few had difficulty in adjusting to the implications of Nazi and Japanese ambitions for the United States after Pearl Harbor. The increased authority of the United States in world affairs revealed for them another side of the wisdom of the Founding Fathers. Dexter Perkins eloquently reminded his readers of the peculiar American virtues in diplomacy and of the civilizing mission they might perform in mitigating the evils of the balance of power and in promoting the rule of international law.[3] This book, a staple of the United States Information Service, developed from lectures at the University of Uppsala, enlightening Europeans on the American approach to foreign policy. Bemis in the later editions of his influential textbook and in a combative piece for the *Virginia Quarterly Review* accepted the challenge of the isolationists after the war and employed his erudition to align George Washington, Thomas Jefferson, and James Monroe with the United Nations and the North Atlantic Treaty.[4] Curtis P. Nettels seemed to have been a minority voice among historians of early America in pleading against the passage of the treaty on the grounds that Washington would have disapproved it.[5]

The second generation of scholars came into its professional maturity in the wake of that war. Many of them were former students of Bemis and Bailey who identified realism with what later would be known as the "consensus" interpretation of the American past. While the third generation of critics preferred to equate this approach to an Eisenhower fuzziness or to unseemly fears of McCarthyism, the postwar scholars drew their picture of history from the optimism of World War II when the prospect of a Pax Americana was an exciting challenge to diplomatic historians. They followed the paths of the founding fathers and went beyond them in many ways. Their exploitation of multiarchival research was more thorough; their understanding of the interplay of domestic and foreign affairs, of the psychological dimensions involved, or of the roles of public opinion and elite groups was more sophisticated than that of their predecessors.

The studies of Alexander DeConde concerning Franco-American relations in the Federalist era and of Bradford Perkins in his trilogy on Anglo-American relations from 1795 to the Monroe Doctrine were noteworthy for their ability to relate diplomacy to the larger political scene.[6] Insights and techniques from other disciplines became part of the scholarly baggage of diplomatic historians. In examining causes of the War of 1812 the idea of national honor and the need to preserve the Republican party were the materials of intellectual history and even of psychohistory in the writings of Norman K. Risjord and Roger H. Brown.[7] Historians have also made full use of biographical information generated by the support of the National Historical Publications Commission after World War II. Princeton's Jefferson papers, Columbia's Hamilton, Chicago's and Virginia's Madison, Yale's and the American Philosophical Society's Franklin, and Harvard's Adams Family inspired not only reevaluations of those major figures but also new views of lesser diplomatists. George Dangerfield's *Livingston* is a model of excellence in biography.[8]

What has been particularly striking about their work has been their acceptance of the ideological framework of the founders. Although the former are more sensitive to nuances of behavior and have admirably filled many hiatuses in information, the main lines remain unchanged. America emerged in the writings of the second generation of professional diplomatic historians much as it had been in the first: namely, a special breed of nation, fighting for its survival in a hostile world and succeeding because of a combination of inherent moral virtues, a particular racial composition, the special circumstances of geography, and the good fortune of rivalries among the larger powers of Europe. Scholars who have attempted to fit American diplomatic history into a different frame, such as Seymour M. Lipset and Robert R. Palmer, usually were drawn from a different discipline or from another field of history.[9] Richard B. Morris's valiant try to recast the postrevolutionary experience in the model of a contemporary emerging nation lacked credibility.[10]

There has been considerable harmony between historians of the early national period with such political scientists as Hans J. Morgenthau whose search for realism matched theirs.[11] To express American virtures in terms of the sterile moralistic pieties in the manner of the older generation was embarrassing to a nation caught up in the leadership of an imperfect world. The postwar historians discovered that the diplomatists from Washington to Monroe fitted the spirit of the 1950s better than did the makers of foreign policy from Jackson to Wilson; the Founding Fathers were realists who knew the limits of morality in politics as well as the limits of their own power. Hence, the arguments among historians were often over who was the greater realist: Hamilton or Jefferson, Madison or Monroe, Franklin or Jay. Dumas Malone and Albert H. Bowman celebrated Jefferson's essential wisdom in foreign policy while Gilbert L. Lycan and Helene J. Looze were joyful combatants on behalf of Hamilton.[12] Lawrence S. Kaplan was less concerned with Hamilton's judgment than with Jefferson's errors in his relations with France.[13] Gerald Stourzh's study of Hamilton, perhaps the most discerning of all recent examinations of Hamilton, found qualities which most often others had missed.[14] The debate over revolutionary diplomacy continued as Richard Morris elevated John Jay to first rank, and Cecil B. Currey exposed Benjamin Franklin as a realist in a different tradition: he would triumph personally in the Revolution whichever side won.[15]

Thomas J. McCormick claims that too many historians have become obsessed with a "metaphysical" "realism-idealism" which has created an artificial and sterile polarity.[16] It has diverted the diplomatic historian, he asserts, from developing comparative analyses of contemporary societies, and from looking for new frames for understanding foreign relations. Yet it is worth observing that the revisionists of the 1960s, the so-called New Left, have shied away from the early national period. Although McCormick may be correct in his charges about the realist-idealist debate and about the parochialism of diplomatic historians, the New Left has not distinguished itself for any reevaluations of the diplomacy of the early period. The record of revisionist historiography is meager compared with its contribution to the understanding of the cold war.

This lacuna is all the more surprising considering the labors of William Appleman Williams, an inspirational figure to the New Left.[17] To him diplomacy was the handmaiden of a coherent expansionist search for markets. In an important article in the *William and Mary Quarterly* in 1958 Williams claimed that all the Founding Fathers shared an interest in replacing British mercantilism with American, and that Madison deserves more credit than Hamilton in promoting American industry; Hamilton, in this view was tied too much to Britain. Whatever the merits of the argument, his disciples have failed to develop it for the Federalist or Jeffersonian periods. Indeed, the only major contributors to the theme of American imperialism, although from a non-Marxist perspective, are veterans of another generation: Arthur B. Darling who dwelled on the power struggle over the Mississippi Valley between Europe and America, and Richard W. Van Alstyne who observed the continuities in American expansionism.[18]

JEFFERSONIAN HISTORIOGRAPHY

By sifting through the heap of publications on foreign affairs which piles up annually, one can find some evidence in the historiography of the diplomacy of the new nation of all the current flowing today, from character studies to local history, from comparative analysis to quantitative methods. A modest beginning has been made in the use of quantitative techniques. Mary Ryan has examined party formation in the Federalist period with implications for partisan roles in the foreign policy debate during the quasi-war with France.[19] Ronald L. Hatzenbuehler has employed cluster bloc analysis scaling and an index of cohesion in the study of roll calls relating to foreign policy in the House of Representatives during the first session of the Twelfth Congress.[20] Even the less likely area of state history has yielded some insights into foreign affairs. Such studies as Richard R. Beeman's on Virginia in the 1790s and Victor A. Sapio's on Pennsylvania in 1812 have the merit of looking beyond the national level to find the local roots of foreign policy.[21] But these are all marginal in their impact.

Surprisingly, the Progressive school of interpretation is missing from the list for the most part, despite the temptations of a Hamilton-Jefferson dualism. Indeed, if it appears at all it is largely a pale reflection of that conflict. Hamilton's Anglophilia or Jefferson's Francophilia are essentially character defects which may damage the national interest but are not basically part of the agrarian-industrial class struggle characterizing most of the Progressive approach. Charles E. Neu places Julius Pratt and Arthur Whitaker into the Progressive mold, considering the primacy they gave to the Western agrarian as opposed to the Eastern merchant in the shaping of American foreign policy.[22] Yet, diplomacy does not emerge as a class activity since the objectives of foreign policies mesh. Indeed, foreign affairs has a flattening effect on all differences as East and West, Federalist and Jeffersonian, all seem to seek an isolationist America independent of political connections to the Old World but prepared to profit from both its political difficulties and economic needs. Small wonder then that the consensus history predominates.

Given the relative immunity of diplomatic history to the prevailing schools of this century it is understandable that the first generations of national history still bear the stamp of the founding fathers, and in the case of Henry Adams a founding grandfather, of the profession. A scholar must begin to study the Revolution with the work of Edward S. Corwin and Samuel Flagg Bemis, and can never discard their contributions.[23] The judgments of Bemis and Whitaker on the diplomacy of the Confederal and Federalist periods vis-à-vis Great Britain and Spain remain standards.[24] And no one can approach Jeffersonian foreign policy or the War of 1812 without stepping into the long shadow of Henry Adams whose nine-volume history was completed before the turn of the twentieth century.[25]

Even the major statements on Western influence upon the War of 1812, such as those of Pratt and George R. Taylor, date back to the first third of the twentieth century.[26] As for the Monroe Doctrine, Dexter Perkins's identification with the subject has not dimmed with the passage of time. Rather, it has been brightened by his own exegetical reviews of the doctrine.[27] While the great Progressive historians—Charles A. Beard, Frederick Jackson Turner, and Arthur M. Schlesinger, Sr.—may be treated with respect by students of economic, Western, and social history, respectively, they are victims of a generation gap. They do not speak to subsequent generations in the way their contemporaries in diplomatic history address their children and grandchildren.

14

RECENT HISTORIOGRAPH- ICAL TRENDS

Isolationism has long been a term that has been more assumed than examined in American historiography. It has been an integral part of the American exceptionalism that separated America's history from that of the Old World.

Scholars in early American diplomatic history of every generation have taken isolationism into account in their writings. J. Fred Rippy and Angie Debo wrote on "The Historical Background of the American Policy of Isolation," *Smith College Studies in History* 9 (1924), over sixty years ago.

Even when Albert K. Weinberg, "The Historical Meaning of the American Doctrine of Isolation," *American Political Science Review* 34 (September 1940): 539-47, suggests doubts about its validity, he also suggests that it cannot be ignored. Max Savelle regards isolationism as fundamental to America's development in his "Colonial Origins of American Diplomatic Principles," *Pacific Historical Review* 3 (Aug. 1934): 334-50, and later in his monumental *The Origins of American Diplomacy: The International History of Angloamerica* (New York, 1967). The theme runs through the works of Samuel Flagg Bemis, notably *The Diplomacy of the American Revolution*, 3d ed. (Bloomington, Ind., 1951), and is reflected in Lawrence S. Kaplan's survey, *Colonies into Nation: American Diplomacy, 1763-1801* (New York, 1972). Variations on the theme are found in Felix Gilbert, *To the Farewell Address: Ideas of Early American Foreign Policy* (Princeton, N.J., 1961), where he considers American isolationism as an instrument to show the way to a brave new world. Countering Gilbert's thesis is James Hutson's view in "Intellectual Foundation of Early American Diplomacy," *Diplomatic History* 1 (Winter 1977): 1-19, and in *John Adams and the Diplomacy of the American Revolution* (Lexington, Ky., 1980). Hutson accepts the idea of isolationism while claiming that it was founded on the assumption of Old World power politics, not New World idealism.

The validity, even the reality, of isolationism was challenged by a school of revisionist historians, led by William Appleman Williams. His "The Legend of Isolationism," in *Science and Society* 18 (Winter 1954): 1-20, refers to the 1920s rather than to the age of Jefferson, but there is a consistency in his writings about American foreign policy that has strong resonance in the eighteenth as well as twentieth centuries. If expansionism characterized America's behavior, isolationism had no meaning. This is implicit in his "The Age of Mercantilism: An Interpretation of the American Political Economy, 1763-1828," *William and Mary Quarterly*, 3d ser., 15 (Oct. 1958): 419-37, and may be found as well in Walter LaFeber, "Foreign Policy of a New Nation: Franklin, Madison, and the 'Dream of a New Land' to Fulfill with People in Self-Control, 1750-1804," in W. A. Williams, ed., *From Colony to Empire: Essays in the History of American Foreign Relations* (New York, 1972), 9-38. From an ideological rather than economic perspective, Alexander DeConde in the third volume of his trilogy, *This Affair of Louisiana* (New York, 1976), accepts the idea of expansionism, if not imperialism, anticipating a Manifest Destiny for America. However, none of the above deal specifically with the issue of abstention from European commitments in their critiques of isolationism.

In the last generation there have been important, often exciting, contributions to the literature of the Age of Jefferson. There will be more, as the publications of the works of the Founding Fathers from Jefferson to Charles Carroll, encouraged after World War II by the National Historical Publications Commission, come to completion. In addition to Hutson's study of John Adams, three books in particular stand out for their contributions to the historiography of the American Revolution: William Stinchcombe, *The American Revolution and the French Alliance* (Syracuse, N.Y., 1969), shows the important involvement of the Continental Congress in foreign policy; Jonathan R. Dull, *The French Navy and American Independence: A Study of Arms and Diplomacy* (Princeton, N.J., 1975), emphasizes the role of Spain rather than the role of Saratoga in securing the French alliance; and Orville T. Murphy, *Charles, Gravier, Comte de Vergennes: French Diplomacy on the Eve of the Revolution, 1719-1787* (Albany, N.Y., 1982), presents an authoritative and sympathetic account of Vergennes's support of the American cause. Two bicentennial symposia organized by the U.S. Capitol Historical Society and edited by Ronald Hoffman and Peter J. Albert, *Diplomacy and Revolution: The Franco-American Alliance of 1778* (Charlottesville, Va., 1981), and *Peace and the Peacemakers: The Treaty of 1783* (Charlottesville, Va., 1986), offer new insights into the two important treaties of the American Revolution. Dull has produced a new and impressive synthesis of the diplomacy of the Revolution that touches areas uncovered in the earlier works of Bemis and Morris, in *A Diplomatic History of the American Revolution* (New Haven, Conn., 1985).

There is even less to note in the scholarship of the Confederation era. Neither the standard "Critical Period" volumes of the nineteenth century nor the contemporary progressive interpretations of Merrill Jensen, *The New Nation: A History of the United States during the Confederation, 1781-1789* (New York, 1950), make much room for foreign relations. For John Fiske, *Critical Period in American History* (Boston, 1888), at least weakness in the conduct of foreign relations is a part of the crisis. Jensen would minimize this problem. The one book that does center on diplomacy in the Confederation is Frederick W. Marks III, *Independence on Trial: Foreign Affairs and the Making of the Constitution* (Baton Rouge, La., 1973). Although peripheral to his major interests, Jack N. Rakove, *The Beginnings of National Politics: An Interpretative History of the Continental Congress* (New York, 1979), examines Congress's problems with the conduct of foreign relations. Robert Rhodes Crout's studies on the interaction of French commercial needs and the American connection yields important information on Franco-American relations in this period.

The Federalist era continues to appeal. Burton I. Kaufman, ed., *Washington's Farewell Address: The View from the Twentieth Century* (Chicago, 1969), surveys the changing interpretations. Jerald A. Combs, *The*

Jay Treaty: Political Battleground of the Founding Fathers (Berkeley, Calif., 1970), unlike Bemis, analyzes the argument over the treaty primarily in terms of each party's conception of the national interest, and minimizes the roles of personalities in the conflict. Albert Hall Bowman, *The Struggle for Neutrality: Franco-American Diplomacy during the Federalist Era* (Knoxville, Tenn., 1974), emphasizes the Federalist bias against France in the Jay Treaty and shows how the French foreign office looked at American policy. William Stinchcombe, *The XYZ Affair* (Westport, Conn., 1981), is the first full examination of this crisis, with respect to both the conflict between Federalists and Republicans and between the United States and France.

The long shadow of Henry Adams will always inhibit new interpretations of the Jefferson presidency. Burton Spivak's *Jefferson's English Crisis: Commerce, Embargo and the Republican Revolution* (Charlottesville, Va., 1979) offers a major reevaluation of Jefferson's views on the embargo. The key to this interpretation is the evolution of the embargo from a precautionary preparation for war to an act of coercion, with the side benefit of removing America from noxious British commercial connections. Clifford L. Egan, *Neither Peace nor War: Franco-American Relations, 1803–1812* (Baton Rouge, La., 1983), attempts to deal with an area of forming relations not covered by the work of DeConde or Perkins. Albert H. Bowman, using French archives extensively, is currently undertaking a larger task of dealing with the years and the materials that Henry Adams had written about with such authority a century ago.

The causes of the War of 1812, if not the diplomacy of that war, has not been neglected in the last decade. The dominance of Julius W. Pratt, *The Expansionists of 1812* (New York, 1925), with a western expansionist interpretation that challenged Adams's *History* has been in turn modified by Bradford Perkins, *Prologue to War* (Berkeley, Calif., 1961), and Reginald Horsman, *The Causes of the War of 1812* (Philadelphia, 1962), which returned attention to maritime causes. Roger H. Brown, *The Republic in Peril* (New York, 1964), focuses on party rather than section with the Republican fear of republicanism itself at stake as a factor in the coming of the war. Brown's attention to congressional behavior is reinforced by the work of Ronald L. Hatzenbuehler and Robert L. Ivie, *Congress Declares War: Rhetoric, Leadership, and Partisanship in the Early Republic* (Kent, Ohio, 1983), in examining the dynamics behind Congress's declaration of war. J. C. A. Stagg, *Mr. Madison's War: Politics, Diplomacy, and Warfare in the Early American Republic, 1783–1830* (Princeton, N.J., 1983), returns the debate to western grounds as he explained Madison's wish to invade Canada because of its commercial importance for Britain. Two important surveys of the literature cover most of the interpretations written before

1970: Warren H. Goodman, "The Origins of the War of 1812: A Survey of Changing Interpretations," *Mississippi Valley Historical Review* 28 (Sept. 1941): 171–86, and Clifford L. Egan, "The Origins of the War of 1812: Three Decades of Historical Writing," *Military Affairs* 38 (Apr. 1974): 72–75.

The diplomacy of the war itself has never received in the past two generations the detailed if unsophisticated treatment provided by Frank A. Updyke, *The Diplomacy of the War of 1812* (Baltimore, Md., 1915). Far more satisfactory but still marginal to his interests is Bradford Perkins, *Castlereagh and Adams* (Berkeley, Calif., 1964). Fred L. Engelman, *The Peace of Christmas Eve* (New York, 1962), is a narrowly focused but readable and convincing account of the negotiations behind the Treaty of Ghent.

Studies of the foreign relations of the Era of Good Feelings have not advanced beyond the standards of the past generation: George Dangerfield, *Era of Good Feelings* (New York, 1952); Samuel Flagg Bemis's monumental *John Quincy Adams and the Foundations of American Foreign Policy* (New York, 1949); Arthur P. Whitaker, *The United States and the Independence of Latin America, 1800–1830* (Berkeley, Calif., 1949). Dexter Perkins's studies of the Monroe Doctrine remain authoritative. The one major challenge to its approach is Ernest R. May, *The Making of the Monroe Doctrine* (Cambridge, Mass., 1975). From his examination of bureaucratic politics May concludes that Adams and his colleagues were motivated more by presidential aspirations than by fears of European invasion.

It is obvious that the continuing flow of studies in the Age of Jefferson has not yet changed radically the understanding of United States foreign relations that may be found in Samuel Flagg Bemis and Grace Gardner Griffin, eds., *Guide to the Diplomatic History of the United States, 1775–1921* (Washington, D.C., 1935), written over half a century ago. Recent scholarship has filled crevices, reinforced perceptions, and revised earlier judgments, but has not replaced the interpretations of the past. If new interpretations are made, they seem to be confined to the narrower or lesser issues.

This consideration has led Jonathan R. Dull to identify the historiography of the earliest years of the nation's history as "not a battleground of conflicting interpretations but a wasteland of outdated scholarship" in "American Foreign Relations before the Constitution: A Historiographical Wasteland," in Gerald K. Haines and J. Samuel Walker, *American Foreign Relations: A Historiographical Review* (Westport, Conn., 1918), 1. Charles S. Maier in "Marking Time: The Historiography of International Relations," in Michael Kammen, ed., *The Past Before Us: Contemporary Historical Writing in the United States* (Ithaca, N.Y., 1980), 377, is more moderate in his language. Still, it is clear that he considers the work of historians of the Age of Jefferson to be uninspired if not pedestrian.

The charges are exaggerated. The relevant chapters in Haines and Walker and the survey of Jerald A. Combs, *American Diplomatic History: Two Centuries of Changing Interpretations* (Berkeley, Calif., 1983), disclose that the Age of Jefferson has not fired the imagination of this generation's diplomatic historians, and that most of the contributions of the first generation of diplomatic historians remain in place. They also reveal that significant analyses continue to be made of the major questions of the period. The valuable bibliographical essays written by William Stinchcombe, Albert Bowman, Bradford Perkins, and Lester Langley in Richard Dean Burns, *SHAFR Guide to American Foreign Relations since 1700* (Santa Barbara, Calif., 1983), and the comprehensive bibliographical essay in Reginald Horsman, *The Diplomacy of the New Republic, 1776–1815* (Arlington, Ill., 1985), not only discuss the scholarship of the current generation but point to directions that the next generation may follow.

NOTES

CHAPTER 2

1. See Gilbert Chinard, *Thomas Jefferson: Apostle of Americanism* (Boston, Mass., 1929); Dumas Malone, *Jefferson and His Time,* 6 vols. (Boston, Mass., 1948–); Merrill D. Peterson, *Thomas Jefferson and the New Nation* (New York, 1970).

2. Quoted in Henry S. Randall, *The Life of Thomas Jefferson,* 3 vols. (New York, 1858), 3:508.

3. Hamilton to Edward Carrington, 20 May 1792, in Harold C. Syrett and Jacob E. Cooke, eds., *The Papers of Alexander Hamilton,* 26 vols. (New York, 1961–79), 11:439.

4. See, for example, Henry Cabot Lodge, *Alexander Hamilton* (Boston, Mass., 1882); Claude G. Bowers, *Jefferson and Hamilton: The Struggle for Democracy in America* (Chautauqua, N.Y., 1927).

5. *William and Mary Quarterly,* 3d ser., 12 (Apr. 1955): 333.

6. The Syrett edition of Hamilton indirectly acknowledges the year as 1755 in *Papers of Hamilton* 1:7n.1; Broadus Mitchell, *Alexander Hamilton: Youth to Maturity 1755–1788* (New York, 1957), accepts it in the title. On the other hand, Robert Hendrickson, *Hamilton (1757–1789),* vol. 1 (New York, 1976), pointedly disagrees.

7. Jefferson to Monroe, 8 Jan. 1804, in Paul L. Ford, *The Works of Thomas Jefferson,* 12 vols. (New York, 1904), 10:60–61.

8. Thomas Paine, "Common Sense," in Moncure Conway, ed., *The Writings of Thomas Paine,* 4 vols. (New York, 1967), 1:88–89.

9. Merrill D. Peterson, "Thomas Jefferson and Commercial Policy, 1783–1793," *William and Mary Quarterly,* 3d ser., 22 (Oct. 1965): 609.

10. Jefferson to T. M. Randolph, 2 Feb. 1800, in Andrew A. Lipscomb and Albert E. Bergh, eds., *The Writings of Thomas Jefferson,* 20 vols. (Washington, D.C., 1903), 10:151.

11. Jefferson to Col. John Taylor, 1 Aug. 1807, ibid., 11:305.

12. Jefferson to Thomas Leiper, 21 Aug. 1807, Ford, *Works of Jefferson* 10:483–84.

13. Article 11 of Treaty of Alliance in David Hunter Miller, *Treaties and Other International Acts of the United States of America,* 8 vols. (Washington, D.C., 1931–48), 2:239.

14. Jefferson to Madison, 28 Apr. 1793, Ford, *Works of Jefferson* 7:301, 302.

15. Jefferson to Edmond Genet, 17 June 1793, ibid. See Article 24 of Treaty of Amity and Commerce, in Miller, *Treaties* 2:19–20; Articles 24 and 25 of Jay's Treaty, ibid., 2:262.

16. Pierre Adet to Minister of Foreign Affairs, 31 Dec. 1796, in Frederick Jackson Turner, ed., "Correspondence of the French Ministers to the United States, 1791–1797," *American Historical Association, Annual Report, 1903* (Washington, D.C., 1904), 982–83.

17. Jefferson to Elbridge Gerry, 26 Jan. 1799, Ford, *Works of Thomas Jefferson* 7:18.

18. Jefferson to Paine, 18 Mar. 1801, Lipscomb, *Writings of Jefferson* 10:223–24.

19. Gerald Stourzh, *Alexander Hamilton and the Idea of Republican Government* (Stanford, Calif., 1970), 198–99.

20. Jefferson to Madison, 19 May 1793, Lipscomb, *Writings of Jefferson* 9:97.

21. Jefferson, "Anas," ibid., 1:362.

22. Harry Ammon, *The Genet Mission* (New York, 1973), 84–85; Albert H. Bowman, *The*

NOTES TO CHAPTER 3

Struggle for Neutrality: Franco-American Diplomacy during the Federalist Era (Knoxville, Tenn., 1974), 88.

23. Jefferson to Madison, 3 Mar. 1798, Lipscomb, *Writings of Jefferson* 9:433.

24. Jefferson to Philip Mazzei, 24 Apr. 1796, Ford, *Works of Jefferson* 8:240–41.

25. Jefferson to William B. Giles, 27 Apr. 1795, Lipscomb, *Writings of Jefferson* 9:305.

26. Jefferson to William Short, 3 Jan. 1793, ibid., 9:10; Jefferson to Tench Coxe, 1 May 1794, ibid., 9:285.

27. Dumas Malone, *Jefferson and His Time*, vol. 3, *Jefferson and the Ordeal of Liberty* (Boston, Mass., 1926), 46.

28. Jefferson to Abigail Adams, 25 Sept. 1785, in Julian P. Boyd et al., eds., *The Papers of Thomas Jefferson* (Princeton, N.J., 1950–), 8:548–49.

29. Marie Kimball, *Thomas Jefferson's Cook Book* (Richmond, Va., 1949), 2.

30. See reference to Dolly's "renowned for its beefsteak," in Charles McC. Weis and Frederick A. Pottle, eds., *Boswell in Extremes 1776–1778* (New York, 1970), 286. Boyd, *Papers of Jefferson* 9:350–51, in his exegesis found that Jefferson would have preferred dining at the Adams's home that night.

31. I raised this issue briefly in chapter 1, "Thomas Jefferson: The Idealist as Realist."

32. Jefferson to Gouverneur Morris, 7 Nov. 1792, Ford, *Works of Jefferson* 7:175.

33. Jefferson to Morris, 12 Mar. 1793, in Paul L. Ford, ed., *The Writings of Thomas Jefferson,* 10 vols. (New York, 1892–99), 6:199.

34. Thomas A. Bailey, *A Diplomatic History of the American People,* 9th ed. (Englewood Cliffs, N.J., 1974), 34. See also John Bassett Moore, *A Digest of International Law,* 8 vols. (Washington, D.C., 1906), 1:120; Charles Cheyney Hyde, *International Law Chiefly as Interpreted and Applied by the United States,* 2 vols. (Boston, Mass., 1922), 1:67–68.

35. 21 Feb. 1923, *Congressional Record—Senate,* 67th Cong., 4th sess., 4160.

36. Secretary of State Charles Evans Hughes to President of the American Federation of Labor (Gompers), *Foreign Relations of the United States, 1923* 2:760–64; Senate Committee on Foreign Relations, *The United States and Communist China in 1949 and 1950: The Question of Rapprochement and Recognition,* 93d Cong., 1st sess., Jan. 1973, 12–13.

CHAPTER 3

1. John Lothrop Motley, *The Rise of the Dutch Republic: A History,* 2 vols. (New York, 1898), 1:iii–iv.

2. Charles Francis Adams, ed., *The Works of John Adams,* 10 vols. (Boston, 1850–56), 7:399–400.

3. Lyman H. Butterfield et al., eds., *Diary and Autobiography of John Adams,* 4 vols. (Cambridge, Mass., 1961), 3:201.

4. Andrew A. Lipscomb and Albert E. Bergh, eds., *The Writings of Thomas Jefferson,* 20 vols. (Washington, D.C., 1903), 1:115–16.

5. Adams to Jefferson, 28 Oct. 1787, in Julian P. Boyd et al., eds., *The Papers of Thomas Jefferson* (Princeton, N.J., 1950–), 12:292; Adams to Jay, 15 Nov. 1787, Adams, *Works of John Adams* 8:460.

6. Abigail Adams to John Quincy Adams, 12 Oct. 1787, in the Adams Papers, reel 370, Massachusetts Historical Society, Boston.

7. See Merrill Jensen, *The New Nation: A History of the United States during the Confederation, 1781–1789* (New York, 1950), 383.

8. Jefferson to John Jay, 26 Sept. 1786, Boyd, *Papers of Jefferson* 10:406.

9. James C. Riley, "Foreign Credit and Fiscal Stability: Dutch Investment in the United States, 1781–1794," *Journal of American History* 65 (Dec. 1978): 672ff.; Merrill D. Peterson, *Thomas Jefferson and the New Nation* (New York, 1970), 362–63; *Journals of the Continental Congress* 23 (2 Oct. 1787): 590–93.

10. Willink and van Staphorst to Jefferson, 31 Jan. 1788, Boyd, *Papers of Jefferson* 12:542ff.

11. Jefferson's Opinion on Fiscal Policy, 26 Aug. 1970, ibid., 17:425.

12. Jefferson to Jay, 12 Mar. 1789, ibid., 14:645.

13. Jefferson to Alexander Donald, 28 July 1787, ibid., 11:633.

14. Adams to Jefferson, 12 Feb. 1788, ibid., 12:581.

15. Adams to James Warren, 9 Dec. 1780, in W. C. Ford, ed., "Warren-Adams Letters," *Massachusetts Historical Society Collections* (Boston, Mass., 1925), 73, no. 2:154.

16. "Facts Concerning American Paper Money," 1767, in Albert H. Smyth, ed., *The Writings of Benjamin Franklin*, 10 vols. (New York, 1907), 5:9.

17. Franklin to Charles W. F. Dumas, 6 Aug. 1781, ibid., 8:292.

18. Adams to Warren, 9 Dec. 1780, "Warren-Adams Letters," 2:154.

19. Adams to Robert Morris, 21 May 1783, Adams, *Works of John Adams* 8:59.

20. Adams to Robert R. Livingston, 23 July 1783, ibid., 8:112.

21. Adams to Livingston, 7 July 1783, ibid., 8:85.

22. Madison to James Monroe, 21 June 1786, in William T. Hutchinson and William M. Rachal, eds., *The Papers of James Madison*, (Chicago, Ill., 1962–), 9:82.

23. From *The North-American*, no. 2, 8 Oct. 1783, ibid., 7:321.

24. From *The Continentalist*, no. 5, 18 Apr. 1782, in Harold C. Syrett and Jacob E. Cooke, eds., *The Papers of Alexander Hamilton*, 26 vols. (New York, 1961–79), 3:78.

25. Jefferson to Jay, 11 Oct. 1785, Boyd, *Papers of Jefferson* 8:608.

26. Jay to Jefferson, 14 July 1786, ibid., 10:135.

27. Jefferson to Adams, 19 Nov. 1785, ibid., 9:43.

28. Jefferson to Monroe, 11 Dec. 1785, ibid., 9:95.

29. Paul G. Sifton, ed., "Otto's *Mémoire* to Vergennes, 1785," *William and Mary Quarterly*, 3d ser., 22 (Oct. 1965): 643.

30. Jefferson to Madison, 11 Nov. 1784, Boyd, *Papers of Jefferson* 7:506; Jefferson to Samuel Osgood, 5 Oct. 1785, ibid., 8:589.

31. Jefferson to Jay, 21 June 1787, ibid., 11:491; Jefferson to Edward Carrington, 4 Aug. 1787, ibid., 11:679.

32. Jefferson to John Sullivan, 5 Oct. 1787, ibid., 12:209.

33. Jefferson to Benjamin Vaughan, 2 July 1787, ibid., 11:533.

34. Jefferson to George Washington, 14 Aug. 1787, ibid., 12:37–38.

35. Jefferson to Jay, 3 Nov. 1787, ibid, 12:310.

36. Jefferson to Vaughan, 2 July 1787, ibid., 11:533.

37. Quoted in Edward Handler, *America and Europe in the Political Thought of John Adams* (Cambridge, Mass., 1964), 115.

38. See commentary in Boyd, *Papers of Jefferson* 13:xxxiii.

39. Quoted in Handler, *Political Thought of John Adams*, 112.

40. Adams to Jefferson, 10 Nov. 1787, Boyd, *Papers of Jefferson* 12:335.

41. Jefferson to G. K. van Hogendorp, 25 Aug. 1786, ibid., 10:299.

42. Washington to Henry Knox, 5 Feb. 1788, in J. C. Fitzpatrick, ed., *The Writings of George Washington*, 19 vols. (Washington, D.C., 1931–44), 29:401.

43. Washington to Reverend Francis Adrian Vanderkemp, 28 May 1788, ibid., 29:505; Adams to Jefferson, 10 Nov. 1787, Boyd, *Papers of Jefferson* 12:335.

44. Jefferson to Abigail Adams, 1 July 1787, Boyd, *Papers of Jefferson* 12:33.

NOTES TO CHAPTER 4

45. Jefferson to David Humphreys, 14 Aug. 1787, ibid., 12:33.

46. Smyth, *Writings of Franklin,* 30 June 1787, 9:603; Max Farrand, ed., *Records of the Federal Convention,* 20 July 1787, 4 vols. (New Haven, Conn., 1937), 2:68. This point is repeated in Patrick Henry's comments on 9 June 1788, during the debate on the Constitution at the Virginia state convention, in Jonathan Elliot, ed., *The Debates of the State Conventions,* 5 vols. (Philadelphia, Pa., 1836–45), 3:160.

47. Jefferson to William Stephens Smith, 13 Nov. 1787, Boyd, *Papers of Jefferson* 12:356.

48. 17 June 1788, Hutchinson & Rachal, *Papers of James Madison* 11:126.

49. 17 June 1788, Elliot, *Debates* 2:234.

50. See William H. Riker, "Dutch and American Federalism," *Journal of the History of Ideas* 18 (Oct. 1957): 495.

51. Farrand, *Records,* 29 June 1787, 1:478; 28 June, 1787, 1:457. Madison underscores Holland's special influence in the *Federalist,* No. 20.

52. Elliot, *Debates,* 12 June 1788, 3:290; 11 June 1788, 3:275.

53. Ibid., 17 June 1788, 2:224.

54. See J. W. Schulte Nordholt, "The Example of the Dutch Republic for American Federalism," *Bijdragen en Mededelingen Betreffende de Geschiedenis der Nederlanden* 94 (1979): 437–49.

55. See Simon Schama, *Patriots and Liberators: Revolution in the Netherlands, 1780–1813* (New York, 1977), 61; Robert R. Palmer, *The Age of the Democratic Revolution: The Challenge* (Princeton, N.J., 1959), 325ff. J. W. Schulte Nordholt, "Gijsbert van Hogendorp in America, 1783–1784," *Acta Historiae Neerlandicae* 10 (1978): 139, found van Hogendorp one of the few disappointed Americanophiles, preferring the Constitution to the Articles.

56. Jefferson to Adams, 27 Sept. 1787. Boyd, *Papers of Jefferson* 12:189.

CHAPTER 4

1. H. C. Allen, *Great Britain and the United States: A History of Anglo-American Relations, 1783–1952* (New York, 1955), 23.

2. Adams to John Jay, 3 Dec. 1785, in Charles Francis Adams, ed., *The Works of John Adams,* 10 vols. (Boston, 1850–56), 8:355.

3. John Quincy Adams to Louisa Adams, 28 Oct. 1814, in Worthington C. Ford, ed., *Writings of John Quincy Adams,* 7 vols. (New York, 1913–17), 5:175.

4. Bradford Perkins, *Prologue to War: England and the United States, 1805–1812* (Berkeley, Calif., 1961), 275.

5. Quoted in Bradford Perkins, *Castlereagh and Adams: England and the United States, 1812–1823* (Berkeley, Calif., 1964), 209.

6. Bradford Perkins, *The First Rapprochement: England and the United States, 1795–1805* (Philadelphia, 1955).

7. Jefferson to Du Pont, 18 Apr. 1802, in Andrew A. Lipscomb and Albert E. Bergh, eds., *The Writings of Thomas Jefferson,* 20 vols. (Washington, D. C., 1903), 10:313.

8. Hamilton to Washington, 15 Sept. 1790, in Harold C. Syrett and Jacob E. Cooke, eds., *The Papers of Alexander Hamilton,* 26 vols. (New York, 1961–79), 7:46–47.

9. Julian P. Boyd, *Number 7: Alexander Hamilton's Secret Attempts to Control American Foreign Policy* (Princeton, N.J., 1964).

10. Quoted in Samuel Flagg Bemis, *Jay's Treaty: A Study in Commerce and Diplomacy* (New Haven, Conn., 1962), 337.

11. Quoted in Perkins, *First Rapprochement,* 104.

12. Quoted in Perkins, *Prologue to War*, 176.

13. Ibid., 73.

14. Ibid., 138.

15. See Robert Ernst, *Rufus King: American Federalist* (Chapel Hill, N.C., 1968), 314; Theodore Welch, *Theodore Sedgwick, Federalist: A Political Portrait* (Middletown, Conn., 1965), 247.

16. Quoted in Samuel Eliot Morison, *Harrison Gray Otis, 1765–1848: The Urbane Federalist* (Boston, Mass., 1969), 321–22.

17. Ibid., 323.

18. Ibid., 323–24.

19. Quoted in Perkins, *Prologue to War*, 436.

20. Quoted in Roger H. Brown, *The Republic in Peril: 1812* (New York, 1964), 96.

21. Samuel Eliot Morison et al., *Dissent in Three American Wars* (Cambridge, Mass., 1970), 18.

22. Quoted in J. S. Martell, "A Sidelight on Federalist Strategy During the War of 1812," *American Historical Review* 43 (Apr. 1938): 558.

23. Quoted in Morison, *Dissent in Three American Wars*, 24.

24. Charles K. Webster, ed., *Britain and the Independence of Latin America*, 2 vols. (London, 1938), 1:42.

CHAPTER 5

1. Paul A. Varg, *Foreign Policies of the Founding Fathers* (Lansing, Mich., 1963), 72.

2. Cecilia Kenyon, "Alexander Hamilton: Rousseau of the Right," *Political Science Quarterly* 73 (June 1958): 171–78; Albert H. Bowman, "Jefferson, Hamilton and American Foreign Policy," ibid., 71 (Mar. 1956): 18–41.

3. Bowman, "Jefferson, Hamilton," 21–22.

4. Gilbert L. Lycan, *Alexander Hamilton and American Foreign Policy: A Design for Greatness* (Norman, Okla., 1970), 417–18.

5. Dumas Malone, "Jefferson, Hamilton, and the Constitution," in W. H. Nelson, ed., *Theory and Practice in American Politics* (Chicago, Ill., 1964), 14.

6. John C. Miller, *The Federalist Era, 1789–1801* (New York, 1960), 12–13.

7. Merrill D. Peterson, "Thomas Jefferson and Commercial Policy, 1783–1793," *William and Mary Quarterly*, 3d ser., 22 (Oct. 1965): 592.

8. Jefferson to Monroe, 17 June 1785, in Julian P. Boyd et al., eds., *The Papers of Thomas Jefferson* (Princeton, N.J., 1950–), 7:231.

9. Dumas Malone, *Jefferson and His Time*, vol. 2, *Jefferson and the Rights of Man* (Boston, 1951), 174.

10. See discussion in ibid., 172–74.

11. Jefferson to Joseph Jones, 4 Aug. 1787, Boyd, *Papers of Jefferson* 12:34.

12. Jefferson to Madison, 20 Dec. 1787, ibid., 12:439.

13. Robert R. Davis, "The Foundations of American Diplomatic Treaty Etiquette," *Foreign Service Journal*, Mar. 1968, 21–22.

14. Jefferson's "Opinion on the Powers of the Senate Respecting Diplomatic Appointments," 24 Apr. 1790, Boyd, *Papers of Jefferson* 16:379.

15. Jacob E. Cooke, "The Compromise of 1790," *William and Mary Quarterly*, 3d ser., 27 (Oct. 1970): 524, challenges Jefferson's "exaggerated claim that [the bargain] was responsible for the passage of the residence and assumption measures."

16. Jefferson to Edward Rutledge, 4 July 1790, Boyd, *Papers of Jefferson* 16:601.

NOTES TO CHAPTER 6

17. Julian P. Boyd, *Number 7: Alexander Hamilton's Secret Attempts to Control American Foreign Policy* (Princeton, N.J., 1964), 64–65.

18. Hamilton to Washington, 15 Sept. 1790, in Harold C. Syrett and Jacob E. Cooke, eds., *The Papers of Alexander Hamilton,* 26 vols. (New York, 1961–79), 7:46–47.

19. Jefferson to Madison, 19 Dec. 1800, in Andrew A. Lipscomb and Albert E. Bergh, eds., *The Writings of Thomas Jefferson,* 20 vols. (Washington, D.C., 1903), 10:185.

20. Hamilton to Theodore Sedgwick, 22 Dec. 1800, in Henry Cabot Lodge, ed., *The Works of Alexander Hamilton,* 10 vols. (New York, 1904), 10:397–98.

CHAPTER 6

1. "Isolationism" first appeared in print in 1922. See Mitford M. Mathews, ed., *A Dictionary of Americanisms on Historical Principles* (Chicago, Ill., 1951), 1:891.

2. Felix Gilbert, *To the Farewell Address: Ideas of Early American Foreign Policy* (Princeton, N.J., 1961), 46ff.

3. W. C. Ford et al., eds., *The Journals of the Continental Congress,* 34 vols. (Washington, D.C., 1904–37), 3:392.

4. John Adams to John Winthrop, 23 June 1776, in Edmund C. Burnett, ed., *Letters of Members of Continental Congress,* 8 vols. (Washington, D.C., 1921–36), 1:502.

5. "Plan of Treaties," *Journals of the Continental Congress* 6:768–78.

6. Harrison et al., Committee of Secret Correspondence to the Commissioner at Paris, Baltimore, 30 Dec. 1776, in Francis Wharton, ed., *Revolutionary Diplomatic Correspondence of the United States,* 6 vols. (Washington, D.C., 1889), 2:240.

7. Silas Deane memoir to French foreign minister, 30 Dec. 1776, in Archives du Ministère des affaires étrangères, Paris, correspondance politique, États-Unis, 1:15, transcript in Library of Congress.

8. Arthur Lee to Baron Schulenberg, 10 June 1777, in Wharton, *Revolutionary Diplomatic Correspondence* 2:334.

9. David Hunter Miller, *Treaties and Other International Acts of the United States of America,* 8 vols. (Washington, D.C., 1931–48), 2:39.

10. Committee of Commissioners, 4 May 1778, in Wharton, *Revolutionary Diplomatic Correspondence* 2:569.

11. Article 2 of Treaty of Alliance, in Miller, *Treaties* 2:36–37.

12. *Journals of the Continental Congress* 20 (8 and 11 June 1781): 615–17, 627–28.

13. Robert Morris to Benjamin Franklin, 5 Dec. 1781, in Robert Morris Papers, Library of Congress.

14. Morris to Franklin, 1 July 1782, Morris Papers.

15. John Jay to Robert Livingston, 3 Apr. 1782, in Jay Papers, Library of Congress.

16. Hamilton's remarks on the Provisional Peace Treaty in the Continental Congress, Philadelphia, 19 Mar. 1783, in Harold C. Syrett and Jacob E. Cooke, eds., *The Papers of Alexander Hamilton,* 26 vols. (New York, 1961–79), 3:294–95.

17. Debates in the Congress of the Confederation, 19 Mar. 1783, in Gaillard Hunt, ed., *Writings of James Madison,* 9 vols. (New York, 1900–1910), 1:404–5.

18. Debates in the Congress of the Confederation, 12 Mar. 1783, ibid., 1:406.

19. Motion on the Provisional Peace Treaty in the Continental Congress, 19 Mar. 1783, Syrett, *Papers of Hamilton* 3:296–97.

20. Debates in the Congress of the Confederation, 9–10 Jan. 1783, Hunt, *Writings of Madison* 1:306–97.

21. Debates in the Congress of the Confederation, 13 Jan. 1783, ibid., 3:309.

22. William Stinchcombe observes that "the French-American defensive alliance ended in fact when the news arrived of the termination of hostilities between France and Great Britain in March, 1783," in *The American Revolution and the French Alliance* (Syracuse, N.Y., 1969), 200.

23. Reports of Secretary Jay, respecting French and American consuls, 4 July 1786, in *The Diplomatic Correspondence of the United States of America from the Signing of the Definitive Treaty of Peace to the Adoption of the Constitution, March 4, 1789,* 3 vols. (Washington, D.C., 1837), 1:226–27. See discussion in Samuel Flagg Bemis, "John Jay," in Bemis, ed., *The American Secretaries of State and Their Diplomacy,* 10 vols. (New York, 1928), 1:258; and Dumas Malone, *Jefferson and His Time,* vol. 2, *Jefferson and the Rights of Man* (Boston, Mass., 1951), 199–201.

24. Elbridge Gerry to Rufus King, 21 Mar. 1785, Gerry Papers, Library of Congress.

25. Jefferson to William Short, 28 July 1791, in Paul L. Ford, ed., *The Writings of Thomas Jefferson,* 10 vols. (New York, 1892–99), 5:362–63.

26. See discussion in Charles M. Thomas, *American Neutrality in 1793: A Study in Cabinet government* (New York, 1931), 46–47; Charles S. Hyneman, *The First American Neutrality: A Study of the American Understanding of Neutral Obligations during the Years 1792 to 1815* (Urbana, Ill., 1934), 12–13.

27. Jefferson to Gouverneur Morris, 12 Mar. 1793, Ford, *Writings of Jefferson* 6:199.

28. Letters of Helvidius, No. 3, Hunt, *Writings of Madison* 6:167.

29. Monroe to Jefferson, 3 Sept. 1793, in Stanislaus M. Hamilton, ed., *The Writings of James Monroe,* 7 vols. (New York, 1898–1903), 1:274.

30. Eugene P. Link, *Democratic-Republican Societies, 1790–1800* (New York, 1942), 20, identifies them with Sons of Liberty and contemporary British radical clubs.

31. Jefferson to Madison, 28 Apr. 1793, in Ford, *Writings of Jefferson* 6:232.

32. Jefferson to Edmond Genet, 17 June 1793, in Andrew A. Lipscomb and Albert E. Bergh, eds., *The Writings of Thomas Jefferson,* 20 vols. (Washington, D.C., 1903), 9:131–37.

33. Jefferson to W. B. Giles, 27 Apr. 1795, in Ford, *Writings of Jefferson* 8:172. Particularly noteworthy was Jefferson's impulse to give up his retirement in 1795 to dine in London with General Pichegru and to "hail the dawn of liberty & republicanism in that island."

34. Madison to Jefferson, 25 Dec. 1796; to Colonel James Madison, 27 Nov. 1796, in Madison Papers, Library of Congress.

35. Jefferson to Thomas Pinckney, 29 May 1797, Lipscomb, *Writings of Jefferson* 9:389–90.

36. Monroe to Jefferson, 16 June 1798, Hamilton, *Writings of Monroe* 3:126.

37. Jefferson to Edmund Pendleton, 29 Jan. 1799, Ford, *Writings of Jefferson* 7:337.

38. Madison to Jefferson, 15 Apr. 1798, Hunt, *Writings of Madison* 6:315.

39. Jefferson, "Anas," 31 Oct. 1792, in Lipscomb, *Writings of Jefferson* 1:320–22; unpublished article for the *Gazette of the United States,* Mar.-Apr. 1793, in Syrett, *Papers of Hamilton* 14:268.

40. *Annals of Congress,* 5th Cong., 2d sess., H.R., 6 July 1798, 2126.

41. Philadelphia *General Advertiser,* 12 July 1798.

42. *General Advertiser,* 26 Feb. 1798.

43. *General Advertiser,* 10 July 1798.

44. Jefferson to Gerry, 26 Jan. 1799, Ford, *Writings of Jefferson* 7:328.

45. Madison to Jefferson, 24 Apr. 1800, Hunt, *Writings of Madison* 6:408.

46. Jefferson to John Breckinridge, 29 Jan. 1800, in Ford, *Writings of Jefferson* 7:417–18.

47. Jefferson to Madison, 19 Dec. 1800, in Lipscomb, *Writings of Jefferson* 10:185.

48. Thomas Paine to Jefferson, 1 and 4 Oct. 1800, Jefferson Papers, Library of Congress; Joel Barlow to Jefferson, 3 Oct. 1800, ibid. Many of Paine's views were made public in ex-

tracts of his letters written in October 1800 and appear in the *National Intelligencer*, 26 Jan. and 11 Feb. 1801.

49. Jefferson to George Logan, 21 Mar. 1801, in Ford, *Writings of Jefferson*, 8:23.

CHAPTER 7

1. Vernon L. Parrington, *Main Currents in American Thought* . . . (New York, 1927–30), 2:10.

2. William Cullen Bryant, "The Embargo or Sketches of the Times; a Satire," in Tremaine McDowell, ed., *William Cullen Bryant: Representative Selections* (New York, 1935), 341ff.

3. See, for example: Dumas Malone, *Jefferson and His Time*, vol. 2, *Jefferson and the Rights of Man* (Boston, Mass., 1951); Gilbert Chinard, *Thomas Jefferson: The Apostle of Americanism* (Boston, Mass., 1929); Merrill D. Peterson, *The Jefferson Image in the American Mind* (New York, 1960).

4. Adrienne Koch, *The Philosophy of Thomas Jefferson* (New York, 1943), 44–45.

5. Idéologie was the name coined by Destutt de Tracy to express the philosophical movement based largely on the sensationalist theory of knowledge. Denoting no particular school, it encompassed most of the philosophers of the Revolution in its fold with the exception of the Rousseauist and the Terrorist. For the purposes of this article, the term applies to all members of the pro-American intelligentsia in the Napoleonic era.

6. Gilbert Chinard, *Volney et l'Amérique* (Baltimore, Md., 1923), 139, in Durand Echeverria, *Mirage in the West: A History of the French Image of American Society to 1815* (Princeton, N.J., 1957), 276.

7. See chapter 8, "Jefferson, the Napoleonic Wars, and the Balance of Power." The familiar Federalist view of Jefferson reveals a weak character subjected to French influence. In the article above, his support of France is seen as a product of his conception of the European balance of power.

8. Marie Kimball, *Jefferson: The Scene of Europe, 1784–1789* (New York, 1950), 82ff.

9. Jefferson to Madison, 12 Jan. 1789, in Julian P. Boyd et al., eds., *The Papers of Thomas Jefferson* (Princeton, N.J., 1950–), 14:437.

10. Alfred Whitney Griswold, *Farming and Democracy* (New York, 1948), 23–31.

11. Robert R. Palmer, "The Dubious Democrat: Thomas Jefferson in Bourbon France," *Political Science Quarterly* 72 (1957): 388–404.

12. Autobiography, in Andrew A. Lipscomb and Albert E. Bergh, eds., *The Writings of Thomas Jefferson*, 20 vols. (Washington, D.C., 1903), 1:154–57.

13. Jefferson to William Short, 3 Jan. 1793, ibid., 9:10; Jefferson to Thomas Randolph, 7 Jan. 1793, ibid., 9:13.

14. Charles Hunter Van Duzer, "Contributions of the Ideologues to French Revolutionary Thought," *The Johns Hopkins University Studies in Historical and Political Science* (Baltimore, Md., 1935) 53:80–83.

15. Chinard, *Volney et l'Amérique*, 43.

16. Mildred Stahl Fletcher, "Louisiana as a Factor in French Diplomacy from 1763 to 1800," *Mississippi Valley Historical Review* 17 (1930): 367–77; E. Wilson Lyon, *Louisiana in French Diplomacy, 1759–1804* (Norman, Okla., 1934), 88–98. Jefferson to Démeunier, 29 Apr. 1795, in Paul L. Ford, ed., *The Works of Thomas Jefferson,* 12 vols. (New York, 1904), 8:173–75. Démeunier, former editor of the *Encyclopédie Méthodique,* was then an exile in London. It is noteworthy that Jefferson never made much of a distinction between the Thermidorians and the men of the Directory.

17. Among American statesmen only Hamilton understood that the Convention of Morte-

fontaine "plays into the hands of France, by the precedent of those principles of navigation which she is at this moment desirous of making the basis of a league of the northern powers against England"; Hamilton to Theodore Sedgwick, 12 Dec. 1800, in Henry Cabot Lodge, ed., *The Works of Alexander Hamilton,* 10 vols. (New York. 1904), 10:397. Yet Hamilton, like the more moderate Federalists and like Jefferson himself, considered the convention to be less harmful than other possible solutions. See Arthur B. Darling, *Our Rising Empire, 1763–1803* (New Haven, 1940), 379.

18. Charles Lebrun, the third consul, sounded the keynote of France's ambitions at the signing of the convention when he proposed the toast: "To the Union of America with the powers of the North for securing the freedom of the high seas." *Gazette nationale ou le moniteur universel,* 6 Oct. 1800, 14. Quoted by George F. Hoar, "A Famous Fête," American Antiquarian Society, *Proceedings,* new ser. (Worcester, Mass., 1898), 12:257. See also Arthur A. Richmond, "Napoleon and the Armed Neutrality of 1800; A Diplomatic Challenge to British Sea Power," Royal United Service Institution, *Journal* 104, no. 614 (1959): 1–9.

19. Louis André Pichon, the French minister to the United States, reported, however, that the exigencies of domestic politics would prevent Jefferson from doing anything more than applauding from afar French success in the war with Britain. Chances of Jefferson's joining the league were slight, in Pichon's estimation. Pichon to the Minister of Foreign Affairs, 4 May 1801, Archives du Ministère des affaires étrangères, Paris, correspondance politique, États-Unis, 12 July 1801, ibid., foll. 177–84.

20. Pichon to the Minister of Foreign Affairs, 1 Dec. 1801, ibid., foll. 433–436vo. It was Pichon's duty to assure Jefferson that France had given up all designs upon Louisiana.

21. Thomas Paine to Jefferson, 1 and 4 Oct. 1800; Barlow to Jefferson, 4 Oct. 1800, Jefferson Papers, 107, Library of Congress. James Woodress, *A Yankee's Odyssey: The Life of Joel Barlow* (Philadelphia, Pa., 1958), 207–8, believes that Barlow's interest in a "Maritime Convention" was stimulated primarily by the economic benefits it would bring the United States.

22. Van Duzer, "Contributions of the Ideologues," 143–48.

23. Echeverria, *Mirage in the West,* 227.

24. Van Duzer, "Contributions of the Ideologues," 148–49.

25. Lafayette to Jefferson, 10 Feb. 1800, in Gilbert Chinard, ed., *The Letters of Lafayette and Jefferson . . .* (Baltimore, Md., 1929), 210; Lafayette to Jefferson, 21 June 1801, ibid., 213.

26. Gilbert Chinard, *Jefferson et les idéologues, d'après sa correspondance inédite avec Destutt de Tracy, Cabinis, J. B. Say et Auguste Comte* (Baltimore, Md., 1925), 13.

27. Jefferson to Robert Livingston, 18 Apr. 1802, Lipscomb, *Writings of Jefferson* 10:313.

28. Jefferson to Livingston, 5 May 1802, Jefferson Papers, 113, Lib. Cong. The president mentioned that he had allowed Du Pont to read the threatening letter of 18 April.

29. Jefferson to Du Pont, 25 Apr. 1802, in Lipscomb & Bergh, *Writings of Jefferson* 10:316–19.

30. Du Pont to Jefferson, 30 Apr. 1802, in Gilbert Chinard, ed., *The Correspondence of Jefferson and Du Pont de Nemours, with an Introduction on Jefferson and the Physiocrats* (Baltimore, Md., 1931), 48–54.

31. Monroe to Jefferson, 20 Sept. 1802, Jefferson Papers, 134, Lib. Cong. Jefferson himself had been elected to the National Institute in 1801. See Comte de Franqueville, *Le premier siècle de l'institut de France* (Paris, 1895), 2:55.

32. Jefferson to Monroe, 8 Jan. 1804, Ford, *Works of Jefferson* 10:60–61.

33. Jefferson to T. M. Randolph, 2 Feb. 1800, Lipscomb, *Writings of Jefferson* 10:150. He expressed in particular his disappointment in the "views and principles" of Sieyès, Volney, and Lafayette after they supported Bonaparte.

34. Jefferson to Volney, 20 Apr. 1802, Jefferson Papers, 122; Lib. Cong.; Jefferson to

NOTES TO CHAPTER 7

Mme. de Corny, 31 Jan. 1803, in Gilbert Chinard, ed., *Trois amitiés françaises de Jefferson, d'après sa correspondance inédite avec madame de Brehan, de Tessé, et de Corny* (Paris, 1927), 212; Jefferson to Cabanis, 12 July 1803, in Lipscomb, *Writings of Jefferson* 10:405.

35. After his retirement, Jefferson personally translated Destutt de Tracy's *Treatise on Political Economy* from the unpublished French original, and wrote a prospectus for it, praising the work.

36. "My occupations permit me only to ask questions. They deny me the time, if I had the information, to answer them. Perhaps, as worthy of the attention of the author of the Traité d'Économie Politique, I shall find them answered in that work. If they are not, the reason will have been that you wrote for Europe; while I shall have asked them because I think for America." Jefferson to J. B. Say, 4 Feb. 1804, in Lipscomb, *Writings of Jefferson* 11:3. "These investigations are very meta-physical, profound, and demonstrative, and will give satisfaction to minds in the habit of abstract speculation." This is part of the prospectus to Destutt de Tracy's *Treatise on Political Economy* warning American readers about the abstract parts of the work. Jefferson to Joseph Mulligan, 6 Apr. 1816, ibid., 14:462.

37. Jefferson to Lafayette, 4 Nov. 1803, in Chinard, *Letters of Lafayette and Jefferson*, 225–26; Jefferson to William Claiborne, 25 May 1806, in Chinard, *Correspondence of Jefferson and Du Pont*, 98.

38. Du Pont to Jefferson, 12 May 1803, in Chinard, ed., *Correspondence of Jefferson and Du Pont*, 73; Jefferson to Du Pont, 19 Jan. 1804, ibid., 81. Du Pont was appeased by Jefferson's reasoning but the Louisianans were not. They presented a memorial to Congress in 1804 indignantly complaining about the arbitrary executive and judicial powers vested in the governor.

39. See Van Duzer, "Contributions of the Ideologues," 151–63.

40. Lafayette to Jefferson, 20 Feb. 1807, Chinard, *Letters of Lafayette and Jefferson*, 253. Lafayette lamented the fate of good liberals forced into exile, but thought that these "jolts and bars" would not disturb the liberal impulses given France by the United States.

41. Lafayette to Jefferson, 1 Sept. 1803, ibid., 224. Typically, Lafayette blamed Britain, not Bonaparte, for violating the Treaty of Amiens and renewing the war.

42. Lafayette to Jefferson, 31 Mar. 1803, ibid., 218.

43. Du Pont to Jefferson, 10 Mar. 1806, 12 July 1807, 13 Aug. 1807, 23 July 1808, Chinard, *Correspondence of Jefferson and Du Pont*, 108, 112, 120, 128.

44. Du Pont called the embargo an act of courage. Du Pont to Jefferson, 24 July 1808, ibid., 135. Mme. de Staël was one of the few French liberals to urge Jefferson to take a stand against Napoleon during the War of 1812. In his reply, Jefferson deplored Napoleon's acts but declared Britain to be the greater threat to the United States. Mme. de Staël to Jefferson, 10 Nov. 1812, in Marie G. Kimball, "Unpublished Correspondence of Mme. de Staël with Thomas Jefferson," *North American Review* 208 (1918): 66–68; Jefferson to Mme. de Staël, 24 May 1813, Lipscomb, *Writings of Jefferson* 13:237–45. See chapter 8, "Jefferson, the Napoleonic Wars, and the Balance of Power."

45. Lafayette to Jefferson, 16 Sept. 1809, in Chinard, *Letters of Lafayette and Jefferson*, 289.

46. Lafayette to Jefferson, 18 Nov. 1809, ibid., 294.

47. Adams to Jefferson, 16 Dec. 1816, in Lester J. Cappon, ed., *The Adams-Jefferson Letters: The Complete Correspondence between Thomas Jefferson and Abigail and John Adams* (Chapel Hill, N.C., 1959), 2:500–501.

48. Jefferson to Adams, 28 Oct. 1813, ibid., 2:391.

49. Jefferson to Baron Quesnai de Rochemont, 18 May 1818, Jefferson Papers, University of Virginia. "I am not satisfied that the mass of mind in France and the countries North of that

has taken a solid direction, which may be momentarily checked, but will ultimately attain its determined object, that of a government in which the people by their representatives have an effectual control."

50. Gallatin, one of the United States peace commissioners in France in 1815, reported the flourishing of revolutionary legacy which the Revolution was unable to destroy: the people's independence of priest and noble. Lafayette to Jefferson, 6 Sept. and 27 Nov. 1815, Jefferson Papers, 24 and 205, Lib. Cong. Lafayette also submitted reports to Jefferson which, characteristically, were much more optimistic than Gallatin's. Lafayette to Jefferson, 10 Dec. 1817, and 20 July 1820, Chinard, *Letters of Lafayette and Jefferson,* 381, 398.

51. Jefferson was sure that the French would "finally establish for themselves a government of rational and well-tempered liberty. So much science cannot be lost; so much light shed over them can never fail to produce some good, in the end." Jefferson to Albert Gallatin, 16 Oct. 1815, Lipscomb, *Writings of Jefferson* 14:359.

52. Jefferson to Adams, 5 July 1814, Cappon, *Adams-Jefferson Letters* 2:431; Jefferson to Adams, 4 Sept. 1823, ibid., 2:596.

CHAPTER 8

1. W. Stull Holt, "Uncle Sam as Deer, Jackal, and Lion; or the United States in Power Politics," *Pacific Spectator* 3 (1949): 47–48.

2. Jefferson to Benjamin Rush, 4 Oct. 1803, in Andrew A. Lipscomb and Albert E. Bergh, eds., *The Writings of Thomas Jefferson,* 20 vols. (Washington, D.C., 1903), 10:422.

3. Jefferson to Edward Rutledge, 4 July 1790, ibid., 8:61.

4. Monroe and William Pinkney had been dispatched to London in 1806 to make a treaty with Britain upon the expiration of Jay's Treaty of 1794. The result was so unacceptable to Jefferson that he refused to present it to the Senate.

5. Albert Gallatin to Jefferson, 13 Apr. 1807, Jefferson Papers, 166, Library of Congress; Jefferson to Madison, 21 Apr. 1807, Lipscomb, *Writings of Jefferson* 11:193.

6. Proclamation of 2 July 1807, in James D. Richardson, ed., *A Compilation of the Messages and Papers of the Presidents, 1789–1897,* 10 vols. (Washington, D.C., 1896–99), 1:423.

7. Jefferson to Du Pont, 14 July 1807, in Gilbert Chinard, ed., *The Correspondence of Jefferson and Du Pont de Nemours, with an Introduction on Jefferson and the Physiocrats* (Baltimore, Md.,1931), 116; Jefferson to Lafayette, 14 July 1807, Lipscomb, *Writings of Jefferson* 11:279; Turreau to Talleyrand, 18 July 1807, Archives du Ministère des affaires étrangères, Paris, correspondance politique, États-Unis, 60:166–71 (hereafter cited as Correspondance politique). When Jefferson failed to take a strong stand with the British, Turreau bitterly gave up all hope for a people "who have no idea of glory, grandeur, and justice"; 4 Sept. 1807, ibid., foll. 199–201.

8. William Tatham to Jefferson, 1 July 1807; Tatham to Jefferson, 3 July 1807, Jefferson Papers, 167, Lib. Cong. Both presented reasons for moderation, and Jefferson, in turn, advised Governor Cabell of Virginia to exercise discretion in applying the proclamation against British ships in Norfolk. Jefferson to Cabell, 19 and 24 July 1807, Lipscomb, *Writings of Jefferson* 11:288–90, 294–96.

9. Jefferson to George Clinton, 6 July 1807, ibid., 11:258. Henry Adams claimed that Jefferson would not have delayed calling the Congress into emergency session if he had really wanted war. Adams, *History of the United States during the Administrations of Jefferson and Madison,* 9 vols. (New York, 1889–91), 4:34–35.

10. Adams, *History* 4:39–40.

NOTES TO CHAPTER 8

11. Jefferson to G. K. van Hogendorp, 13 Oct. 1785, Lipscomb, *Writings of Jefferson* 5:183. Louis M. Sears seems to have regarded the embargo as a natural outgrowth of Jefferson's philosophy of life and not as a measure of opportunism, as Adams emphasized. Sears, *Jefferson and the Embargo* (Durham, N.C., 1927), 1–2. Sears gives too great a role to Jefferson's pacifism, however, as a cause of the embargo. See also Irving Brant, *James Madison: Secretary of State, 1800–1809* (Indianapolis, Ind., 1953), 397–403, and Leonard D. White, *The Jeffersonians: A Study in Administrative History, 1801–1829* (New York, 1951), 423–24.

12. Three out of the four documents attached to the message dealt with French violations of American neutrality.

13. In November 1807 Jefferson thought that if no wheat reached England by May, she would be starved into submission. W. E. Dodd, "Napoleon Breaks Thomas Jefferson," *American Mercury* 5 (1925): 311; Schuyler D. Hoslett, "Jefferson and England: The Embargo as a Measure of Coercion," *Americana* 34 (1940): 39. Jefferson was gratified in the following spring to learn of complaints in Liverpool about the embargo's effects. Jefferson to Caesar A. Rodney, 24 Apr. 1808, Lipscomb, *Writings of Jefferson* 12:36.

14. Turreau to Champagny, 28 June 28, 1808, Correspondance politique, 51:166–77. Turreau was reporting this information to Talleyrand's successor as minister of foreign affairs.

15. Adams, *History* 4:232. Pickering was the leading figure in the campaign to prove that Napoleon personally dictated the embargo to Jefferson. See Hervey P. Prentiss, *Timothy Pickering as the Leader of New England Federalism 1800–1815* (Salem, Mass., 1934).

16. Jefferson to Col. John Taylor, 1 Aug. 1807, Lipscomb, *Writings of Jefferson* 11:305.

17. Jefferson expressed these sentiments in reply to the suggestion that Bonaparte was possibly Providence's instrument for punishing the crimes of kings. Leiper to Jefferson, 20 Aug. 1807, Jefferson Papers, 170, Lib. Cong.; Jefferson to Leiper, 21 Aug. 1807, Paul L. Ford, ed., *The Works of Thomas Jefferson,* 12 vols. (New York, 1904), 10:483–84.

18. Despite the obvious guile, Jefferson was still interested in a maritime pact upholding neutral rights. He corresponded intermittently with Alexander of Russia on the subject and dispatched the Short mission in 1808 in the hope of stimulating Russian interest. He would not have America join such a league, but he thought that it, like the Continental System, served American interests. Jefferson to Paine, 26 Mar. 1806, Ford, *Works of Jefferson* 10:247; Jefferson to Alexander I, 19 Apr. 1806, ibid., 10:249–51; Jefferson to William Duane, 20 July 1807, Lipscomb, *Writings of Jefferson* 11:292; Jefferson to Paine, 9 Oct. 1807, ibid., 11:378.

19. John Armstrong to Champagny, 8 Feb. 1808, Correspondance politique, 61:36–36vo; Turreau to Champagny, 28 June 1808, ibid., foll. 166–77.

20. Armstrong to Champagny, 4 and 8 Feb. 1808, ibid., foll. 32–33, 36–36vo. Armstrong's hopes for Florida depended upon a promise the French made, before they knew of the embargo, in return for an alliance.

21. I. J. Cox, "Pan-American Policy of Jefferson and Wilkinson," *Mississippi Valley Historical Review* 1 (1914): 212. Cox claims that Jefferson's desire for Florida influenced his whole relationship with Bonaparte.

22. Turreau to Champagny, 28 June 1808, Correspondance politique, 61:166–77.

23. Jefferson to Madison, 31 May 1808, Lipscomb, *Writings of Jefferson* 12:70; Jefferson to Gallatin, 4 July 1808, ibid., 12:79; Jefferson to Madison, 12 Aug. 1808, ibid., 12:126.

24. Jefferson to Henry Dearborn, 12 Aug. 1808, ibid., 12:125. Always optimistic in this period, Jefferson wondered if France's difficulties in Spain might make this the proper time to take action against Spanish America.

25. Turreau to Champagny, 3 July 1809, Correspondance politique, 61:238–47vo.

26. Sears, *Jefferson and the Embargo,* 318.

27. Federalists and their sympathizers made no secret of their belief that Jefferson con-

trolled Madison's decisions. While Jefferson offered his advice on many issues, there was no conscious effort on his part to dictate policy and no uniform practice of acceptance on Madison's part. See Roy J. Honeywell, "President Jefferson and His Successor," *American Historical Review* 46 (Oct. 1940): 64–75. During the War of 1812 Jefferson reduced his correspondence with Madison to avoid charges of meddling. He was human enough, however, to resent the times when he did offer advice and Madison refused it. Jefferson to Monroe, 30 May 1813, Lipscomb, *Writings of Jefferson* 13:250–52; Jefferson to Madison, 18 June 1813, ibid., 13:259–60.

28. Jefferson to Caesar A. Rodney, 10 Feb. 1810, ibid., 12:357–58; Jefferson to Robert Patterson, 11 Sept. 1811, ibid., 13:87.

29. Jefferson to Madison, 19 and 27 Apr. 1809, ibid., 12:274, 276–77; Jefferson to John Langdon, 5 Mar. 1810, ibid., 12:375. Jefferson's emphasis.

30. Jefferson to W. C. Nicholas, 25 May 1809, Ford, *Works of Jefferson* 11:107–8; Jefferson to Madison, 16 June 1809, ibid., 11:112.

31. A. T. Mahan, *Sea Power in its Relations to the War of 1812,* 12 vols. (London, 1905), 1:235–41.

32. Jefferson to Philip Mazzei, 29 Dec. 1813, Jefferson Papers, 200, Lib. Cong.

33. Madison to Jefferson, 18 Mar. 1811, and 25 May 1812, in Gaillard Hunt, *The Writings of James Madison,* 9 vols. (New York, 1900–1910), 8:134–35, 190–91.

34. C. C. Tansill, "Robert Smith," in Samuel Flagg Bemis, ed., *The American Secretaries of State and Their Diplomacy,* 10 vols. (New York, 1928) 3:177. See also Irving Brant, *James Madison: The President, 1809–1812* (Indianapolis, Ind., 1956), 481–83. Brant places most of the blame, however, on Federalist and British leadership.

35. Jefferson to John Wayles Eppes, 5 Jan. 1811, Ford, *Works of Jefferson* 11:160–61. See Julius W. Pratt, *Expansionists of 1812* (New York, 1925), 69–75.

36. Jefferson to John Adams, 11 June 1812, Lipscomb, *Writings of Jefferson* 13:161.

37. Jefferson to Madison, 29 June 1812, ibid., 13:172; Jefferson to Madison, 26 Mar. 1812, Jefferson Papers, 195, Lib. Cong.

38. The failure of the Erskine Agreement so soon after the failure of the embargo increased his pessimism about future Anglo-American relations. Jefferson to Madison, 17 Aug. 1809, Lipscomb, *Writings of Jefferson* 12:305–6. Jefferson still thought that the embargo had been the instrument that kept us from "a gripe of the paw" of the Mammoth and "the flounce of the tail" of the Leviathan. But part of the nation rebelled against that program, and "from that moment, I have seen no system which could keep us entirely aloof from these agents of destruction." Jefferson to Walter Jones, 5 Mar. 1810, ibid., 12:372–73.

39. Jefferson to William Duane, 4 Aug. 1812, ibid., 13:180–81.

40. Jefferson to Gen. Thaddeus Kosciusko, 28 June 1812, ibid., 13:169. Jefferson had long believed that England's industrial system would fall apart once its American sources of supply were cut off. As late as the summer of 1814 he still had visions of starving workers eager to help America punish their ruling classes for the loss of their livelihoods. See Jefferson to Thomas Cooper, 10 Sept. 1814, ibid., 14:186.

41. Jefferson to Thomas Letre, 8 Aug. 1812, ibid., 13:185–86.

42. Jefferson to Robert Wright, 8 Aug. 1812, ibid., 13:184.

43. Jefferson to Duane, 4 Aug. 1812, ibid., 13:181.

44. Monroe's report to the President, 12 July 1813, in Walter Lowrie et al., eds., *American State Papers* (Washington, D.C., 1833–61), *Foreign Relations* (6 vols.), 3:609–12.

45. The Senate failed by only two votes to include France in its declaration of war against Britain. France, for her part, showed no disposition to treat her republican colleague any more graciously than she had before the United States entered the war.

46. Jefferson to Wright, 8 Aug. 1812, Lipscomb, *Writings of Jefferson* 13:184–85.

47. Mme. de Staël was the only French liberal to urge Jefferson to take a stand against Napoleon and to warn him against supporting France's war effort. Jefferson's reply was the standard one deploring Napoleon's acts but seeing Britain's as more injurious to the United States. Mme. de Staël to Jefferson, 10 Nov. 1812, in Marie G. Kimball, "Unpublished Correspondence of Mme. de Staël with Thomas Jefferson," *North American Review* 208 (1918): 66–68; Jefferson to Mme. de Staël, 24 May 1813, Lipscomb, *Writings of Jefferson* 13:237–245.

48. Jefferson to T. M. Randolph, 14 Nov. 1813, Jefferson Papers, 200, Lib. Cong.

49. Jefferson to James Ronaldson, 12 Jan. 1813, Lipscomb, *Writings of Jefferson* 13:205–6. A year later Jefferson changed his mind about a French invasion of Russia when he realized that a Napoleonic victory would "lay at his feet the whole continent of Europe." Jefferson to Thomas Leiper, 1 Jan. 1814, ibid., 14:43–44.

50. Jefferson to Mrs. Trist, 10 June 1814, Jefferson Papers, Massachusetts Historical Society.

51. The Republican journalist, William Duane, had even assumed that the old master would replace James Monroe as secretary of state after the fiasco in Canada. Jefferson was gratified by this show of loyalty and deemed it honorable "for the general of yesterday to act as a corporal today, if his service can be useful to his country." But he claimed that he was too old to be of service. William Duane to Jefferson, 20 Sept. 1812, Jefferson Papers, 196, Lib. Cong.; Jefferson to Duane, 1 Oct. 1812, Lipscomb, *Writings of Jefferson* 13:186–87.

52. Jefferson to Leiper, 4 Jan. 1814, Jefferson Papers, 200, Lib. Cong.

53. George Logan to Jefferson, 18 Sept. and 9 Dec. 1813, ibid.

54. Logan to Jefferson, 18 Sept. 1813, ibid.

55. Jefferson to Logan, 3 Oct. 1813, Lipscomb, *Writings of Jefferson* 13:384–87.

56. It appeared in *Poulson's American Daily Advertiser*, Philadelphia, 6 Dec. 1813.

57. Leiper to Jefferson, 9 Dec. 1813, Jefferson Papers, 200, Lib. Cong.

58. Jefferson to Leiper, 1 Jan. 1814, Lipscomb, *Writings of Jefferson* 14: 41–45. Jefferson did not give his opinions specifically on America's ties with France in the Logan letter, as he had in less publicized ones. In the Leiper letter he actually enlarged on the evils of Bonapartism. He hoped for a stalemate but implied that British defeat would be his second choice.

59. It is worth noting that Jefferson's cry of betrayal did not signify the severance of his relations with Logan. Jefferson never wanted to lose a friend; he went out of his way to renew ties with Logan as he had done with others—Paine, Monroe, William Short—who had abused his friendship on various occasions. It is possible that Logan had not realized what he had done. He actually wrote Jefferson, thanking him for what he obviously considered to be support of his views. Logan to Jefferson, 9 Dec. 1813, Jefferson Papers, 200, Lib. Cong. Not until after the war did Jefferson express to Logan his resentment over the incident, and then he couched it in gentle terms. Jefferson to Logan, 19 May 1816, Ford, *Works of Jefferson* 11:525–26.

60. Jefferson to John Melish, 10 Dec. 1814, Lipscomb, *Writings of Jefferson* 14:219.

61. Jefferson to Thomas Cooper, 10 Sept. 1814, ibid., 14:186; Jefferson to William Crawford, 11 Feb. 1815, ibid., 14:240; Jefferson to Monroe, 1 Jan. 1815, ibid., 14:226–27.

62. Jefferson to William Short, 18 Nov. 1814, ibid., 14:212–13; Jefferson to John Adams, 5 July 1814, ibid., 14:146–47; Jefferson to Caesar Rodney, 16 Mar. 1815, ibid., 14:285–86.

63. Jefferson to Madison, 23 Mar. 1815, ibid., 14:291–92.

64. Jefferson to Correa de Serra, 28 June 1815, ibid., 14:330; Jefferson to Adams, 10 Aug. 1815, ibid., 14:345; Jefferson to Mazzei, 9 Aug. 1815, Ford, *Works of Jefferson* 11:483.

65. Jefferson to Du Pont, 15 May 1815, Lipscomb, *Writings of Jefferson* 14:197–98; Jefferson to Adams, 10 June and 11 Aug. 1815, ibid., 14:299–300, 346.

66. Jefferson to Madison, 27 Aug. 1805, ibid., 11:87; Jefferson to Monroe, 4 May 1806, ibid., 11:111.

CHAPTER 9

1. *Poulson's American Daily Advertiser,* 5 Jan. 1813.
2. Samuel Austin, *The Apology of Patriots or the Heresy of the Friends of Washington and Peace Policy Defended* (Worcester, Mass., 1812), pamphlet, William L. Clements Library, University of Michigan.
3. Timothy Pickering to William Reed, 3 Mar. 1812; Pickering to Reed, 31 Jan. 1812, Pickering Papers, Massachusetts Historical Society.
4. Samuel Taggart to Pickering, 24 Apr. 1812; Pickering to Taggart, 1 May 1812, ibid.
5. *Annals of Congress,* 12th Cong., 1st sess., Appendix, 2219–20, 2222.
6. Memorandum, Mar. 1836, in Henry Adams, *Life of Albert Gallatin* (Philadelphia, Pa., 1879), 461; Madison to Henry Wheaton, 26 Feb. 1827, in Gaillard Hunt, ed., *Writings of James Madison,* 9 vols. (New York, 1900–1910), 9:273–74.
7. Adams to William Eustis, 26 Oct. 1811, in Worthington C. Ford, ed., *The Writings of John Quincy Adams,* 7 vols. (New York, 1913–17), 4:261.
8. Speech on report of House Foreign Relations Committee, 12 Dec. 1811, in Robert L. Meriwether, ed., *The Papers of John C. Calhoun* (Columbia, S.C., 1959), 1:83–85.
9. Speech on the bill to raise an additional military force, 31 Dec. 1811, in James F. Hopkins, ed., *The Papers of Henry Clay* (Lexington, Ky., 1959–), 1:607.
10. Jefferson to James Maury, 25 Apr. 1812, Jefferson Papers, Library of Congress.
11. William Jones to Jonathan Roberts, 10 June 1812, William Jones Papers, Uselma Clark Smith Collection, Historical Society of Pennsylvania.
12. Madison to Jefferson, 18 Mar. 1811, Hunt, *Writings of Madison* 8:134–35.
13. Louis Sérurier to Cadore, 10 Apr. and 30 June 1811, Archives du Ministère des affaires étrangères, Paris, correspondance politique, États-Unis, 65:166–68, 265–68, photostats, Manuscript Division, Library of Congress (hereafter cited as Correspondance politique). It should perhaps be pointed out that Monroe was "acting" secretary of state from early April until late November 1811.
14. Joel Barlow to Count Bassano, 30 Apr. 1812, ibid., 69:47; Henry Adams, *History of the United States during the Administrations of Jefferson and Madison,* 9 vols. (New York, 1889–91), 6:193.
15. Adams, *History* 6:195–201, 232.
16. Emmrich-Joseph, duc de Dalberg, to Bassano, 28 May 1812, including "Examen des rapports entre la France et les États-Unis en 1812," Correspondance politique, 69:80–89; Dalberg to Bassano, 12 June 1812, ibid., 136–37.
17. Dictated in Conseil d'administration du commerce, 29 Apr. 1811, J. B. P. Vaillant et al., eds., *Correspondance de Napoléon Ier,* 32 vols. (Paris, 1858–70), 22:122–24; Napoleon to Bassano, 23 and 28 Aug. 1811, ibid., 432, 448; Barlow to Dalberg, 5 June 1812, Correspondance politique, 69:121.
18. *Annals of Congress,* 13th Cong., 1st sess., 281 (18 June 1813).
19. Ibid., 12th Cong., 1st sess., 270 (12 June 1812); 286–87 (15 June 1812); 296–97 (17 June 1812); 1637 (4 June 1812).
20. Jonathan Roberts to Matthew Roberts, 23 May 1812, Jonathan Roberts Papers, Gratz Collection, Historical Society of Pennsylvania.
21. Fragment of a letter written in 1812, Monroe Papers, New York Public Library.

NOTES TO CHAPTER 9

22. William Jones to Jonathan Roberts, 10 June 1812, Jones Papers.

23. Madison to Jefferson, 25 May 1812, Hunt, *Writings of Madison* 8:191.

24. William Jones to Jonathan Roberts, 27 May 1812, Roberts Papers.

25. Sérurier to Bassano, 12 Jan. 1812, Correspondance politique, 67:123–31.

26. Monroe to Col. John Taylor, 13 June 1812, in Stanislaus M. Hamilton, ed., *The Writings of James Monroe,* 7 vols (New York, 1898–1903), 5:211.

27. *National Intelligencer,* 14 Apr. 1812.

28. Monroe to [Lord Auckland?], autumn, 1811, Hamilton, *Writings of Monroe* 5:192–93; Monroe to Taylor, 13 June 1812, ibid., 5:211.

29. Cincinnati *Spy,* 2 May and 6 June 1812.

30. John Connelly to Roberts, 21 May 1812, Roberts Papers. Colonel Connelly was a prominent Philadelphia commission merchant.

31. Napoleon crossed the Neimen River on 23 June 1812.

32. Madison to Henry Wheaton, 26 Feb. 1827, Hunt, *Writings of Madison* 9:274. Bradford Perkins, *Prologue to War: England and the United States, 1805–1812* (Berkeley, Calif., 1961), 406, cited this letter to emphasize not only the coincidental nature of the two acts but also the absence of any American desire to aid Napoleon. One might add that Madison did look upon the coincidence as a happy one because Napoleon's action appeared to be beneficial to the United States. See also Adams, *History* 6:265–66.

33. Cincinnati *Liberty Hall,* 2 June 1812.

34. William Jones to Jonathan Roberts, 10 June 1812, Jones Papers.

35. Jonathan Russell to John Smith, 2 Aug. 1811, Samuel Smith Papers, Manuscript Division, Library of Congress. See Edward Fox to Jonathan Roberts, 4 May 1812, Roberts Papers, for an example.

36. William Cobbett, *Letters on the Late War between the United States and Great Britain* (New York, 1815), 17, pamphlet, William L. Clements Library, University of Michigan.

37. *Niles' Weekly Register* 2 (1 Aug. 1812): 364.

38. *Annals of Congress,* 12th Cong., 1st sess., 1287 (9 Apr. 1812).

39. The Virginia Resolutions were presented to the Senate on 3 Feb. 1812. See *Annals of Congress,* 12th Cong., 1st sess., 112–13. The Ohio Resolutions, drawn up on 26 Dec. 1811, and forwarded to the president on 1 Jan. 1812, may be found in Department of State Miscellaneous Letters, 1 Jan. to 30 June 1812, National Archives.

40. "Resolutions of the Citizens and Inhabitants of Richmond, Manchester, and Their Vicinities in the State of Virginia, approving the late measures of the national administration—May 30," Department of State Miscellaneous Letters, 1 Jan. to 30 June 1812.

41. Cincinnati *Liberty Hall,* 29 Apr. 1812; Richmond *Enquirer,* 12 Apr. 1812.

42. President's message to the Congress, 1 June 1812, in James D. Richardson, ed., *A Compilation of the Messages and Papers of the Presidents, 1789–1897,* 10 vols. (Washington, D.C., 1896–99), 1:505.

43. Foreign Relations Committee Report on the Causes and Reasons for War, 3 June 1812, Meriwether, *Papers of Calhoun* 1:120; *Annals of Congress,* 12th Cong., 1st sess., 1552 (25 June 1812).

44. Adams, *History* 6:232–33.

45. George Harrison to Jonathan Roberts, 31 May 1812, Roberts Papers; Jefferson to William Duane, 20 Apr. 1812, Jefferson Papers, Lib. Cong.

46. Monroe to Barlow, 24 Feb. 1812; Monroe to Russell, 26 June 1812, Hamilton, *Writings of Monroe* 5:199, 212–13.

47. Alexander Dallas, *An Exposition of the Causes and Character of the Late War with Great Britain* (Philadelphia, Pa., 1815), 52.

CHAPTER 10

1. Bradford Perkins, *Castlereagh and Adams: England and the United States, 1812–1823* (Berkeley, Calif., 1964); Harry L. Coles, *The War of 1812* (Chicago, Ill., 1965); Patrick C. T. White, *A Nation on Trial: America and the War of 1812* (New York, 1965); Reginald Horsman, *War of 1812* (New York, 1969).

2. Henry Adams, *History of the United States during the Administrations of Jefferson and Madison*, 9 vols. (New York, 1889–91); Fred L. Engelman, *The Peace of Christmas Eve* (New York, 1962).

3. *Annals of Congress,* 12th Cong., 1st sess., 270–97 (13, 15, 16 June 1812); ibid., 13th Cong., 1st and 2d sess., 170–311 (16–19, 21 June 1813); ibid., 13th Cong., 2d sess., 890–927 (11, 12 Jan. 1814).

4. James D. Richardson, ed., *A Compilation of the Messages and Papers of the Presidents, 1789–1897,* 10 vols. (Washington, D.C., 1896–99), 1:499–505; Monroe to Joel Barlow, 24 Feb. 1812; Monroe to Jonathan Russell, 26 June 1812, in Stanislaus M. Hamilton, ed., *The Writings of James Monroe,* 7 vols. (New York, 1898–1903), 5:199, 212–13. See also *National Intelligencer,* 4 Aug. 1812; Report of James Monroe on the French decree (St. Cloud) of 28 Apr. 1811, 12 July 1813, Walter Lowrie et al., eds., *American State Papers* (Washington, D.C., 1833–1861), *Foreign Relations* (6 vols.), 3:609–12.

5. Jefferson to William Duane, 4 Aug. 1812, Andrew A. Lipscomb and Albert E. Bergh, eds., *The Writings of Thomas Jefferson,* 20 vols. (Washington, D.C., 1903), 13:180–81.

6. See chapter 9, "France and Madison's Decision for War, 1812." One American, John M. Taylor of Philadelphia, thought it reasonable for Napoleon to give America "as many ships of war as a fair valuation as will pay for the property Sequestered, Burned, etc."; Taylor to David B. Warden, 30 Nov. 1812, Viscount Melville Papers, William L. Clements Library, University of Michigan; Henry Clay to the House of Representatives, 7 Dec. 1812, *Annals of Congress,* 12th Cong., 2d sess., 301 (7 Dec. 1812); Joel Barlow to Duke of Bassano, 17 July 1812, Despatches from United States Ministers to France, No. 13, microfilm copies, National Archives.

7. Lawrence S. Kaplan, *Jefferson and France: An Essay on Politics and Political Ideas* (New Haven, Conn., 1967), 137–38.

8. Louis Sérurier to Bassano, 14 Oct. 1812, Washington, Dispatch No. 72, Louis Sérurier Papers, Centre de microfilm des archives de Seine et Oise.

9. Ibid., 28 Sept. 1812, No. 70.

10. For John Adams's concept of alliance, see Felix Gilbert, *To the Farewell Address: Ideas of Early American Foreign Policy* (Princeton, N.J., 1961), 45–54.

11. Adams, *History* 6:219.

12. *National Intelligencer,* 31 Mar. 1814, 19 May 1814; Philadelphia *Aurora,* 2 June, 1 Sept. 1814; Richmond *Enquirer,* 3 July 1812, 6 Apr. 1814; *Niles' Weekly Register,* 31 July 1813, 5 Dec. 1812; Warren (Ohio) *Trump of Fame,* 16 Feb. 1814.

13. Barlow to James Madison, 26 Sept. 1812, Paris (private), James Madison Papers, Manuscript Division, Library of Congress. See also Irving Brant, "Joel Barlow, Madison's Stubborn Minister," *William and Mary Quarterly,* 3d ser., 15 (Oct. 1958): 446–47.

14. Sérurier to Bassano, 19 June 1812, No. 59; 6 July 1812, No. 61, Sérurier Papers.

15. Sérurier to Bassano, 17 Dec. 1812, No. 80; 14 Feb. 1813, No. 86; 20 Feb. 1813, No. 87; 1 Mar. 1813, No. 88; 6 Mar. 1813, No. 89, Sérurier Papers.

16. George Libaire, ed., *With Napoleon in Russia: The Memoirs of General de Caulaincourt, Duke of Vicenza* (New York, 1935), 371–72.

NOTES TO CHAPTER 10

17. Monroe to William Crawford, 29 May 1813, Department of State Instructions to United States Ministers, Records of the Department of State, RG 59, National Archives.

18. Napoleon to Barlow, Nov. 1812, Joel Barlow Papers, Houghton Library, Harvard University.

19. Crawford to Monroe, 19 Nov. 1813, No. 11, Despatches; Crawford to Monroe, 16 Sept. 1813, No. 4, Despatches.

20. *Journal de Paris*, 29 July 1812, reprinted in the Richmond *Enquirer*, 6 Oct. 1812.

21. The prefect of Calais gave this advice to Americans who were returning home from France at the outbreak of the war. London *Courier*, 29 July 1812, reprinted in *Poulson's American Daily Advertiser*, 22 Sept. 1812.

22. Sérurier to Bassano, 7 Oct. 1812, No. 76, Sérurier Papers.

23. Crawford to Bassano, 11 Sept. 1813, No. 4, Despatches.

24. Crawford to Duke of Vicenza, 18 Jan. 1814, No. 35, Despatches.

25. Report of Ministry of Foreign Affairs to Emperor, 4 Jan. 1814, Archives du Ministère des affaires étrangères, Paris, correspondance politique, États-Unis, 71:10–10v, photostats, Manuscript Division, Library of Congress (hereafter cited as Correspondance politique); Report of Ministry of Foreign Affairs to Emperor, 24 Jan. 1814, ibid., 69:33–34v. Note the similarity of recommendations to those made in 1812 under the title of "Examen des rapports entre la France et les États-Unis en 1812," in Emmrich-Joseph, duc de Dalberg, to Bassano, 28 May 1812, ibid., 80-89. In the intervening eighteen months Barlow had made somewhat informal attempts to have the indemnities paid out of a fund created by revenues from licenses for American trade with the French Empire. It would have involved a 20 percent reduction in France's tariff and a complicated relationship with French merchants who, in return for assuming some of the financial burdens, would have received special trade privileges in the American trade. Both Napoleon and Crawford were dissatisfied with this plan. See outline of a convention of indemnity, 15 Oct. 1812, ibid., 272–73; Crawford to Monroe, 1 Dec. 1813, No. 12, Despatches.

26. Richmond *Enquirer*, 30 Mar., 6 Apr., 4 May 1814; *National Intelligencer*, 19 May 1814.

27. Richmond *Enquirer*, 2 Apr. 1814.

28. Richmond *Enquirer*, 18, 28 May, 4, 14 June 1814; *National Intelligencer*, 21 May 1814.

29. Crawford to Charles Maurice de Talleyrand, 26 May, 1 June, 12 July 1814, William Crawford Papers, Manuscript Division, Library of Congress. Crawford to Monroe, 16 Dec. 1814, No. 35, Despatches, expresses his disappointment to the secretary of state in detail.

30. Crawford complained of a specious distinction France made between letter of marque and privateer which was used to justify discrimination against American vessels. Crawford to Arnail-François de Jaucourt, 30 Nov. 1814, Crawford Papers.

31. Crawford to Henry Clay, 15 May, 9 Oct. 1814, in James F. Hopkins, ed., *The Papers of Henry Clay* (Lexington, Ky., 1959–), 1:910–11, 943.

32. Crawford to Monroe, 11 Apr. 1814, No. 17, Despatches. Monroe thought that "it is even probable that our relations with France may be improved by this event." Monroe to Crawford, 25 June 1814, Diplomatic Instructions of the Department of State, Records of the Department of State, RG 59, National Archives.

33. Crawford to Monroe, 16 Dec. 1814, No. 35, Despatches.

34. Engelman, *The Peace of Christmas Eve*, 249.

35. Duke of Wellington to Jaucourt, 22 Jan. 1815, Correspondance politique, 72:15–15v.

36. In instructions to Sérurier special attention was paid to the importance of maintaining France's neutral stance and of avoiding offense to the British. See Instructions to Sérurier, 8 Sept. 1814, ibid., 176v; Jaucourt to Sérurier, 8 Nov. 1814, ibid., 253–54.

37. Crawford to American Commissioners at Ghent, 20 May 1814, enclosing letter pre-

sented by the Marquis de Lafayette to Emperor Alexander, 26 May 1814, Hopkins, *Papers of Clay* 1:926–27.

38. Crawford to Monroe, 17 Aug. 1814, No. 25 (private), Despatches; Levett Harris to Albert Gallatin, 21 Aug. 1814, copy book, Levett Harris Papers, William L. Clements Library, University of Michigan.

39. John Randolph of Roanoke, an ardent opponent of the war and of Madison, saw Russian mediation from the beginning as a stroke of luck for the administration. Randolph to Josiah Quincy, 23 May 1813, John Randolph Papers, Manuscript Division, Library of Congress. Madison himself made no secret of his expectations of Russian friendship in the contest with England. Madison to John Nicholas, 2 Apr. 1813, Madison Papers. See also *National Intelligencer,* 17 Feb. 1814; Richmond *Enquirer,* 4 June 1814. See Perkins, *Castlereagh and Adams,* 65, for Britain's view of Russian friendship for the United States. See also Crawford to the American Commissioners at Ghent, 13 May 1814, Hopkins, *Papers of Clay* 1:907.

40. Goulburn Memorandum, 4 Sept. 1814, Henry Goulburn Papers, William L. Clements Library, University of Michigan.

41. John Quincy Adams to Crawford, 17 Nov. 1814, Worthington C. Ford, ed., *The Writings of John Quincy Adams,* 7 vols. (New York, 1913–17), 5:195; John Quincy Adams to Louisa Catherine Adams, 18 Nov. 1814, ibid., 196–97.

42. Alexander Dallas to William Jones, 13 Aug. 1814, William Jones Papers, Uselma Clark Smith Collection, Historical Society of Pennsylvania.

43. Introduction (1845), Sérurier Papers.

CHAPTER 11

1. See in particular Samuel Flagg Bemis, *Pinckney's Treaty: A Study of America's Advantage from Europe's Distress, 1783–1800* (Baltimore, Md., 1926), and *A Diplomatic History of the United States,* 5th ed. (New York, 1965), 167.

2. Louis Sérurier to Duke of Bassano, 6 Mar. 1813, Archives du Ministère des affaires étrangères, Paris, correspondance politique, États-Unis, 7:103v, photostats, Manuscript Division, Library of Congress (hereafter cited as Correspondance politique).

3. Henry Adams, *History of the United States during the Administrations of Jefferson and Madison,* 9 vols. (New York, 1889–91), 5:331.

4. Irving Brant, "Joel Barlow, Madison's Stubborn Minister," *William and Mary Quarterly,* 3d ser., 15 (Oct. 1958): 438.

5. See Joseph B. Cobb, *Leisure Labors or Miscellanies Historical, Literary, and Political* (New York, 1858), 143.

6. Philip Jackson Green, "William H. Crawford and the War of 1812," *Georgia Historical Quarterly* 26 (Mar. 1942): 27–29.

7. For the former see *Poulson's American Daily Advertiser,* 15 Jan. 1812; for the latter, Timothy Pickering to Samuel Taggart, 1 May 1812, Pickering Papers, Massachusetts Historical Society.

8. *National Intelligencer,* 4 Aug. 1812.

9. William H. Crawford to Monroe, 27 Sept. 1812, in Adams, *History* 6:395–96.

10. Crawford to Sylvanus Bourne, 5 Nov. 1813, quoted in J. E. D. Shipp, *Giant Days, or the Life and Times of William H. Crawford* (Americus, Ga., 1909), 119.

11. Crawford to Bassano, 11 Sept. 1813, No. 14, Despatches from United States to Ministers to France, microfilm copies, National Archives.

12. Crawford to Monroe, 15 Aug. 1813, ibid.

13. Crawford to Duke of Vicence, 4 Jan. 1814, Crawford Papers, Library of Congress.

NOTES TO CHAPTER 12

14. Crawford to Bassano, 11 Sept. 1813, ibid.
15. Crawford to Vicence, 18 Jan. 1814, ibid.
16. Crawford to Vicence, 18 Jan. 1814, ibid.
17. Crawford to Talleyrand, 26 May 1814; Crawford to Talleyrand, 1 June 1814; Crawford to Talleyrand, 12 July 1814, ibid.
18. Crawford to Monroe, 17 Aug. 1814, No. 14, ibid.
19. Crawford to Jaucourt, 3 and 30 Nov. 1814, Crawford Papers, Lib. Cong.; Crawford to Monroe, 12 Dec. 1814, No. 15, Despatches, expresses his disappointment in detail to the secretary of state.
20. Crawford to Henry Clay, 9 Oct. 1814, in James F. Hopkins, ed., *The Papers of Henry Clay* (Lexington, Ky., 1959–), 1:943.
21. Crawford to Clay, 15 May 1814, ibid., 1:910–11.
22. Philip Jackson Green, *The Life of William Harris Crawford* (Charlotte, N.C., 1965), observes Crawford's confidence in the skill of the commissioners.
23. Crawford to Clay, 10 June 1814, Hopkins, *Papers of Clay* 1:934–35; Clay to Crawford, 2 July 1814, ibid., 1:938–39; Monroe to Adams, Bayard, Clay, and Russell, 28 Jan. 1814, Department of State Instructions to United States Ministers, Records of the Department of State, RG 59, Crawford Papers, National Archives.
24. Crawford to Talleyrand, 12 July 1814; Crawford to Jaucourt, 30 Nov. 1814, Instructions.
25. Crawford to Clay, 9 July 1814, Hopkins, *Papers of Clay* 1:945–46.
26. Crawford to the American Commissioners at Ghent, 13 May 1814, ibid., 1:914.
27. Crawford to the American Commissioners at Ghent, 28 May 1814, enclosing letter presented to Czar Alexander I by Lafayette, 26 May 1814, ibid., 1:926–27.
28. 29 June 1814, in James D. Richardson, ed., *A Compilation of the Messages and Papers of the Presidents, 1789–1897,* 10 vols. (Washington, D.C., 1896–99), 1:534–44; Crawford to Talleyrand and to ministers of maritime states in Paris, 22 Aug. 1814, No. 15, Despatches. He reported the wide circulation he had given to the president's proclamation while noting at the same time that he was not optimistic about its results, 10 Sept. 1814, ibid.
29. Clancarty to Gambier, 4 Sept. 1814, Henry Goulburn Papers, William L. Clements Library, University of Michigan.
30. American Commissioners to British Commissioners, 24 Aug. 1814; Goulburn Memorandum, 4 Sept. 1814, ibid.
31. Monroe to Crawford, 11 Aug. 1814, Crawford Papers (private letter telling of the president's agreement to permit his retirement, but urging him to remain at his post until the end of the conflict).
32. Crawford to Monroe, 21 Mar. 1815, No. 16, Despatches. Speculations about the meaning of Napoleon's return to Paris: Crawford to Monroe, 15 Apr. 1815, 16, Despatches. Report of an inconclusive talk being held on April 3 with the duke of Vicence on the subject of indemnity.
33. Crawford to Monroe, 15 Apr. 1815 (private), ibid.
34. Louis-Guillaume Otto to Vicence, 22 Apr. 1815, Correspondance politique, 72:81–82.
35. Crawford to Otto, 3 May 1815, Crawford Papers.
36. Chase C. Mooney, *William H. Crawford, 1772–1834* (Lexington, Ky., 1974), 76.

CHAPTER 12

1. James H. Hopkins, ed., *The Papers of Henry Clay* (Lexington, Ky., 1959–), 2:520.

2. Quoted in José de Onis, *The United States as Seen by Spanish Writers* (New York, 1952), 24.

3. Monroe to Joel R. Poinsett, 30 Apr. 1811, in William R. Manning, ed., *Diplomatic Correspondence of the United States Concerning the Independence of the Latin-American Nations,* 3 vols. (New York, 1925), 1:ii.

4. Charles Francis Adams, ed., *The Memoirs of John Quincy Adams,* 12 vols. (Philadelphia, Pa., 1874–77), 5:176.

5. *Miranda's Diary,* in W. S. Robertson, *The Life of Miranda,* 2 vols. (Chapel Hill, N.C., 1929), 1:296.

6. *Miranda's Diary,* 300.

7. *Miranda's Diary,* 301.

8. Cabinet meeting, 22 Oct. 1807, in "Anas," in Andrew A. Lipscomb and Albert E. Bergh, eds., *The Writings of Thomas Jefferson,* 20 vols. (Washington, D.C., 1903), 1:484–85.

9. Quoted in J. Fred Rippy, *Joel R. Poinsett, Versatile American* (Durham, N.C., 1935), 18–19.

10. "Diary of José Bernardo Gutierrez de Lara, 1811–1812," *American Historical Review* 34 (Jan. 1929): 283.

11. Ibid., 72.

12. H. W. S. Cleveland, ed., *Voyages of a Merchant Mariner, Compiled from the Journals and Letters of Richard J. Cleveland* (New York, 1886), 187–93.

13. Quoted in John B. McMaster, *The Life and Times of Stephen Girard, Mariner and Merchant,* 2 vols. (Philadelphia, Pa., 1918), 2:171.

14. Ibid., 2:162–63.

15. William D. Robinson, *A Cursory View of Spanish America* (Georgetown, D.C., 1815), 20.

16. Manuel Torres, *An Exposition of the Commerce of Spanish America with Some Observations on Its Importance to the United States* (Philadelphia, Pa., 1816), 11, 14.

17. Hopkins, *Papers of Clay* 2:522.

18. Samuel Flagg Bemis, "Early Diplomatic Missions from Buenos Aires to the United States, 1811–24," in Bemis, ed., *American Foreign Policy and the Blessings of Liberty and Other Essays* (New Haven, Conn., 1962), 344.

19. Samuel Flagg Bemis, *John Quincy Adams and the Foundations of American Foreign Policy* (New York, 1949), 344.

20. Manning, *Diplomatic Correspondence* 1:433–34.

21. Adams, *Memoirs* 4:45.

22. Ibid., 5:46.

23. Ibid., 5:86, 94–95, 104 (1, 4 May 1820). See Bemis, *John Quincy Adams,* 352.

24. *Annals of Congress,* 16th Cong., 1st sess., 2228 (10 May 1820).

25. Quoted in Samuel Flagg Bemis, "John Quincy Adams," in Bemis, ed., *The American Secretaries of State and Their Diplomacy,* 10 vols. (New York: 1928), 4:45.

26. Adams, *Memoirs* 6:24–25. See Bradford Perkins, *Castlereagh and Adams: England and the United States, 1812–1823* (Berkeley, Calif., 1964), 299.

CHAPTER 13

1. In addition to his editing of "Correspondence of the French Ministers to the United States, 1791–1797," *American Historical Association, Annual Report,* 1903 (Washington, D.C., 1904), Turner published several articles on the West in French diplomacy drawn from

NOTES TO CHAPTER 13

the above documents. See, for example, "The Origin of Genet's Projected Attack on Louisiana and the Florida," *American Historical Review* 3 (July 1898): 650–71, and "The Policy of France toward the Mississippi Valley in the Period of Washington and Adams," *American Historical Review* 10 (Jan. 1905): 249–79.

2. Samuel Flagg Bemis, *Pinckney's Treaty: A Study of America's Advantage from Europe's Distress, 1783–1800* (Baltimore, Md., 1926); Dexter Perkins, *The Monroe Doctrine, 1823–1826* (Cambridge, Mass., 1927); Julius W. Pratt, *Expansionists of 1812* (New York: 1925).

3. Dexter Perkins, *The American Approach to Foreign Policy* (Cambridge, Mass., 1952).

4. Samuel Flagg Bemis, "The Shifting Strategy of American Defense and Diplomacy," *Virginia Quarterly Review* 24 (Summer 1948): 321–35.

5. Nettels's testimony, *Hearings,* Senate Committee on Foreign Relations, 81st Cong., 1st sess., pt. 2:1107.

6. Alexander DeConde, *Entangling Alliance: Politics & Diplomacy under George Washington* (Durham, N.C., Press, 1959), and *The Quasi-War: The Politics and Diplomacy of the Undeclared War with France, 1797–1801* (New York, 1966); Bradford Perkins, *The First Rapprochement: England and the United States, 1795–1805* (Philadelphia, 1955), *Prologue to War: England and the United States, 1805–1812* (Berkeley, Calif., 1961), and *Castlereagh and Adams: England and the United States, 1812–1823* (Berkeley, Calif., 1964).

7. Norman K. Risjord, "1812: Conservatives, War Hawks, and the Nation's Honor," *William and Mary Quarterly* 17 (Apr. 1961): 196–210; Roger H. Brown, *The Republic in Peril: 1812* (New York, 1964).

8. George Dangerfield, *Chancellor Robert R. Livingston of New York, 1746–1813* (New York, 1960).

9. Seymour Martin Lipset, *The First New Nation: The United States in Historical and Comparative Perspective* (New York, 1963); Robert R. Palmer, *The Age of the Democratic Revolution,* 2 vols. (Princeton, N.J., 1959–64).

10. Richard B. Morris, *The Emerging Nations and the American Revolution* (New York, 1970).

11. See, for example, Hans J. Morgenthau, *In Defense of the National Interest: A Critical Examination of American Foreign Policy* (New York, 1951).

12. Dumas Malone, *Jefferson and His Time,* 6 vols. (Boston, Mass., 1948–81); Albert H. Bowman, "Jefferson, Hamilton and American Foreign Policy," *Political Science Quarterly* 71 (Mar. 1956): 18–41; Gilbert L. Lycan, *Alexander Hamilton and American Foreign Policy: A Design for Greatness* (Norman, Okla., 1970); Helene Johnson Looze, *Alexander Hamilton and the British Orientation of American Foreign Policy* (The Hague, 1969).

13. Lawrence S. Kaplan, *Jefferson and France: An Essay on Politics and Political Ideas* (New Haven, Conn., 1967).

14. Gerald Stourzh, *Alexander Hamilton and the Idea of Republican Government* (Stanford, Calif., 1970).

15. Richard B. Morris, *The Peacemakers: The Great Powers and American Independence* (New York, 1965); Cecil B. Currey, *Code Number 72: Ben Franklin, Patriot or Spy?* (Englewood Cliffs, N.J., 1972).

16. Thomas J. McCormick, "The State of American Diplomatic History," in Herbert J. Bass, ed., *The State of American History* (Chicago, Ill., 1970), 119.

17. William A. Williams, "The Age of Mercantilism: An Interpretation of the American Political Economy, 1763–1828," *William and Mary Quarterly,* 3d ser., 15 (Oct. 1958): 419-37.

18. Arthur B. Darling, *Our Rising Empire, 1763–1803* (New Haven, Conn., 1940); Richard W. Van Alstyne, *The Rising American Empire* (New York, 1960).

NOTES TO CHAPTER 13

19. See Mary Ryan, "Party Formation in the United States Congress, 1789–1796, A Quantitative Analysis," *William and Mary Quarterly,* 3d ser., 27 (Oct. 1971): 523–42.

20. Ronald L. Hatzenbuehler, "Party Unity and the Decision for War in the House of Representatives in 1812," *William and Mary Quarterly,* 3d ser., 29 (July 1972): 367–90.

21. Richard R. Beeman, *The Old Dominion and the New Nation, 1788–1801* (Lexington, Ky., 1972); Victor A. Sapio, *Pennsylvania and the War of 1812* (Lexington, Ky., 1970).

22. Charles E. Neu, "The Changing Interpretive Structure of American Foreign Policy," in John Braeman et al., eds., *Twentieth-Century American Foreign Policy* (Columbus, Ohio, 1971), 10.

23. Edward S. Corwin, *French Policy and the American Alliance of 1778* (Princeton, N.J., 1916); Samuel Flagg Bemis, *The Diplomacy of the American Revolution* (New York, 1935).

24. Bemis, *Jay's Treaty: A Study in Commerce and Diplomacy* (New Haven, Conn., 1962), and *Pinckney's Treaty;* Arthur P. Whitaker, *The Spanish-American Frontier: The Westward Movement and the Spanish Retreat in the Mississippi Valley* (Boston, Mass., 1927); and *The Mississippi Question, 1795–1803* (New York, 1934).

25. Henry Adams, *History of the United States during the Administrations of Jefferson and Madison,* 9 vols. (New York, 1889–91).

26. Pratt, *Expansionists of 1812;* George R. Taylor, "Agrarian Discontent in the Mississippi Valley Preceding the War of 1812," *The Journal of Political Economy* 39 (Aug. 1931): 486–505.

27. D. Perkins, *The Monroe Doctrine,* and *Hands Off: A History of the Monroe Doctrine* (Boston, Mass., 1941).

INDEX

INDEX